# CASENOTE LEGAL BRIEFS

# PRODUCTS LIABILITY

**Adaptable to courses utilizing Owen, Montgomery and Keeton's casebook on Products Liability and Safety**

NORMAN S. GOLDENBERG, SENIOR EDITOR
PETER TENEN, MANAGING EDITOR

STAFF WRITERS

CHRIS YOUKER
KEMP RICHARDSON
RICK BRODY
BILL CARERO
MICHAEL LEKOV
DIANE FOLEY JONES
DAVID KNOCKBLOCK
HOWARD LEVIANT

PUBLISHED BY CASENOTES PUBLISHING CO., INC. 1640 5th ST., SUITE 208 SANTA MONICA, CA 90401

ISBN 0-87457-113-8

# FORMAT OF THE CASENOTE LEGAL BRIEF

**CASE CAPSULE: This bold-faced section (first three paragraphs) highlights the procedural nature of the case, a short summary of the facts, and the rule of law. This is an invaluable quick-review device designed to refresh the student's memory for classroom discussion and exam preparation.**

**NATURE OF CASE: This section identifies the form of action (e.g., breach of contract, negligence, battery), the type of proceeding (e.g., demurrer, appeal from trial court's jury instructions) and the relief sought (e.g., damages, injunction, criminal sanctions).**

**FACT SUMMARY: The fact summary is included to refresh the student's memory. It can be used as a quick reminder of the facts when the student is chosen by an instructor to brief a case.**

**CONCISE RULE OF LAW: This portion of the brief summarizes the general principle of law that the case illustrates. Like the fact summary, it is included to refresh the student's memory. It may be used for instant recall of the court's holding and for classroom discussion or home review.**

**FACTS:** This section contains all relevant facts of the case, including the contentions of the parties and the lower court holdings. It is written in a logical order to give the student a clear understanding of the case. The plaintiff and defendant are identified by their proper names throughout and are always labeled with a (P) or (D).

**ISSUE:** The issue is a concise question that brings out the essence of the opinion as it relates to the section of the casebook in which the case appears. Both substantive and procedural issues are included if relevant to the decision.

**HOLDING AND DECISION:** This section offers a clear and in-depth discussion of the rule of the case and the court's rationale. It is written in easy-to-understand language. When relevant, it includes a thorough discussion of the exceptions listed by the court, the concurring and dissenting opinions, and the names of the judges.

**CONCURRENCE / DISSENT:** All concurrences and dissents are briefed whenever they are included by the casebook editor.

**EDITOR'S ANALYSIS:** This last paragraph gives the student a broad understanding of where the case "fits in" with other cases in the section of the book and with the entire course. It is a hornbook-style discussion indicating whether the case is a majority or minority opinion and comparing the principal case with other cases in the casebook. It may also provide analysis from restatements, uniform codes, and law review articles. The editor's analysis will prove to be invaluable to classroom discussion.

**CROSS-REFERENCE TO OUTLINE:** Wherever possible, following each case is a cross-reference linking the subject matter of the issue to the appropriate place in the *Casenote Law Outline,* which provides further information on the subject.

---

**WINTER v. G.P. PUTNAM'S SONS**

938 F.2d 1033 (1991).

**NATURE OF CASE: Appeal from summary judgment in a products liability action.**

**FACT SUMMARY: Winter (P) relied on a book on mushrooms published by Putnam (D) and became critically ill after eating a poisonous mushroom.**

**CONCISE RULE OF LAW: Strict products liability is not applicable to the expressions contained within a book.**

**FACTS:** Winter (P) purchased The Encyclopedia of Mushrooms, a book published by Putnam (D), to help in collecting and eating wild mushrooms. In 1988, Winter (P), relying on descriptions in the book, ate some wild mushrooms which turned out to be poisonous. Winter (P) became so ill he required a liver transplant. He brought a strict products liability action against Putnam (D), alleging that the book contained erroneous and misleading information that caused his injury. Putnam (D) responded that the information in the book was not a product for purposes of strict products liability, and the trial court granted its motion for summary judgment. The trial court also rejected Winter's (P) actions for negligence and misrepresentation. Winter (P) appealed.

**ISSUE:** Is strict products liability applicable to the expressions contained within a book?

**HOLDING AND DECISION:** (Sneed, J.) No. Strict products liability is not applicable to the expressions contained within a book. Products liability is geared toward tangible objects. The expression of ideas is governed by copyright, libel, and misrepresentation laws. The Restatement (Second) of Torts lists examples of the items that are covered by §402A strict liability. All are tangible items, such as tires or automobiles. There is no indication that the doctrine should be expanded beyond this area. Furthermore, there is a strong public interest in the unfettered exchange of ideas. The threat of liability without fault could seriously inhibit persons who wish to share thoughts and ideas with others. Although some courts have held that aeronautical charts are products for purposes of strict liability, these charts are highly technical tools which resemble compasses. The Encyclopedia of Mushrooms, published by Putnam (D), is a book of pure thought and expression and therefore does not constitute a product for purposes of strict liability. Additionally, publishers do not owe a duty to investigate the contents of books that they distribute. Therefore, a negligence action may not be maintained by Winter (P) against Putnam (D). Affirmed.

**EDITOR'S ANALYSIS:** This decision is in accord with the rulings in most jurisdictions. See Alm v. Nostrand Reinhold Co., Inc., 480 N.E. 2d 1263 (Ill. 1985). The court also stated that since the publisher is not a guarantor of the accuracy of an author's statements, an action for negligent misrepresentation could not be maintained. The elements of negligent misrepresentation are stated in § 311 of the Restatement (Second) of Torts.

***[For more information on misrepresentation, see Casenote Law Outline on Torts, Chapter 12, § III, Negligent Misrepresentation.]***

# NOTE TO THE STUDENT

**OUR GOAL.** It is the goal of Casenotes Publishing Company, Inc. to create and distribute the finest, clearest and most accurate legal briefs available. To this end, we are constantly seeking new ideas, comments and constructive criticism. As a user of *Casenote Legal Briefs,* your suggestions will be highly valued. With all correspondence, please include your complete name, address, and telephone number, including area code and zip code.

**THE TOTAL STUDY SYSTEM.** Casenote Legal Briefs are just one part of the Casenotes TOTAL STUDY SYSTEM. Most briefs are (wherever possible) cross-referenced to the appropriate *Casenote Law Outline,* which will elaborate on the issue at hand. By purchasing a Law Outline together with your Legal Brief, you will have both parts of the Casenotes TOTAL STUDY SYSTEM. (See the advertising in the front of this book for a list of Law Outlines currently available.)

**A NOTE ABOUT LANGUAGE.** Please note that the language used in *Casenote Legal Briefs* in reference to minority groups and women reflects terminology used within the historical context of the time in which the respective courts wrote the opinions. We at Casenotes Publishing Co., Inc. are well aware of and very sensitive to the desires of all people to be treated with dignity and to be referred to as they prefer. Because such preferences change from time to time, and because the language of the courts reflects the time period in which opinions were written, our case briefs will not necessarily reflect contemporary references. We appreciate your understanding and invite your comments.

**A NOTE REGARDING NEW EDITIONS.** As of our press date, this Casenote Legal Brief is current and includes briefs of all cases in the current version of the casebook, divided into chapters that correspond to that edition of the casebook. However, occasionally a new edition of the casebook comes out in the interim, and sometimes the casebook author will make changes in the sequence of the cases in the chapters, add or delete cases, or change the chapter titles. Should you be using this Legal Brief in conjuction with a casebook that was issued later than this book, you can receive all of the newer cases, which are available free from us, by sending in the "Supplement Request Form" in this section of the book (please follow all instructions on that form). The Supplement(s) will contain all the missing cases, and will bring your Casenote Legal Brief up to date.

**EDITOR'S NOTE.** Casenote Legal Briefs are intended to supplement the student's casebook, not replace it. There is no substitute for the student's own mastery of this important learning and study technique. If used properly, *Casenote Legal Briefs* are an effective law study aid that will serve to reinforce the student's understanding of the cases.

REV 4-97

REF. # 1431-97-1197

# SUPPLEMENT REQUEST FORM

At the time this book was printed, a brief was included for every major case in the casebook and for every existing supplement to the casebook. However, if a new supplement to the casebook (or a new edition of the casebook) has been published since this publication was printed and if that casebook supplement (or new edition of the casebook) was available for sale at the time you purchased this Casenote Legal Briefs book, we will be pleased to provide you the new cases contained therein AT NO CHARGE when you send us a stamped, self-addressed envelope.

TO OBTAIN YOUR FREE SUPPLEMENT MATERIAL, **YOU MUST FOLLOW THE INSTRUCTIONS BELOW PRECISELY** OR YOUR REQUEST WILL NOT BE ACKNOWLEDGED!

1. Please check if there is in fact an existing supplement and, if so, that the cases are not already included in your Casenote Legal Briefs. Check the main table of cases as well as the supplement table of cases, if any.
2. **REMOVE THIS ENTIRE PAGE FROM THE BOOK.** You MUST send this ORIGINAL page to receive your supplement. This page acts as your proof of purchase and contains the reference number necessary to fill your supplement request properly. No photocopy of this page or written request will be honored or answered. Any request from which the reference number has been removed, altered or obliterated will not be honored.
3. ✶ Prepare a STAMPED self-addressed envelope for return mailing. Be sure to use a FULL SIZE (9 X 12) ENVELOPE (MANILA TYPE) so that the supplement will fit and AFFIX ENOUGH POSTAGE TO COVER 3 OZ. **ANY SUPPLEMENT REQUEST NOT ACCOMPANIED BY A STAMPED SELF-ADDRESSED ENVELOPE WILL ABSOLUTELY NOT BE FILLED OR ACKNOWLEDGED.**
4. MULTIPLE SUPPLEMENT REQUESTS: If you are ordering more than one supplement, we suggest that you enclose a stamped, self-addressed envelope for each supplement requested. If you enclose only one envelope for a multiple request, your order may not be filled immediately should any supplement which you requested still be in production. In other words, your order will be held by us until it can be filled completely.
5. Casenotes prints two kinds of supplements. A "New Edition" supplement is issued when a new edition of your casebook is published. A "New Edition" supplement gives you all major cases found in the new edition of the casebook which did not appear in the previous edition. A regular "supplement" is issued when a paperback supplement to your casebook is published. If the box at the lower right is stamped, then the "New Edition" supplement was provided to your bookstore and is *not* available from Casenotes; however, Casenotes will still send you any regular "supplements" which have been printed either before or after the new edition of your casebook appeared and which, according to the reference number at the top of this page, have not been included in this book. If the box is not stamped, Casenotes will send you any supplements, "New Edition" and/or regular, needed to completely update your Casenote Legal Briefs.

✶☞ ***NOTE:*** **REQUESTS FOR SUPPLEMENTS WILL NOT BE FILLED UNLESS THESE INSTRUCTIONS ARE COMPLIED WITH!**

6. Fill in the following information:

Full title of CASEBOOK **PRODUCTS LIABILITY**

CASEBOOK author's name **Owen, Keeton and Montgomery**

Copyright year of new edition or new paperback supplement ____

Name and location of bookstore where this Casenote Legal Brief was purchased ____

Name and location of law school you attend ____

Any comments regarding Casenote Legal Briefs ____

NOTE: IF THIS BOX IS STAMPED, NO NEW EDITION SUPPLEMENT CAN BE OBTAINED BY MAIL.

PUBLISHED BY **CASENOTES PUBLISHING CO., INC. 1640 5th ST, SUITE 208 SANTA MONICA, CA 90401**

**PLEASE PRINT**

**NAME** ____ **PHONE** ____ **DATE** ____

**ADDRESS/CITY/STATE/ZIP** ____

## A GLOSSARY OF COMMON LATIN WORDS AND PHRASES ENCOUNTERED IN THE LAW

**A FORTIORI:** Because one fact exists or has been proven, therefore a second fact that is related to the first fact must also exist.

**A PRIORI:** From the cause to the effect. A term of logic used to denote that when one generally accepted truth is shown to be a cause, another particular effect must necessarily follow.

**AB INITIO:** From the beginning; a condition which has existed throughout, as in a marriage which was void ab initio.

**ACTUS REUS:** The wrongful act; in criminal law, such action sufficient to trigger criminal liability.

**AD VALOREM:** According to value; an ad valorem tax is imposed upon an item located within the taxing jurisdiction calculated by the value of such item.

**AMICUS CURIAE:** Friend of the court. Its most common usage takes the form of an amicus curiae brief, filed by a person who is not a party to an action but is nonetheless allowed to offer an argument supporting his legal interests.

**ARGUENDO:** In arguing. A statement, possibly hypothetical, made for the purpose of argument, is one made arguendo.

**BILL QUIA TIMET:** A bill to quiet title (establish ownership) to real property.

**BONA FIDE:** True, honest, or genuine. May refer to a person's legal position based on good faith or lacking notice of fraud (such as a bona fide purchaser for value) or to the authenticity of a particular document (such as a bona fide last will and testament).

**CAUSA MORTIS:** With approaching death in mind. A gift causa mortis is a gift given by a party who feels certain that death is imminent.

**CAVEAT EMPTOR:** Let the buyer beware. This maxim is reflected in the rule of law that a buyer purchases at his own risk because it is his responsibility to examine, judge, test, and otherwise inspect what he is buying.

**CERTIORARI:** A writ of review. Petitions for review of a case by the United States Supreme Court are most often done by means of a writ of certiorari.

**CONTRA:** On the other hand. Opposite. Contrary to.

**CORAM NOBIS:** Before us; writs of error directed to the court that originally rendered the judgment.

**CORAM VOBIS:** Before you; writs of error directed by an appellate court to a lower court to correct a factual error.

**CORPUS DELICTI:** The body of the crime; the requisite elements of a crime amounting to objective proof that a crime has been committed.

**CUM TESTAMENTO ANNEXO, ADMINISTRATOR (ADMINISTRATOR C.T.A.):** With will annexed; an administrator c.t.a. settles an estate pursuant to a will in which he is not appointed.

**DE BONIS NON, ADMINISTRATOR (ADMINISTRATOR D.B.N.):** Of goods not administered; an administrator d.b.n. settles a partially settled estate.

**DE FACTO:** In fact; in reality; actually. Existing in fact but not officially approved or engendered.

**DE JURE:** By right; lawful. Describes a condition that is legitimate "as a matter of law," in contrast to the term "de facto," which connotes something existing in fact but not legally sanctioned or authorized. For example, de facto segregation refers to segregation brought about by housing patterns, etc., whereas de jure segregation refers to segregation created by law.

**DE MINIMUS:** Of minimal importance; insignificant; a trifle; not worth bothering about.

**DE NOVO:** Anew; a second time; afresh. A trial de novo is a new trial held at the appellate level as if the case originated there and the trial at a lower level had not taken place.

**DICTA:** Generally used as an abbreviated form of obiter dicta, a term describing those portions of a judicial opinion incidental or not necessary to resolution of the specific question before the court. Such nonessential statements and remarks are not considered to be binding precedent.

**DUCES TECUM:** Refers to a particular type of writ or subpoena requesting a party or organization to produce certain documents in their possession.

**EN BANC:** Full bench. Where a court sits with all justices present rather than the usual quorum.

**EX PARTE:** For one side or one party only. An ex parte proceeding is one undertaken for the benefit of only one party, without notice to, or an appearance by, an adverse party.

**EX POST FACTO:** After the fact. An ex post facto law is a law that retroactively changes the consequences of a prior act.

**EX REL.:** Abbreviated form of the term ex relatione, meaning, upon relation or information. When the state brings an action in which it has no interest against an individual at the instigation of one who has a private interest in the matter.

**FORUM NON CONVENIENS:** Inconvenient forum. Although a court may have jurisdiction over the case, the action should be tried in a more conveniently located court, one to which parties and witnesses may more easily travel, for example.

**GUARDIAN AD LITEM:** A guardian of an infant as to litigation, appointed to represent the infant and pursue his/her rights.

**HABEAS CORPUS:** You have the body. The modern writ of habeas corpus is a writ directing that a person (body) being detained (such as a prisoner) be brought before the court so that the legality of his detention can be judicially ascertained.

**IN CAMERA:** In private, in chambers. When a hearing is held before a judge in his chambers or when all spectators are excluded from the courtroom.

**IN FORMA PAUPERIS:** In the manner of a pauper. A party who proceeds in forma pauperis because of his poverty is one who is allowed to bring suit without liability for costs.

**INFRA:** Below, under. A word referring the reader to a later part of a book. (The opposite of supra.)

**IN LOCO PARENTIS:** In the place of a parent.

**IN PARI DELICTO:** Equally wrong; a court of equity will not grant requested relief to an applicant who is in pari delicto, or as much at fault in the transactions giving rise to the controversy as is the opponent of the applicant.

**IN PARI MATERIA:** On like subject matter or upon the same matter. Statutes relating to the same person or things are said to be in pari materia. It is a general rule of statutory construction that such statutes should be construed together, i.e., looked at as if they together constituted one law.

**IN PERSONAM:** Against the person. Jurisdiction over the person of an individual.

**IN RE:** In the matter of. Used to designate a proceeding involving an estate or other property.

**IN REM:** A term that signifies an action against the res, or thing. An action in rem is basically one that is taken directly against property, as distinguished from an action in personam, i.e., against the person.

**INTER ALIA:** Among other things. Used to show that the whole of a statement, pleading, list, statute, etc., has not been set forth in its entirety.

**INTER PARTES:** Between the parties. May refer to contracts, conveyances or other transactions having legal significance.

**INTER VIVOS:** Between the living. An inter vivos gift is a gift made by a living grantor, as distinguished from bequests contained in a will, which pass upon the death of the testator.

**IPSO FACTO:** By the mere fact itself.

**JUS:** Law or the entire body of law.

**LEX LOCI:** The law of the place; the notion that the rights of parties to a legal proceeding are governed by the law of the place where those rights arose.

**MALUM IN SE:** Evil or wrong in and of itself; inherently wrong. This term describes an act that is wrong by its very nature, as opposed to one which would not be wrong but for the fact that there is a specific legal prohibition against it (malum prohibitum).

**MALUM PROHIBITUM:** Wrong because prohibited, but not inherently evil. Used to describe something that is wrong because it is expressly forbidden by law but that is not in and of itself evil, e.g., speeding.

**MANDAMUS:** We command. A writ directing an official to take a certain action.

**MENS REA:** A guilty mind; a criminal intent. A term used to signify the mental state that accompanies a crime or other prohibited act. Some crimes require only a general mens rea (general intent to do the prohibited act), but others, like assault with intent to murder, require the existence of a specific mens rea.

**MODUS OPERANDI:** Method of operating; generally refers to the manner or style of a criminal in committing crimes, admissible in appropriate cases as evidence of the identity of a defendant.

**NEXUS:** A connection to.

**NISI PRIUS:** A court of first impression. A nisi prius court is one where issues of fact are tried before a judge or jury.

**N.O.V. (NON OBSTANTE VEREDICTO):** Notwithstanding the verdict. A judgment n.o.v. is a judgment given in favor of one party despite the fact that a verdict was returned in favor of the other party, the justification being that the verdict either had no reasonable support in fact or was contrary to law.

**NUNC PRO TUNC:** Now for then. This phrase refers to actions that may be taken and will then have full retroactive effect.

**PENDENTE LITE:** Pending the suit; pending litigation underway.

**PER CAPITA:** By head; beneficiaries of an estate, if they take in equal shares, take per capita.

**PER CURIAM:** By the court; signifies an opinion ostensibly written "by the whole court" and with no identified author.

**PER SE:** By itself, in itself; inherently.

**PER STIRPES:** By representation. Used primarily in the law of wills to describe the method of distribution where a person, generally because of death, is unable to take that which is left to him by the will of another, and therefore his heirs divide such property between them rather than take under the will individually.

**PRIMA FACIE:** On its face, at first sight. A prima facie case is one that is sufficient on its face, meaning that the evidence supporting it is adequate to establish the case until contradicted or overcome by other evidence.

**PRO TANTO:** For so much; as far as it goes. Often used in eminent domain cases when a property owner receives partial payment for his land without prejudice to his right to bring suit for the full amount he claims his land to be worth.

**QUANTUM MERUIT:** As much as he deserves. Refers to recovery based on the doctrine of unjust enrichment in those cases in which a party has rendered valuable services or furnished materials that were accepted and enjoyed by another under circumstances that would reasonably notify the recipient that the rendering party expected to be paid. In essence, the law implies a contract to pay the reasonable value of the services or materials furnished.

**QUASI:** Almost like; as if; nearly. This term is essentially used to signify that one subject or thing is almost analogous to another but that material differences between them do exist. For example, a quasi-criminal proceeding is one that is not strictly criminal but shares enough of the same characteristics to require some of the same safeguards (e.g., procedural due process must be followed in a parol hearing).

**QUID PRO QUO:** Something for something. In contract law, the consideration, something of value, passed between the parties to render the contract binding.

**RES GESTAE:** Things done; in evidence law, this principle justifies the admission of a statement that would otherwise be hearsay when it is made so closely to the event in question as to be said to be a part of it, or with such spontaneity as not to have the possibility of falsehood.

**RES IPSA LOQUITUR:** The thing speaks for itself. This doctrine gives rise to a rebuttable presumption of negligence when the instrumentality causing the injury was within the exclusive control of the defendant, and the injury was one that does not normally occur unless a person has been negligent.

**RES JUDICATA:** A matter adjudged. Doctrine which provides that once a court of competent jurisdiction has rendered a final judgment or decree on the merits, that judgment or decree is conclusive upon the parties to the case and prevents them from engaging in any other litigation on the points and issues determined therein.

**RESPONDEAT SUPERIOR:** Let the master reply. This doctrine holds the master liable for the wrongful acts of his servant (or the principal for his agent) in those cases in which the servant (or agent) was acting within the scope of his authority at the time of the injury.

**STARE DECISIS:** To stand by or adhere to that which has been decided. The common law doctrine of stare decisis attempts to give security and certainty to the law by following the policy that once a principle of law as applicable to a certain set of facts has been set forth in a decision, it forms a precedent which will subsequently be followed, even though a different decision might be made were it the first time the question had arisen. Of course, stare decisis is not an inviolable principle and is departed from in instances where there is good cause (e.g., considerations of public policy led the Supreme Court to disregard prior decisions sanctioning segregation).

**SUPRA:** Above. A word referring a reader to an earlier part of a book.

**ULTRA VIRES:** Beyond the power. This phrase is most commonly used to refer to actions taken by a corporation that are beyond the power or legal authority of the corporation.

## ADDENDUM OF FRENCH DERIVATIVES

**IN PAIS:** Not pursuant to legal proceedings.

**CHATTEL:** Tangible personal property.

**CY PRES:** Doctrine permitting courts to apply trust funds to purposes not expressed in the trust but necessary to carry out the settlor's intent.

**PER AUTRE VIE:** For another's life; in property law, an estate may be granted that will terminate upon the death of someone other than the grantee.

**PROFIT A PRENDRE:** A license to remove minerals or other produce from land.

**VOIR DIRE:** Process of questioning jurors as to their predispositions about the case or parties to a proceeding in order to identify those jurors displaying bias or prejudice.

# LAW OUTLINES from CASENOTE™

# *the Ultimate Outline*

- ***WRITTEN BY NATIONALLY RECOGNIZED AUTHORITIES IN THEIR FIELD.***
- ***FEATURING A FLEXIBLE, SUBJECT-ORIENTED APPROACH.***
- ***CONTAINS: TABLE OF CONTENTS; CAPSULE OUTLINE; FULL OUTLINE; EXAM PREPARATION; GLOSSARY; TABLE OF CASES; TABLE OF AUTHORITIES; CASEBOOK CROSS REFERENCE CHART; INDEX.***
- ***THE TOTAL LAW SUMMARY UTILIZING THE MOST COMPREHENSIVE STUDY APPROACH IN THE MOST EFFECTIVE, EASY-TO-READ FORMAT.***

| REF # | SUBJECT | AUTHORS | RETAIL PRICE |
|---|---|---|---|
| | | | (effective 7/1/97) |
| #5260 | **ADMINISTRATIVE LAW** | by **Charles H. Koch, Jr.,** Dudley W. Woodbridge Professor of Law, College of William and Mary. **Sidney A. Shapiro,** John M. Rounds Professor of Law, University of Kansas. (1996) | **$19.95** |
| #5040 | **CIVIL PROCEDURE** | by **John B. Oakley,** Professor of Law, University of California, Davis. **Rex R. Perschbacher,** Professor of Law & Associate Dean, Academic Affairs, University of California, Davis. (1996) | **$20.95** |
| | **COMMERCIAL LAW** | (*see* **5700 SALES ● 5710 SECURED TRANS. ● 5720 NEG. INSTRUMENTS & PMT. SYST.**) | |
| #5070 | **CONFLICT OF LAWS** | by **Luther L. McDougal, III,** W.R. Irby Professor of Law, Tulane University. **Robert L. Felix,** James P. Mozingo, III Prof. of Law, Univ. of S. Carolina. (1996) | **$19.95** |
| #5080 | **CONSTITUTIONAL LAW** | by **Gary Goodpaster,** Prof. of Law, Univ. of California, Davis. (1997 ) | **$21.95** |
| #5010 | **CONTRACTS** | by **Daniel Wm. Fessler,** Professor of Law, University of California, Davis. (1996) | **$19.95** |
| #5050 | **CORPORATIONS** AND ALTERNATIVE BUSINESS VEHICLES | by **Lewis D. Solomon,** Arthur Selwin Miller Research Prof. of Law, George Washington Univ. **Daniel Wm. Fessler,** Prof. of Law, University of California, Davis. **Arthur E. Wilmarth, Jr.,** Assoc. Prof. of Law, George Washington University. (1997) | **$21.95** |
| #5020 | **CRIMINAL LAW** | by **Joshua Dressler,** Professor of Law, McGeorge School of Law. (1996) | **$19.95** |
| #5200 | **CRIMINAL PROCEDURE** | by **Joshua Dressler,** Prof. of Law, McGeorge School of Law. (1997) | **$18.95** |
| #5800 | **ESTATE & GIFT TAX** INCLUDING THE FEDERAL GENERATION-SKIPPING TAX | by **Joseph M. Dodge,** W.H. Francis Prof. of Law, University of Texas at Austin. (1993) | **$19.95** |
| #5060 | **EVIDENCE** | by **Kenneth Graham, Jr.,** Professor of Law, University of California, Los Angeles. (1996) | **$21.95** |
| #5400 | **FEDERAL COURTS** | by **Howard P. Fink,** Isadore and Ida Topper Prof. of Law, Ohio State University. **Linda S. Mullenix,** Bernard J. Ward Centennial Prof. of Law, Univ. of Texas. (1997) | **$20.95** |
| #5210 | **FEDERAL INCOME TAXATION** | by **Joseph M. Dodge,** W.H. Francis Professor of Law, University of Texas at Austin (1994). | **$20.95** |
| #5300 | **LEGAL RESEARCH** | by **Nancy L. Schultz,** Associate Professor of Law, Chapman University. **Louis J. Sirico, Jr.,** Professor of Law, Villanova University. (1996) | **$19.95** |
| #5720 | **NEGOTIABLE INST. & PMT. SYST.** | by **Donald B. King,** Professor of Law, Saint Louis University **Peter Winship,** James Cleo Thompson, Sr. Trustee Prof., SMU. (1995) | **$20.95** |
| #5030 | **PROPERTY** | by **Sheldon F. Kurtz,** Percy Bordwell Professor of Law, University of Iowa, and **Patricia Cain,** Professor of Law, University of Iowa | **$20.95** |
| #5700 | **SALES** | by **Robert E. Scott,** Dean and Lewis F. Powell, Jr. Professor of Law, University of Virginia. **Donald B. King,** Professor of Law, Saint Louis University. (1992 w/'96 supp.) | **$19.95** |
| #5710 | **SECURED TRANSACTIONS** | by **Donald B. King,** Professor of Law, Saint Louis University. (1995 w/'96 supp.) | **$18.95** |
| #5000 | **TORTS** | by **George C. Christie,** James B. Duke Professor of Law, Duke University. **Jerry J. Phillips,** W.P. Toms Professor of Law & Chair, Committee on Admissions, University of Tennessee. (1996) | **$20.95** |
| #5220 | **WILLS, TRUSTS & ESTATES** | by **William M. McGovern,** Professor of Law, University of California, Los Angeles. (1996) | **$20.95** |

rev. 2/1/97

# CASENOTE™ LEGAL BRIEFS

*PRICE LIST — EFFECTIVE JULY 1, 1997 • PRICES SUBJECT TO CHANGE WITHOUT NOTICE*

| Ref. No. | Course | Adaptable to Courses Utilizing | Retail Price |
|---|---|---|---|
| 1265 | ADMINISTRATIVE LAW | BONFIELD & ASIMOV | 17.00 |
| 1263 | ADMINISTRATIVE LAW | BREYER, STEWART & SUNSTEIN | 19.00 |
| 1266 | ADMINISTRATIVE LAW | CASS, DIVER & BEERMAN | 17.00 |
| 1260 | ADMINISTRATIVE LAW | GELLHORN, B., S., R., S. & F. | 17.00 |
| 1264 | ADMINISTRATIVE LAW | MASHAW, MERRILL & SHANE | 18.50 |
| 1267 | ADMINISTRATIVE LAW | REESE | 17.00 |
| 1262 | ADMINISTRATIVE LAW | SCHWARTZ | 18.00 |
| 1290 | ADMIRALTY | HEALY & SHARPE | 21.00 |
| 1350 | AGENCY & PARTNERSHIP (ENT.ORG) | CONARD, KNAUSS & SIEGEL | 21.00 |
| 1351 | AGENCY & PARTNERSHIP | HYNES | 20.00 |
| 1281 | ANTITRUST (TRADE REGULATION) | HANDLER, P., G., & W. | 17.50 |
| 1283 | ANTITRUST | SULLIVAN & HOVENKAMP | 18.00 |
| 1611 | BANKING LAW | MACEY & MILLER | 17.00 |
| 1303 | BANKRUPTCY (DEBTOR-CREDITOR) | EISENBERG | 19.00 |
| 1040 | CIVIL PROCEDURE | COUND, F., M. & S | 20.00 |
| 1043 | CIVIL PROCEDURE | FIELD, KAPLAN & CLERMONT | 20.00 |
| 1041 | CIVIL PROCEDURE | HAZARD, TAIT & FLETCHER | 19.00 |
| 1047 | CIVIL PROCEDURE | MARCUS, REDISH & SHERMAN | 19.00 |
| 1044 | CIVIL PROCEDURE | ROSENBERG, S. & D. | 20.00 |
| 1046 | CIVIL PROCEDURE | YEAZELL | 17.00 |
| 1311 | COMM'L LAW | FARNSWORTH, H., R., H. & M. | 19.00 |
| 1312 | COMM'L LAW | JORDAN & WARREN | 19.00 |
| 1310 | COMM'L LAW (SALES/SEC.TR./PAY.LAW [Sys.]) | SPEIDEL, SUMMERS & WHITE | 22.00 |
| 1313 | COMM'L LAW (SALES/SEC.TR./PAY.LAW) | WHALEY | 19.00 |
| 1320 | COMMUNITY PROPERTY | BIRD | 17.50 |
| 1630 | COMPARATIVE LAW | SCHLESINGER, B., D., & H. | 16.00 |
| 1048 | COMPLEX LITIGATION | MARCUS & SHERMAN | 17.00 |
| 1072 | CONFLICTS | BRILMAYER | 17.00 |
| 1071 | CONFLICTS | CRAMTON, C. K., & K. | 17.00 |
| 1070 | CONFLICTS | ROSENBERG, HAY & W. | 20.00 |
| 1086 | CONSTITUTIONAL LAW | BREST & LEVINSON | 18.00 |
| 1082 | CONSTITUTIONAL LAW | COHEN & VARAT | 21.00 |
| 1088 | CONSTITUTIONAL LAW | FARBER, ESKRIDGE & FRICKEY | 18.00 |
| 1080 | CONSTITUTIONAL LAW | GUNTHER & SULLIVAN | 20.00 |
| 1081 | CONSTITUTIONAL LAW | LOCKHART, K., C., S. & F. | 18.00 |
| 1085 | CONSTITUTIONAL LAW | ROTUNDA | 20.00 |
| 1087 | CONSTITUTIONAL LAW | STONE, S., S. & T. | 19.00 |
| 1102 | CONTRACTS | BURTON | 20.00 |
| 1017 | CONTRACTS | CALAMARI, PERILLO & BENDER | 23.00 |
| 1101 | CONTRACTS | CRANDALL & WHALEY | 20.00 |
| 1014 | CONTRACTS | DAWSON, HARVEY & H. | 19.00 |
| 1010 | CONTRACTS | FARNSWORTH & YOUNG | 18.00 |
| 1011 | CONTRACTS | FULLER & EISENBERG | 20.00 |
| 1100 | CONTRACTS | HAMILTON, RAU & WEINTRAUB | 19.00 |
| 1013 | CONTRACTS | KESSLER, GILMORE & KRONMAN | 23.00 |
| 1016 | CONTRACTS | KNAPP & CRYSTAL | 20.50 |
| 1012 | CONTRACTS | MURPHY & SPEIDEL | 22.00 |
| 1018 | CONTRACTS | MURRAY | 22.00 |
| 1015 | CONTRACTS | ROSETT | 21.00 |
| 1019 | CONTRACTS | VERNON | 20.00 |
| 1502 | COPYRIGHT | GOLDSTEIN | 18.00 |
| 1501 | COPYRIGHT | NIMMER, M., M., & N. | 19.50 |
| 1218 | CORPORATE TAXATION | LIND, S. L. & R | 14.00 |
| 1050 | CORPORATIONS | CARY & EISENBERG | 19.00 |
| 1054 | CORPORATIONS | CHOPER,COFFEE, & GILSON | 21.50 |
| 1350 | CORPORATIONS (ENTERPRISE ORG.) | CONARD, KNAUSS & SIEGEL | 21.00 |
| 1053 | CORPORATIONS | HAMILTON | 19.00 |
| 1057 | CORPORATIONS | O'KELLEY & THOMPSON | 18.00 |
| 1056 | CORPORATIONS | SOLOMON, S., B., & W. | 19.00 |
| 1052 | CORPORATIONS | VAGTS | 17.00 |
| 1300 | CREDITOR'S RIGHTS (DEBTOR-CREDITOR) | RIESENFELD | 21.00 |
| 1550 | CRIMINAL JUSTICE | WEINREB | 18.00 |
| 1029 | CRIMINAL LAW | BONNIE, C., J., & L. | 17.00 |
| 1020 | CRIMINAL LAW | BOYCE & PERKINS | 22.00 |
| 1028 | CRIMINAL LAW | DRESSLER | 21.00 |
| 1027 | CRIMINAL LAW | JOHNSON | 20.00 |
| 1021 | CRIMINAL LAW | KADISH & SCHULHOFER | 19.00 |
| 1026 | CRIMINAL LAW | KAPLAN, WEISBERG & BINDER | 18.00 |
| 1023 | CRIMINAL LAW | LAFAVE | 19.00 |
| 1205 | CRIMINAL PROCEDURE | ALLEN, KUHNS & STUNTZ | 17.00 |
| 1202 | CRIMINAL PROCEDURE | HADDAD, Z., S. & B. | 20.00 |
| 1200 | CRIMINAL PROCEDURE | KAMISAR, LAFAVE & ISRAEL | 19.00 |
| 1204 | CRIMINAL PROCEDURE | SALTZBURG & CAPRA | 17.00 |
| 1203 | CRIMINAL PROCEDURE (PROCESS) | WEINREB | 18.50 |
| 1303 | DEBTOR-CREDITOR | EISENBERG | 19.00 |
| 1300 | DEBTOR-CREDITOR (CRED. RTS.) | RIESENFELD | 21.00 |
| 1304 | DEBTOR-CREDITOR | WARREN & WESTBROOK | 19.00 |
| 1224 | DECEDENTS ESTATES | RITCHIE, ALFORD, EFFLAND & D. | 21.00 |
| 1222 | DECEDENTS ESTATES | SCOLES & HALBACH | 21.50 |
| 1231 | DECEDENTS ESTATES (TRUSTS) | WAGGONER, A. & F. | 20.00 |
| | DOMESTIC RELATIONS (*see* FAMILY LAW) | | |
| 3000 | EDUCATION LAW (COURSE OUTLINE) | AQUILA & PETZKE | 25.50 |
| 1670 | EMPLOYMENT DISCRIMINATION | FRIEDMAN & STRICKLER | 17.00 |
| 1671 | EMPLOYMENT DISCRIMINATION | ZIMMER, SULLIVAN, R. & C. | 18.00 |
| 1660 | EMPLOYMENT LAW | ROTHSTEIN, KNAPP & LIEBMAN | 19.50 |
| 1350 | ENTERPRISE ORGANIZATION | CONARD, KNAUSS & SIEGEL | 21.00 |
| 1342 | ENVIRONMENTAL LAW | ANDERSON, MANDELKER & T. | 16.00 |
| 1341 | ENVIRONMENTAL LAW | FINDLEY & FARBER | 18.00 |
| 1345 | ENVIRONMENTAL LAW | MENELL & STEWART | 17.00 |
| 1344 | ENVIRONMENTAL LAW | PERCIVAL, MILLER, S. & L. | 18.00 |
| 1343 | ENVIRONMENTAL LAW | PLATER, ABRAMS & GOLDFARB | 17.00 |
| | EQUITY (*see* REMEDIES) | | |
| 1217 | ESTATE & GIFT TAXATION | BITTKER, CLARK & McCOUCH | 15.00 |
| | ETHICS (*see* PROFESSIONAL RESPONSIBILITY) | | |
| 1065 | EVIDENCE | GREEN & NESSON | 20.00 |
| 1066 | EVIDENCE | MUELLER & KIRKPATRICK | 17.00 |
| 1064 | EVIDENCE | STRONG, BROUN & M. | 22.50 |
| 1062 | EVIDENCE | SUTTON & WELLBORN | 22.00 |
| 1061 | EVIDENCE | WALTZ & PARK | 20.00 |
| 1060 | EVIDENCE | WEINSTEIN, M., A. & B. | 22.50 |
| 1244 | FAMILY LAW (DOMESTIC RELATIONS) | AREEN | 22.00 |
| 1242 | FAMILY LAW (DOMESTIC RELATIONS) | CLARK & GLOWINSKY | 19.00 |
| 1245 | FAMILY LAW (DOMESTIC RELATIONS) | ELLMAN, KURTZ & BARTLETT | 20.00 |
| 1243 | FAMILY LAW (DOMESTIC RELATIONS) | KRAUSE | 24.00 |
| 1240 | FAMILY LAW (DOMESTIC RELATIONS) | WADLINGTON | 20.00 |
| 1231 | FAMILY PROPERTY LAW (WILLS/TRUSTS) | WAGGONER, A. & F. | 20.00 |
| 1362 | FEDERAL COURTS | CURRIE | 17.00 |
| 1360 | FEDERAL COURTS | FALLON, M. & S. (HART & W.) | 19.00 |
| 1360 | FEDERAL COURTS | HART & WECHSLER (FALLON) | 19.00 |
| 1363 | FEDERAL COURTS | LOW & JEFFRIES | 16.00 |
| 1361 | FEDERAL COURTS | McCORMICK, C. & W. | 20.00 |
| 1364 | FEDERAL COURTS | REDISH & NICHOL | 17.00 |
| 1510 | GRATUITOUS TRANSFERS | CLARK, LUSKY & MURPHY | 18.00 |
| 1650 | HEALTH LAW | FURROW, J., J., & S. | 17.50 |
| 1640 | IMMIGRATION LAW | ALEINIKOFF, MARTIN & M. | 16.00 |
| 1641 | IMMIGRATION LAW | LEGOMSKY | 18.00 |
| 1371 | INSURANCE LAW | KEETON | 21.00 |
| 1372 | INSURANCE LAW | YORK, WHELAN & MARTINEZ | 19.00 |
| 1370 | INSURANCE LAW | YOUNG & HOLMES | 17.00 |
| 1394 | INTERNATIONAL BUSINESS TRANSACTIONS | FOLSOM, GORDON & SPANOGLE | 15.00 |
| 1393 | INTERNATIONAL LAW | CARTER & TRIMBLE | 16.00 |
| 1392 | INTERNATIONAL LAW | HENKIN, P., S. & S. | 17.00 |
| 1390 | INTERNATIONAL LAW | OLIVER, F., B., S., & W. | 22.00 |
| 1331 | LABOR LAW | COX, BOK, GORMAN & FINKIN | 19.00 |
| 1332 | LABOR LAW | HARPER & ESTREICHER | 20.00 |
| 1333 | LABOR LAW | LESLIE | 18.50 |
| 1330 | LABOR LAW | MERRIFIELD, S. & C. | 19.00 |
| 1471 | LAND FINANCE (REAL ESTATE TRANS) | BERGER & JOHNSTONE | 18.00 |
| 1620 | LAND FINANCE (REAL ESTATE TRANS) | NELSON & WHITMAN | 19.00 |
| 1452 | LAND USE | CALLIES, FREILICH & ROBERTS | 17.00 |
| 1450 | LAND USE | WRIGHT & GITELMAN | 23.00 |
| 1421 | LEGISLATION | ESKRIDGE & FRICKEY | 15.00 |
| 1480 | MASS MEDIA | FRANKLIN & ANDERSON | 15.00 |
| 1312 | NEGOTIABLE INSTRUMENTS (COMM. LAW) | JORDAN & WARREN | 19.00 |
| 1313 | NEGOTIABLE INSTRUMENTS (COMM. LAW) | WHALEY | 18.00 |
| 1541 | OIL & GAS | KUNTZ, L., A. & S. | 18.00 |
| 1540 | OIL & GAS | MAXWELL, WILLIAMS, M. & K. | 18.00 |
| 1560 | PATENT LAW | FRANCIS & COLLINS | 23.00 |
| 1310 | PAYMENT LAW [SYST.][COMM. LAW] | SPEIDEL, SUMMERS & WHITE | 22.00 |
| 1313 | PAYMENT LAW (COMM.LAW / NEG. INST.) | WHALEY | 19.00 |
| 1431 | PRODUCTS LIABILITY | OWEN, MONTGOMERY & K. | 20.00 |
| 1091 | PROF. RESPONSIBILITY (ETHICS) | GILLERS | 13.00 |
| 1093 | PROF. RESPONSIBILITY (ETHICS) | HAZARD, KONIAK, & CRAMTON | 18.00 |
| 1092 | PROF. RESPONSIBILITY (ETHICS) | MORGAN & ROTUNDA | 13.00 |
| 1030 | PROPERTY | CASNER & LEACH | 21.00 |
| 1031 | PROPERTY | CRIBBET, J., F. & S. | 21.50 |
| 1037 | PROPERTY | DONAHUE, KAUPER & MARTIN | 18.00 |
| 1035 | PROPERTY | DUKEMINIER & KRIER | 18.00 |
| 1034 | PROPERTY | HAAR & LIEBMAN | 20.50 |
| 1036 | PROPERTY | KURTZ & HOVENKAMP | 19.00 |
| 1033 | PROPERTY | NELSON, STOEBUCK, & W. | 20.50 |
| 1032 | PROPERTY | RABIN & KWALL | 20.00 |
| 1038 | PROPERTY | SINGER | 18.50 |
| 1621 | REAL ESTATE TRANSACTIONS | GOLDSTEIN & KORNGOLD | 18.00 |
| 1471 | REAL ESTATE TRANS. & FIN. (LAND FINANCE) | BERGER & JOHNSTONE | 18.00 |
| 1620 | REAL ESTATE TRANSFER & FINANCE | NELSON & WHITMAN | 18.00 |
| 1254 | REMEDIES (EQUITY) | LAYCOCK | 20.00 |
| 1253 | REMEDIES (EQUITY) | LEAVELL, L., N. & K/F. | 21.00 |
| 1252 | REMEDIES (EQUITY) | RE & RE | 23.00 |
| 1255 | REMEDIES (EQUITY) | SHOBEN & TABB | 22.50 |
| 1250 | REMEDIES (EQUITY) | YORK, BAUMAN & RENDLEMAN | 25.00 |
| 1312 | SALES (COMM. LAW) | JORDAN & WARREN | 19.00 |
| 1310 | SALES (COMM. LAW) | SPEIDEL, SUMMERS & WHITE | 22.00 |
| 1313 | SALES (COMM. LAW) | WHALEY | 19.00 |
| 1312 | SECURED TRANS. (COMM. LAW) | JORDAN & WARREN | 19.00 |
| 1310 | SECURED TRANS. | SPEIDEL, SUMMERS & WHITE | 22.00 |
| 1313 | SECURED TRANS. (COMM. LAW) | WHALEY | 19.00 |
| 1272 | SECURITIES REGULATION | COX, HILLMAN, LANGEVOORT | 18.00 |
| 1270 | SECURITIES REGULATION | JENNINGS, MARSH & COFFEE | 18.00 |
| 1680 | SPORTS LAW | WEILER & ROBERTS | 17.50 |
| 1217 | TAXATION (ESTATE & GIFT) | BITTKER, CLARK & McCOUCH | 15.00 |
| 1219 | TAXATION (INDIV. INC.) | BURKE & FRIEL | 19.00 |
| 1212 | TAXATION (FED. INC.) | FREELAND, LIND & STEPHENS | 18.00 |
| 1211 | TAXATION (FED. INC.) | GRAETZ & SCHENK | 17.00 |
| 1210 | TAXATION (FED. INC.) | KLEIN & BANKMAN | 18.00 |
| 1218 | TAXATION (CORPORATE) | LIND, S., L. & R. | 14.00 |
| 1006 | TORTS | DOBBS | 19.00 |
| 1003 | TORTS | EPSTEIN | 20.50 |
| 1004 | TORTS | FRANKLIN & RABIN | 17.50 |
| 1001 | TORTS | HENDERSON, P. & S. | 20.50 |
| 1000 | TORTS | PROSSER, W., S., K., & P. | 24.00 |
| 1005 | TORTS | SHULMAN, JAMES & GRAY | 22.00 |
| 1281 | TRADE REGULATION (ANTITRUST) | HANDLER, P., G., & W. | 17.50 |
| 1230 | TRUSTS | BOGERT, O., H., & H. | 20.50 |
| 1231 | TRUSTS/WILLS (FAMILY PROPERTY LAW) | WAGGONER, A. & F. | 20.00 |
| 1410 | U.C.C | EPSTEIN, MARTIN, H. & N. | 15.00 |
| 1223 | WILLS, TRUSTS & ESTATES | DUKEMINIER & JOHANSON | 19.00 |
| 1220 | WILLS | MECHEM & ATKINSON | 20.00 |
| 1231 | WILLS/TRUSTS (FAMILY PROPERTY LAW) | WAGGONER, A. & F. | 20.00 |

(SERIES XL)

**CASENOTES PUBLISHING CO. INC. ● 1640 FIFTH STREET, SUITE 208 ● SANTA MONICA, CA 90401 ● (310) 395-6500**

E-Mail Address- casenote@westworld.com

Website-http://www.casenotes.com

**PLEASE PURCHASE FROM YOUR LOCAL BOOKSTORE. IF UNAVAILABLE, YOU MAY ORDER DIRECT.***

4TH CLASS POSTAGE (ALLOW TWO WEEKS) $1.00 PER ORDER; 1ST CLASS POSTAGE $3.00 (ONE BOOK), $2.00 EACH (TWO OR MORE BOOKS)

*CALIF. RESIDENTS PLEASE ADD 8¼% SALES TAX

# Notes

## TABLE OF CASES



Continued on next page

# Notes

## TABLE OF CASES (Continued)

# CHAPTER 1
# AN INTRODUCTION TO PRODUCTS LIABILITY AND SAFETY LAW

## QUICK REFERENCE RULES OF LAW

1. **The Judicial Response.** One who sells a product is strictly liable for injuries caused by its product if the product reaches the consumer without substantial change in the condition in which it is sold. (Agostino v. Rockwell Manufacturing Company)

# Notes

## AGOSTINO v. ROCKWELL MANUFACTURING CO.

236 Pa. Super. 434, 345 A.2d 735 (1975).

**NATURE OF CASE: Appeal from nonsuit in strict liability action.**

**FACT SUMMARY: Agostino (P) contended that he had established a prima facie violation of strict liability by showing that a saw which was manufactured by Rockwell (D) was in an unreasonably dangerous condition.**

**CONCISE RULE OF LAW: One who sells a product is strictly liable for injuries caused by its product if the product reaches the consumer without substantial change in the condition in which it is sold.**

**FACTS:** In November 1969, Agostino (P) purchased from Greensburg Lumber & Mill Company (D) a power saw manufactured by Rockwell (D). Agostino (P) was familiar with power saws since he had used them for approximately twenty years in various carpentry jobs. The Rockwell (D) saw that Agostino (P) had purchased was constructed so that after the completion of a cut, a telescopic guard would be automatically released from the housing, covering the blade and thereby preventing the user from being cut. On December 16, 1969, Agostino (P) plugged in the saw, checked the telescopic guard to make sure it was operating properly, and cut two boards. On the third cut, Agostino (P) finished severing the board, but as he attempted to put the saw on a bench the blade grabbed his trousers and cut deeply into his thigh. After dropping the saw on the floor, Agostino (P) noticed that the telescopic guard was not covering the blade but was jammed in the housing. Agostino (P) sued both Greensburg (D) and Rockwell (D) in strict tort liability and was nonsuited on the grounds that he had failed to state a cause of action. Agostino (P) appealed.

**ISSUE:** Is one who sells a product strictly liable for injuries caused by its product if the product reaches the consumer without substantial change in the condition in which it is sold?

**HOLDING AND DECISION:** (Spaeth, J.) Yes. One who sells a product is strictly liable for injuries caused by its product if the product reaches the consumer without substantial change in the condition in which it is sold. To prove a prima facie case, Agostino (P) had to show that the saw had a defect that was unreasonably dangerous to the user, that the defect existed when the saw left Rockwell's (D) plant, and that there was a causal connection between the defect and Agostino's (P) injury. Here, because a malfunction did not occur on the first or second cut does not mean it did not occur on the third. It would be unreasonable to bar recovery because Agostino (P) did not observe the location of the guard at the moment his leg was being lacerated. The jury could have properly inferred from Agostino's (P) testimony that the guard did not function properly. Since there was no evidence of abnormal use or secondary causes, the evidence was sufficient to establish a defective condition unreasonably dangerous to the user. Reversed and remanded.

**EDITOR'S ANALYSIS:** The holding in this case is consistent with § 402A of the Restatement (Second) of Torts. That section provides that: "One who sells any product in a defective condition unreasonably dangerous to the user or to his property is subject to liability for physical harm thereby caused to the ultimate user or consumer, or to his property, if (a) the seller is engaged in the business of selling such a product, and (b) it is expected to and does reach the user or consumer without substantial change in the condition in which it is sold."

**NOTES:**

# Notes

# CHAPTER 2
# NEGLIGENCE

## QUICK REFERENCE RULES OF LAW

1. **The Privacy Obstacle.** A manufacturer of a product which, if negligently constructed is reasonably certain to be dangerous to life, is liable to indirect retail purchasers for injuries caused by such negligent construction. (MacPherson v. Buick Motors Co.)

2. **The Manufacturing Process: Fabrication and Quality Control.** A jury may make a finding of negligence even though expert opinion differs regarding causation. (Jenkins v. General Motors Corp.)

3. **The Manufacturing Process: Fabrication and Quality Control.** A manufacturer has a duty to exercise reasonable care to prevent defective conditions caused by a miscarriage in the manufacturing process. (Ford Motor Co. v. Zahn)

4. **The Design Process: The Product Concept.** Courts should not decide as a matter of law that a product's utility outweighs its risk if the product presents a realistic risk of danger in its use. (Metzgar v. Playskool, Inc.)

5. **The Marketing Process: Warnings and Instructions.** A manufacturer of dangerous products must provide warnings for all incidental and attendant uses. (Boyl v. California Chemical Co.)

# Notes

## MacPHERSON v. BUICK MOTOR CO.

217 N.Y. 382, 111 N.E. 1050 (1916).

**NATURE OF CASE: Action for damages for negligence.**

**FACT SUMMARY: MacPherson (P), who purchased an automobile from a retail dealer who had acquired the car from Buick (D), was injured when a defective wheel gave way causing the car to collapse.**

**CONCISE RULE OF LAW: A manufacturer of a product which, if negligently constructed is reasonably certain to be dangerous to life, is liable to indirect retail purchasers for injuries caused by such negligent construction.**

**FACTS:** Buick (D) manufactured an automobile which it supplied to a retail dealer for resale to the public. The automobile was equipped with a wheel made of defective wood and was purchased by Buick (D) from another manufacturer. MacPherson (P) purchased the automobile from the dealer and while he was driving it, the wheel's spoke gave way, causing the car to collapse. MacPherson (P) sustained personal injuries from the incident and brought this action to recover in negligence therefor. The trial court granted an award of damages, and Buick (D) appealed.

**ISSUE:** Is a manufacturer of a product which, if negligently constructed is reasonably certain to be dangerous to life, liable to indirect retail purchasers for injuries caused by such negligent construction?

**HOLDING AND DECISION:** (Cardozo, J.) Yes. Buick (D) contended that its liability, if any, is limited to any damages due the immediate purchaser of its product. There is ample case law, however, that holds a manufacturer liable for injuries caused by its product to remote purchasers where, for example, poisons were mislabeled, and where a scaffold was dangerously defective. Buick (D) sought to limit the application of these cases to inherently dangerous products. That restriction is no longer meaningful. A manufacturer of a product which, if negligently constructed, is reasonably certain to be dangerous to life is liable to indirect retail purchasers for injuries caused by such negligent construction. A reasonable inspection would have revealed the defect in the wheel in this case, but the inspection was not conducted. This breach of duty gives rise to liability in negligence for MacPherson's (P) injuries. The more probable the danger, the greater the need for caution. Affirmed.

**EDITOR'S ANALYSIS:** This landmark case gives expression to law as it remains even today. Later developments in this area extended liability to users of the products who were not purchasers at all, and in appropriate cases, to bystanders as well. A duty to inspect a product encompasses a duty to inspect the component parts of such a product, and where liability attaches, it cannot be avoided by alleging purchase of a component from another manufacturer.

## JENKINS v. GENERAL MOTORS CORP.

446 F.2d 377 (5th Cir. 1971).

**NATURE OF CASE: Appeal from award of damages for negligence.**

**FACT SUMMARY: General Motors (D) contended that because experts differed as to the cause of in automobile accident in which Jenkins (P) was injured, there was insufficient evidence to submit the case to the jury.**

**CONCISE RULE OF LAW: A jury may make a finding of negligence even though expert opinion differs regarding causation.**

**FACTS:** Jenkins (P) was severely injured when the Corvair automobile in which she was a passenger suddenly veered off the road and landed in a ditch on April 15, 1962. Testimony of Jenkins' (P) witnesses, including the trooper who investigated the accident scene, established that there was no evidence of excessive speed, use of alcoholic beverages, or improper driving. Jenkins (P) and Billy Mixon, the only eyewitnesses to the occurrence, testified that they were driving along when the automobile suddenly veered to the left and became uncontrollable. Subsequently the brakes failed, and the car crashed. Jenkins (P) predicated her action against General Motors (D) on the grounds of negligent failure to properly tighten and inspect a nut on a bolt in the left rear suspension system. Expert opinion at trial differed as to whether the bolt had actually caused the accident, or conversely, had been a result of the accident. A jury returned a verdict for Jenkins (P), and General Motors (D) then brought this appeal arguing that there was insufficient evidence to submit the case to the jury.

**ISSUE:** May a jury make a finding of negligence even though expert opinion differs regarding causation?

**HOLDING AND DECISION:** (Ingraham, J.) Yes. A jury may make a finding of negligence even though expert opinion differs regarding causation. Here, there was conflicting expert testimony at trial regarding the issue of whether the nut on the bolt had failed and caused the accident. The jury was allowed to inspect and even handle the various components of the rear suspension assembly involved, including the bolt and its assembly. The jury was not bound by the evidence introduced by General Motors (D) nor was it forced to accept the testimony of its experts, even if uncontradicted. Thus, the contention of General Motors (D) that there was an absence of probative facts to support the conclusion reached by the jury must be rejected. Affirmed.

**EDITOR'S ANALYSIS:** As this case indicates, products liability cases are often extremely complex, requiring expert witnesses, photographs, exhibits, and films for the jury. The use of expert testimony is often crucial to winning a products liability case. Thus, most attorneys who regularly practice in this area seek expert witnesses who not only are knowledgeable, but also make credible and effective witnesses.

## FORD MOTOR CO. v. ZAHN

265 F.2d 729 (8th Cir. 1959).

**NATURE OF CASE: Appeal from denial of motion for judgment n.o.v. upon award of damages for negligence.**

**FACT SUMMARY: Ford (D) contended that it was not responsible for injuries suffered is a result of Zahn's (P) head striking the sharpened edge of an ashtray.**

**CONCISE RULE OF LAW: A manufacturer has a duty to exercise reasonable care to prevent defective conditions caused by a miscarriage in the manufacturing process.**

**FACTS:** On April 28, 1956, Zahn (P) was riding as a passenger in the front seat of a 1956 Ford automobile that was owned and being driven by Clarence Dailey (D). As the automobile approached a crossroad, Zahn (P) dropped a lighted cigarette on the floor. While Zahn (P) was attempting to retrieve the same from the floor of the vehicle, with his head down, the brakes of the automobile were applied suddenly and with great force, throwing Zahn (P) forward and causing his face to come in contact with an ashtray in the dashboard. Testimony introduced at trial showed that the ashtray had a jagged edge, and that such a defect would be occasioned by a dull cutting die. Zahn (P) then brought this suit for negligence, contending that the sharp edge was a defect which caused his injuries. The jury found for Zahn (P), Ford's (D) motion for a judgment notwithstanding the verdict was denied, and Ford (D) then brought this appeal, contending that it had properly inspected the ashtray, and that the type of damage suffered was not foreseeable.

**ISSUE:** Does a manufacturer have a duty to exercise reasonable care to prevent defective conditions caused by a miscarriage in the manufacturing process?

**HOLDING AND DECISION:** (Matthes, J.) Yes. There is imposed upon the manufacturer of an article for sale or use the duty to exercise reasonable care to prevent defective conditions caused by a miscarriage in the manufacturing process. This duty requires reasonable skill and care in the process of manufacture and for reasonable inspection or tests to discover defects. Here, testimony showed that Ford (D) did not inspect every ashtray, but rather inspected only a sampling of such ashtrays. Regardless of the procedure followed and practiced by Ford (D), the truth is that the defect was not discovered, although it was readily discoverable. Nor was the type of injury unforeseeable. While the risk of danger was perhaps not as great as that which might inhere in a defective wheel or a defective steering mechanism, nevertheless, the fact remains that Zahn (P) did suffer a serious injury, and the jury could properly consider as a circumstance that in this era of fast-moving automobiles, emergencies arise frequently which require the sudden application of brakes which in turn throw the occupants of the automobile forward and against the dashboard. The record reveals that Ford (D) was fully conscious of the necessity of guarding against injuries resulting from such occurrences. Affirmed.

**EDITOR'S ANALYSIS:** Prosser, in his treatise, states that: "Negligence is a matter of risk — that is to say, of recognizable danger of injury. It has been defined as 'conduct which involves an unreasonably great risk of causing damage,' or, more fully, conduct 'which falls below the standard established by law for the protection of others against unreasonably great risk of harm.' " Prosser, Torts, 2d Ed. 119.

**NOTES:**

## METZGAR v. PLAYSKOOL, INC.

U.S. Ct. of App., 30 F. 3d 459 (3rd Cir. 1994).

**NATURE OF CASE: Appeal from summary judgment dismissing wrongful death action.**

**FACT SUMMARY: A court concluded, as a matter of law, that the utility of Playskool's (D) product outweighed its risk of danger.**

**CONCISE RULE OF LAW: Courts should not decide as a matter of law that a product's utility outweighs its risk if the product presents a realistic risk of danger in its use.**

**FACTS:** Metzgar's (P) child choked to death on a top block manufactured by Playskool, Inc. (D). He brought a wrongful death action against Playskool (D), alleging defective design. Based on statistics showing a mortality rate of only one in 720,000 due to choking on small toys, the district court granted summary judgment dismissing the action. Metzgar (P) appealed.

**ISSUE:** Should courts decide as a matter of law that a product's utility outweighs its risk if the product presents a realistic risk of danger in its use?

**HOLDING AND DECISION:** (Mansmann, J.) No. Courts should not decide as a matter of law that a product's utility outweighs its risk if the product presents a realistic risk of danger in its use. A court should engage in a risk-benefit analysis so as to weed out implausible claims of defective design, but the threshold showing of defective design need not be high. So long as a realistic risk of danger is presented, the issue should go to the jury. Here, while only one in 720,000 children die annually due to choking on small toys, that still leaves an average yearly mortality of eleven. This shows a realistic risk of danger. Reversed.

**CONCURRENCE:** (Becker, J.) The evidence would support a jury finding of defective design.

**DISSENT:** (Scalia, J.) Under the court's analysis here, something as simple as a marble could be subject to a defective design claim.

**EDITOR'S ANALYSIS:** Products liability is often known in shorthand form as "strict liability." In fact, strict liability is only a subset of product liability. Defective design may also be brought under a negligence cause of action.

**NOTES:**

## BOYL v. CALIFORNIA CHEMICAL CO.

221 F. Supp. 669 (D. Ore. 1963).

**NATURE OF CASE: Action for negligence.**

**FACT SUMMARY: Boyl (P), who suffered injuries after lying on grass that had previously been sprayed with weed killer, contended that California (D) had failed to provide proper warning labels on its Triox weed killer product.**

**CONCISE RULE OF LAW: A manufacturer of dangerous products must provide warnings for all incidental and attendant uses.**

**FACTS:** California (D), a chemical manufacturer, makes and sells a liquid weed killer called Triox. A major market for Triox is the do-it-yourself garden-type consumer. Substantially 50% of the Triox solution is a chemical compound called sodium arsenite, which is four to six times as toxic to humans as rat poison. During the latter part of May 1960, Boyl (P) purchased a can of Triox to use on her driveway. The can contained several warnings, but did not warn of the long-lasting qualities of the active ingredients in Triox, nor of the lingering risks of the liquid. On Friday, May 27, 1960, Boyl (P) proceeded to apply the Triox to her driveway, and after doing so rinsed out the spray tank and poured the residue on a grassy area of the backyard. On the following Wednesday afternoon, Boyl (P) lay stomach down for a sunning in the rough grass area where she had poured out the Triox rinse. Soon thereafter, Boyl (P) became ill and was hospitalized for three days. She then brought this action against California (D) for negligence, contending that it had not given a proper warning of the hazards of the Triox compound.

**ISSUE:** Must a manufacturer of dangerous products provide warnings for all incidental and attendant uses?

**HOLDING AND DECISION:** (East, J.) Yes. A manufacturer who undertakes to produce and sell to the general public a product with high risk of human harm must provide specification, instruction, and warning, so that it is reasonably safe for ordinary persons to use it, not only for the purposes for which it is produced and intended to be used, but also all other necessarily incidental and attendant uses. The manufacturer also has a duty to give reasonable notice and warning of after or delayed effects or latent or lingering dangers not known or reasonably to be expected by the ordinary user, but which are foreseeably probable to the manufacturer with his expertise. Here, no warning or protective advice whatsoever as to disposal of the fluid or of any risk to unadvised persons from the stability or long-lasting qualities or propensities and lingering risks of the Triox liquid after returning to a dry or solid form was given or even reasonably inferable. The total lack of advice as to disposal of the rinse could mislead a user to conclude that there was no lingering risk after immediate use and air washing. Accordingly, California (D) was negligent toward Boyl (P) in failing to give any reasonable notice or warning of a risk or danger to her personal safety from contact with earth lately contaminated with the Triox solution. Further, such negligence on the part of California (D) was the proximate cause of Boyl's (P) resulting physical malfunctioning and disabilities. Judgment for Boyl (P) in the amount of $7,910.60.

**EDITOR'S ANALYSIS:** Harper and James, in their treatise on the law of torts, state that: "The very concept of negligence presupposes that the actor either does foresee an unreasonable risk of injury, or could foresee it if he conducted himself as a reasonably prudent man. Foreseeability of harm, in turn, unless it is to depend on supernatural revelation, must depend on knowledge." 2, Harper and James, Law of Torts, 907.

**NOTES:**

# CHAPTER 3
# TORTIOUS MISREPRESENTATION

## QUICK REFERENCE RULES OF LAW

**Fraud.** A technically true statement may nevertheless be fraudulent when it does not state matters that materially qualify the statement as made. (St. Joseph Hospital v. Corbetta Construction Co.)

**Strict Liability for Misrepresentation.** A manufacturer or retailer of a product is responsible in tort for all representations upon which the consumer must rely, regardless of a contractual relationship between plaintiff and defendant. (Baxter v. Ford Motor Co.)

**Strict Liability for Misrepresentation.** A misrepresentation of a material fact upon which a person relies is actionable in tort. (Hauter v. Zogarts)

## ST. JOSEPH HOSPITAL v. CORBETTA CONSTRUCTION CO.

Ill. App. Ct., 21 Ill. App. 3d 925, 316 N.E.2d 51 (1974).

**NATURE OF CASE: Appeal from award of damages for fraud in products liability case.**

**NOTES:**

**FACT SUMMARY: Although General Electric (D) knew that its wall paneling was highly inflammable and dangerous, it did not share this information with the contractor who installed the paneling in St. Joseph Hospital (P).**

**CONCISE RULE OF LAW: A technically true statement may nevertheless be fraudulent when it does not state matters that materially qualify the statement as made.**

**FACTS:** General Electric (D) manufactured a wall paneling known as Textolite. In independent tests conducted by Underwriters Laboratories, Textolite was found to be so extremely inflammable and dangerous that Underwriters refused to give it a so-called "flame-spread" rating. GE (D) was informed of the disastrous results of the test. Nevertheless, two months later, it entered into a subcontract with Corbetta Construction (D) to install Textolite on the walls of St. Joseph Hospital (P). In its negotiations with Corbetta (D), GE (D) merely stated that Textolite was "not flame rated." The Hospital (P) subsequently discovered that Textolite had a flame spread rating that was seventeen times the maximum permitted under the Chicago City Code. It sued Corbetta (D) and GE (D) for the cost of replacing the Textolite paneling. The jury awarded damages to the Hospital (P), and GE (D) appealed, arguing that it had correctly informed Corbetta (D) that Textolite was "not rated."

**ISSUE:** May a technically true statement nevertheless be fraudulent when it does not state matters that materially qualify the statement as made?

**HOLDING AND DECISION:** (Hallett, J.) Yes. A technically true statement may nevertheless be fraudulent when it does not state matters that materially qualify the statement as made. In this case, GE (D) concealed the fact that Textolite had actually been flame tested and had tested out a disastrous seventeen times the maximum permitted under the Code. To say merely that Textolite was "not flame rated" was a gross deception. GE (D) is thus liable to the Hospital (P) on the basis of fraud and deceit for not disclosing the real truth, i.e., that Textolite was utterly unfit for use in the Hospital (P). Affirmed.

**EDITOR'S ANALYSIS:** In most jurisdictions, a plaintiff alleging fraud must establish a representation of an existing fact, as well as that fact's materiality and falsity. The plaintiff must also show that the speaker knew of the fact's falsity and intended that it should be acted on by the person to whom it was made. Finally, the plaintiff must show that the statement reached him, that he did not realize it was false, that he relied on it, and that he incurred damages.

## BAXTER v. FORD MOTOR CO.

Wa. Sup. Ct., 12 P.2d 409 (1932).

**NATURE OF CASE: Action to recover damages for personal injuries, based on breach of warranty in tort.**

**FACT SUMMARY: Baxter (P), while driving a car whose windshield, according to representations made by Ford Motor Co. (D), was made of nonshatterable glass, suffered injuries when a pebble struck the windshield, causing small pieces of glass to fly into his eyes.**

**CONCISE RULE OF LAW: A manufacturer or retailer of a product is responsible in tort for all representations upon which the consumer must rely, regardless of a contractual relationship between plaintiff and defendant.**

**FACTS:** Baxter (P) purchased a car from a dealer, who acquired it in town from Ford Motor Co. (D). Baxter (P) was injured when a pebble from a passing car struck the windshield of his car, causing small pieces of glass to fly into his eyes, and resulting in loss of his left eye and damage to his right eye. Ford Motor Co. (D) had made misrepresentations through its advertising that the windshields of its automobiles were constructed of nonshatterable glass. Ford Motor Co. (D) contended, however, that there can be no implied or express warranty without privity of contract, and warranties as to personal property do not attach themselves to, and run with, the article sold. The trial court refused to admit in evidence the printed matter containing Ford's (D) misrepresentations, and entered judgment for Ford Motor Co. (D). Baxter (P) appealed.

**ISSUE:** Can there be an express or implied warranty, based on a manufacturer's representations as to his product, regardless of privity of contract between manufacturer and purchaser?

**HOLDING AND DECISION:** (Herman, J.) Yes. The purchaser has a right to a remedy against the manufacturer because of damages suffered by reason of a failure of goods to comply with the manufacturer's representations as to the existence of qualities that they did not in fact possess, when the absence of such qualities was not readily discoverable, even though there was no privity of contract between the purchaser and the manufacturer. Here, Ford Motor Co. (D) made representations as to the nonshatterability of its windshields, upon which Baxter (P) was forced to rely, as he as a consumer had no means of testing Ford's (D) truthfulness. Ford (D) was therefore under a duty to ascertain that its representations were true, and it is immaterial that it did not in fact know that the representations were false, or that there was in existence no better make of glass. The trial court erred in excluding evidence of the representations from trial and in taking the case from the jury. The rule which long afforded a remedy, independent of contract, to the purchaser of a dangerous article, such as a drug, against the manufacturer who misrepresents its contents, is now extended to all consumer goods. It would be unjust and against public policy to permit manufacturers of goods to create a demand for their products by representing that they possess qualities which they, in fact, do not possess, and then, because there is no privity of contract existing between the consumer and the manufacturer, deny the consumer the right to recover if damages result from the absence of those qualities, when such absence is not readily noticeable.

**EDITOR'S ANALYSIS:** The action in Baxter was based on breach of an express warranty, but the effect of the decision was to hold manufacturers and retailers to strict liability for their misrepresentations. See Restatement (Second) of Torts, § 402B, which holds the manufacturer liable for physical harm to a consumer caused by the latter's justifiable reliance upon the former's misrepresentations, regardless of contractual relationship, fraud, or negligence. However, in order for there to be strict liability, the representation must be made with the expectation that it will reach the plaintiff, and he, in turn, must actually rely upon the representation in his use of the product. The above case is the leading decision in this area, and has been followed almost without exception.

**NOTES:**

## HAUTER v. ZOGARTS

14 Cal. 3d 104, 120 Cal. Rptr. 681, 534 P.2d 377 (1975).

**NATURE OF CASE: Appeal from judgment n.o.v. upon denial of damages for misrepresentation.**

**FACT SUMMARY: Zogarts (D) contended that a statement on its product's package that it was completely safe was a mere statement of fact, the breach of which was not actionable as misrepresentation.**

**CONCISE RULE OF LAW: A misrepresentation of a material fact upon which a person relies is actionable in tort.**

**FACTS:** Zogarts (D) manufactures and sells the "Golfing Gizmo," a training device designed to help unskilled golfers improve their games. The Gizmo works almost like a slingshot, with the golf ball attached to a cord. The product state, "COMPLETELY SAFE BALL WILL NOT HIT PLAYER." In 1966, Louise Hauter (P) purchased a Gizmo and gave it to Fred Hauter, her thirteen-year-old son. On July 14, 1967, Fred Hauter suffered serious injuries, including brain damage, while using the Gizmo. Testimony introduced at trial showed that Fred had hit under the ball with a seven-iron, causing the ball to ricochet into his head. Zogarts (D) contended that the representation of safety was a mere statement of opinion, which was not actionable under the tort of misrepresentation. Following unanimous jury verdict for Zogarts (D), the trial judge granted Hauter's (P) motion for judgment notwithstanding the verdict, and Zogarts (D) appealed.

**ISSUE:** Is a misrepresentation of a material fact upon which a person relies actionable in tort?

**HOLDING AND DECISION:** (Tobriner, J.) Yes. A misrepresentation of a material fact upon which a person relies is actionable in tort. Here, the assertion that the Gizmo was completely safe, that the ball would not hit the player, did not indicate the seller's subjective opinion about the merits of his product but rather factually described an important characteristic of the product. Courts have consistently held similar promises of safety to be representations of fact. Further, courts have come to construe unqualified statements such as the instant one liberally in favor of injured consumers. The materiality of Zogarts' (D) representation can hardly be questioned, for anyone learning to play golf naturally searches for a product that enables him to learn safely. Affirmed.

**EDITOR'S ANALYSIS:** The holding in this case is consistent with the position adopted in the Restatement of Torts. The restatement provides that: "One engaged in the business of selling chattels who, by advertising, labels, or otherwise, makes to the public a misrepresentation of a material fact concerning the character or quality of a chattel sold by him is subject to liability for physical harm to a consumer of the chattel caused by justifiable reliance upon the representation, even though (a) it is not made fraudulently or negligently, and (b) the consumer has not bought the chattel from or entered into any contractual relation with the seller." Restatement (Second) of Torts, § 402B (1965).

**NOTES:**

# CHAPTER 4
# WARRANTY

## QUICK REFERENCE RULES OF LAW

1. **Express Warranty.** Any affirmation of fact or only promise by the seller relating to the goods is an express warranty if the natural tendency of such affirmation or promise is to induce the buyer to purchase the goods, and If the buyer purchases the goods relying thereon. (Lane v. C.A. Swanson & Sons)

2. **Express Warranty.** An affirmation of fact creates an express warranty if it becomes part of the basis of the bargain. (Stang v. Hertz Corp.)

3. **Express Warranty.** A seller's representations regarding the safety of a product become part of the basis of the bargain and will be construed as an express warranty. (Hauter v. Zogarts)

4. **Implied Warranty of Merchantability.** For a product to be merchantable under § 2-314 of the Uniform Commercial Code, the product must be both suitable and safe for its intended purpose. (Maybank v. S.S. Kresge)

5. **Implied Warranty of Fitness for a Particular Purpose.** Whether an implied warranty of fitness for a particular purpose exists in any given case is a question of fact to be determined by the circumstances of the case. (Barb v. Wallace)

6. **Parties and Privity: Proper Defendants and Third Party Beneficiaries.** An employee of the ultimate purchaser of a product who is injured while using the product can sue for breach of warranty, as long as the employee's safety while using the product was part of the basis of the bargain when the product was purchased. (Whitaker v. Lian Feng Machine Co.)

7. **The Problem and Judicial Solution.** The disclaimer of an implied warranty of merchantability imposed by law in transactions for the sale of goods is violative of public policy and void. (Henningsen v. Bloomfield Motors, Inc.)

8. **Disclaimers under the U.C.C.** In order to have a valid disclaimer provision, it must be in clear and distinct language, and prominently set forth in large, bold print in such position as to compel notice. (Dorman v. International Harvester Co.)

9. **Limitations under the U.C.C.** Reasonable agreements which limit or modify remedies will he given effect, but the parties are not free to shape their remedies in an unreasonable or unconscionable way. (McCarty v. E.J. Korvette, Inc.)

10. **Limitations under the U.C.C.** Implied warranties of merchantability and fitness may be discialmed if the disclaimer is conspicuous and mentions merchantability. (Ford Motor Co. v. Moulton)

## LANE v. C.A. SWANSON & SONS

130 Cal. App. 2d 210, 278 P.2d 723 (1955).

**NATURE OF CASE: Appeal from denial of damages for breach of express warranty.**

**FACT SUMMARY: Lane (P) contended that the labeling by Swanson (D) of a product as "Boned Chicken" created an express warranty that no bones would be contained in the product.**

**CONCISE RULE OF LAW: Any affirmation of fact or only promise by the seller relating to the goods is an express warranty if the natural tendency of such affirmation or promise is to induce the buyer to purchase the goods, and If the buyer purchases the goods relying thereon.**

**FACTS:** Lane (P) bought a can of chicken manufactured by Swanson (D). The can stated that it contained "Boned Chicken." In addition, an advertisement placed by Swanson (D) was introduced at trial. The advertisement pictured a can of Swanson (D) Boned Chicken, and beside the can was a description of the contents of the can, including the statement "No bones." Lane (P) contended that there was a bone hidden in the contents of the can that became lodged in his throat, causing severe personal injuries and expense for medical and surgical treatment. Swanson (D) contended that the term "Boned Chicken" was merely descriptive of the manner in which the product was prepared and packaged and that it did not constitute a warranty that the contents of the can were wholly free from bones. The trial court found there was no evidence of an express warranty by Swanson (D) that the contents of the can were free from chicken bones or other foreign substances, and Lane (P) then brought this appeal, contending that the term "Boned Chicken" constituted an express warranty.

**ISSUE:** Is any affirmation of fact or any promise by the seller relating to the goods an express warranty if the natural tendency of such affirmation or promise is to induce the buyer to purchase the goods, and if the buyer purchases the goods relying thereon?

**HOLDING AND DECISION:** (Shinn, J.) Yes. Any affirmation of fact or any promise by the seller relating to the goods is an express warranty if the natural tendency of such affirmation or promise is to induce the buyer to purchase the goods, and if the buyer purchases the goods relying thereon. The tendency of the modern cases is to construe liberally in favor of the buyer language used by the seller in making affirmations respecting the quality of his goods and to enlarge the responsibility of the seller to construe every affirmation by him to be a warranty when such construction is at all reasonable. Here, the term "no bones" would mean to a buyer that no bones whatsoever would be found in the product. Unless it can be said that a small piece of bone is no bone at all when it sticks in one's throat, it cannot be said that a product that contains one or more bone fragments contains no bones. Accordingly, the label on the can, coupled with the representation in the newspaper ads that the contents contained no bones, constituted an express warranty, which was breached. Reversed.

**EDITOR'S ANALYSIS:** The Uniform Commercial Code states that: "Any description of the goods which is made part of the basis of the bargain creates an express warranty that the goods shall conform to the description." In this case, the court held that the representation that the chicken had no bones formed part of the basis of the bargain, and thus gave rise to an express warranty.

**NOTES:**

## STANG v. HERTZ CORP.

83 N.M. 217, 490 P.2d 475 (1971).

**NATURE OF CASE: Appeal from denial of damages for breach of express warranty.**

**FACT SUMMARY: Stang (P) contended that the statement of a Hertz (D) representative that a car had "good tires" constituted an express warranty, which was breached when the tire blew out.**

**CONCISE RULE OF LAW: An affirmation of fact creates an express warranty if it becomes part of the basis of the bargain.**

**FACTS:** This case involves an automobile accident which occurred when a tire blew out. The tire, manufactured by Firestone Tire & Rubber Company (D), was mounted on a car belonging to Hertz (D). The car had been rented by a nun, and Catherine Lavan, also a nun, was a passenger in the car when the blowout occurred. Lavan suffered injuries in the accident, resulting in her death. At trial, evidence was introduced showing that a Hertz (D) representative, in a conversation with one of the nuns, had stated that "you have got good tires." Stang (P) contended that this statement created an express warranty as to the tires, while Hertz (D) contended that it was no more than "puffing." After verdicts in favor of both Firestone (D) and Hertz (D), Stang (P) brought this appeal.

**ISSUE:** Does an affirmation of fact create an express warranty if it becomes part of the basis of the bargain?

**HOLDING AND DECISION:** (Wood, J.) Yes. An affirmation of fact creates an express warranty if it becomes part of the basis of the bargain. The description of the goods also creates an express warranty if the description is made part of the basis of the bargain. Here, there was no evidence that any of the nuns relied on, or in any way considered, the terms of the rental agreement before agreeing to the rental. The comment concerning "good tires" was made after the car had been rented. There was no evidence that either the terms of the rental agreement or the reference to "good tires" was part of the basis of the bargain. Affirmed.

**EDITOR'S ANALYSIS:** The Uniform Commercial Code would seem to be in agreement with the holding in this case. One pertinent section provides that: "It is not necessary to the creation of an express warranty that the seller use formal words such as 'warrant' or 'guarantee' or that he have a specific intention to make a warranty, but an affirmation merely of the value of the goods or a statement purporting to be merely the seller's opinion or commendation of the goods does not create a warranty." U.C.C. § 2-313(2).

**NOTES:**

## HAUTER v. ZOGARTS

14 Cal. 3d 104, 120 Cal. Rptr. 681, 534 P.2d 377 (1975).

**NATURE OF CASE: Appeal from judgment n.o.v. upon denial of damages for misrepresentation.**

**FACT SUMMARY: Zogarts (D) contended that a statement on its product's package that it was completely safe was a mere statement of fact, the breach of which was not actionable as misrepresentation.**

**CONCISE RULE OF LAW: A seller's representations regarding the safety of a product become part of the basis of the bargain and will be construed as an express warranty.**

**FACTS:** Zogarts (D) manufactures and sells the "Golfing Gizmo," a training device designed to help unskilled golfers improve their games. The Gizmo works almost like a slingshot, with the golf ball attached to a cord. The product's instruction booklet states, "COMPLETELY SAFE BALL WILL NOT HIT PLAYER." In 1966, Louise Hauter (P) purchased a Gizmo and gave it to Fred Hauter, her thirteen-year-old son. On July 14, 1967, Fred Hauter suffered serious injuries, including brain damage, while using the Gizmo. Testimony introduced at trial showed that Fred had hit under the ball with a seven-iron, causing the ball to ricochet into his head. Zogarts (D) contended that the representation of safety was a mere statement of opinion, which was not actionable under the tort of misrepresentation. Following unanimous jury verdict for Zogarts (D), the trial judge granted Hauter's (P) motion for judgment notwithstanding the verdict, and Zogarts (D) appealed.

**ISSUE:** Will a seller's representations regarding the safety of a product be construed as an express warranty?

**HOLDING AND DECISION:** (Tobriner, J.) Yes. A seller's representations regarding the safety of a product become part of the basis of the bargain and will be construed as an express warranty. California Commercial Code § 2313 no longer requires that a plaintiff prove his reliance upon specific promises made by the seller. All that must be proven is that such affirmations were made. The statement in the Gizmo's instruction booklet is more than sufficient proof that Zogarts (D) made representations regarding its product's safety which constitute an express warranty. The trial court properly concluded that this express warranty had been breached. Affirmed and remanded to determine damages.

**CONCURRENCE:** (Clark, J.) The record established a breach of express warranty as a matter of law, and no further discussion was necessary.

**EDITOR'S ANALYSIS:** This case illustrates the impact that any statement by a seller can have on the seller's potential liability. Even a statement of opinion can become a warranty under the California U.C.C. § 2313. Protection for a purchaser under this section is greater than that under both the former Uniform Sales Act and the Restatement of Torts.

## MAYBANK v. S.S. KRESGE

46 N.C. App. 687, 266 S.E.2d 409 (1980);
Mod. and Affd. on other grounds, 302 N.C. 129, 273 S.E.2d 681 (1981).

**NATURE OF CASE: Appeal from directed verdict denying damages for product liability.**

**FACT SUMMARY: Maybank (P) appealed from a directed verdict in favor of S.S. Kresge (K-Mart) (D), contending the evidence adduced at trial raised a question for the jury as to whether the flashcube she purchased was fit for its ordinary purpose.**

**CONCISE RULE OF LAW: For a product to be merchantable under § 2-314 of the Uniform Commercial Code (U.C.C.), the product must be both suitable and safe for its intended purpose.**

**FACTS:** Maybank (P) sued K-Mart (D) when a flashcube she purchased from K-Mart (D) exploded in her face, injuring her eye. The carton warned of the risk that damaged flashcubes could shatter. She contended the flashcube was not merchantable under U.C.C. § 2-314. There was no evidence that the cube had been damaged prior to Maybank's (P) use. At the close of Maybank's (P) case, the court directed a verdict for K-Mart (D), and Maybank (P) appealed.

**ISSUE:** For a product to be merchantable under § 2-314 of the U.C.C., must the product be both suitable and safe for its intended purpose?

**HOLDING AND DECISION:** (Vaughn, J.) Yes. For a product to be merchantable under § 2-314 of the U.C.C., the product must be both suitable and safe for its intended purpose. An exploding flashcube does not satisfy the minimum requirements of merchantability set forth in § 2-314. There was no evidence that the cube was damaged, and the warning that a damaged flashcube might shatter did not constitute a sufficient or adequate warning of the danger of an exploding flashcube. An exploding flashcube is not "within the variations permitted by the agreement." The merchantability of the flashcube was a question for the jury. Reversed and remanded.

**EDITOR'S ANALYSIS:** A plaintiff is often faced with a situation where there has been an injury producing failure or malfunction, without being able to pinpoint a cause for the failure. By bringing suit under a U.C.C. § 2-314 warranty theory, the plaintiff can overcome these proximate cause problems. His burden is satisfied by proving the fact of the malfunction itself; there is no need to prove manufacturer's negligence in either the design or manufacture of the product.

**NOTES:**

## BARB v. WALLACE

45 Md. App. 271, 412 A.2d 1314 (1980).

**NATURE OF CASE: Appeal from order granting motion for summary judgment.**

**FACT SUMMARY: Barb (P) appealed from an order granting Wallace's (D) motion for summary judgment, contending that there was a genuine factual dispute as to whether Barb (P) relied on Wallace's (D) skill or judgment in purchasing the engine.**

**CONCISE RULE OF LAW: Whether an implied warranty of fitness for a particular purpose exists in any given case is a question of fact to be determined by the circumstances of the case.**

**FACTS:** Barb (P) bought a small, used, gasoline-powered engine from Wallace (D) for use in a go-cart. Barb (P) told Wallace (D) that the engine would be used in a go-cart, and the evidence indicated that Wallace (D) told him that the engine could be used in a go-cart. Barb (P) indicated at the time of purchase that he was taking a course in auto mechanics and had worked on small engines. When Barb (P) attempted to start the engine, it exploded, injuring him. Barb (P) sued Wallace (D) on various grounds, including breach of implied warranty for a particular purpose under U.C.C. § 2-315, Wallace (D) successfully moved for summary judgment, and Barb (P) appealed, contending there was a factual dispute as to whether he relied on Wallace's (D) skill or judgment in purchasing the engine.

**ISSUE:** Is the question of whether an implied warranty of fitness for a particular purpose exists in any given case a question of fact?

**HOLDING AND DECISION:** (Couch, J.) Yes. Whether an implied warranty of fitness for a particular purpose exists in any given case is a question of fact to be determined by the circumstances of the case. There is evidence that Wallace (D) told Barb (P) that the engine was appropriate for use in a go-cart. The fact that Barb (P) had some experience with engines does not preclude the possibility that he relied on Wallace's (D) representations as to the engine. A question of fact was presented. (The court noted that § 2-315 is not limited in application to merchants only.) Reversed and remanded.

**EDITOR'S ANALYSIS:** There is some overlap between the implied warranty of merchantability and the implied warranty of fitness for a particular purpose, and the courts are split as to whether a U.C.C. § 2-315 action will lie where one under § 2-314 does. Note that there is also overlap between the implied warranty for a particular purpose and a product's express warranties.

## WHITAKER v. LIAN FENG MACHINE CO.

156 Ill. App. 3d 316,108 Ill. Dec. 895, 509 N.E.2d 591 (1987).

**NATURE OF CASE: Appeal from dismissal of implied warranty causes of action.**

**FACT SUMMARY: Whitaker (P) appealed the trial court's decision dismissing the breach of implied warranty counts of this action on grounds of lack of privity, contending the employee of the ultimate purchaser of a product could recover from the seller for breach of warranty.**

**CONCISE RULE OF LAW: An employee of the ultimate purchaser of a product who is injured while using the product can sue for breach of warranty, as long as the employee's safety while using the product was part of the basis of the bargain when the product was purchased.**

**FACTS:** Whitaker (P) cut his hand while using a bandsaw manufactured by Fian (D). The importer (D) and distributor (D) who sold the bandsaw to Whitaker's (P) employer, DuPage, were also sued. The trial court granted the motions of the importer and distributor (D) to dismiss the breach of implied warranty counts of Whitaker's (P) action based upon lack of privity, and Whitaker (P) appealed.

**ISSUE:** Can the employee of the ultimate purchaser of a product recover from the seller for breach of warranty?

**HOLDING AND DECISION:** (White, J.) Yes. An employee of the ultimate purchaser of a product who is injured while using the product can sue for breach of warranty, as long as the employee's safety while using the product was part of the basis of the bargain when the product was purchased. Although case law appears to be split on this issue, the alternative version of U.C.C. § 2-318, adopted in this jurisdiction, does not establish any limitation on the rights of persons in "horizontal privity" to recover for breach of warranty. It has been left to the courts to determine to what extent warranty coverage should be extended to nonpurchasing users. It was alleged in the present case that DuPage bargained for a bandsaw with safety features designed for the benefit of its employees using the saw. Whitaker (P) alleged facts which, if proven, would show that Fian et al. (D) implicitly or explicitly promised to provide a bandsaw safe to use. Therefore, Whitaker's (P) breach of implied warranty causes of action are not barred by lack of privity. Reversed and remanded.

**EDITOR'S ANALYSIS:** While some courts have adopted the court's reasoning in the present case, other courts have attempted to rationalize the expansion of protected persons under U.C.C. § 2-318, on public policy grounds. See McNully v. Nicholson Mfg. Co., 313 A.2d 913 (1983), where the court held that employees are in the "business family" of their employers, allowing them to bring a breach of warranty action.

## HENNINGSEN v. BLOOMFIELD MOTORS, INC.

32 N.J. 358, 161 A.2d 69 (1960).

**NATURE OF CASE: Appeal from award of damages for breach of implied warranty.**

**FACT SUMMARY: Henningsen (P) purchased from Bloomfield (D) an automobile manufactured by Chrysler which allegedly was defective and caused an accident in which Henningsen's (P) wife was injured while driving it.**

**CONCISE RULE OF LAW: The disclaimer of an implied warranty of merchantability imposed by law in transactions for the sale of goods is violative of public policy and void.**

**FACTS:** Henningsen (P) purchased a Plymouth automobile from Bloomfield (D), a retailer. The car was manufactured by Chrysler and sold pursuant to a standardized form contract. The reverse side of the form contained a lengthy disclaimer of all warranties save the expressed ninety-day warranty against defects in materials and workmanship directed only to the original purchaser. Henningsen (P) did not read the fine print disclaimer. While Henningsen's (P) wife was driving the vehicle, an alleged defect in the car caused an accident resulting in Mrs. Henningsen's being injured. Henningsen (P) filed a complaint against Bloomfield (D) and Chrysler (D) for negligence and breach of implied warranty of merchantability. The negligence counts were dismissed, but verdicts were returned for breach of implied warranty. On the basis of the disclaimer, Bloomfield (D) and Chrysler (D) appealed.

**ISSUE:** Is the disclaimer of an implied warranty of merchantability imposed by law in transactions for the sale of goods violative of public policy and void?

**HOLDING AND DECISION:** (Francis, J.) Yes. The doctrine that a person is bound by his signed agreement, in the absence of fraud, does not stand in the way of relief. Freedom of contract is not such an immutable doctrine as to admit of no qualification in the area of law involved in this case. In this case, there is a gross inequality of bargaining position in the use of a standardized form contract. It purports to take away from the purchaser the right to recover for personal injuries caused by defects and give him only a right to have defects cured at the factory. This is unjust. The disclaimer of an implied warranty of merchantability imposed by law in transactions for the sale of goods is violative of public policy and void. Affirmed.

**EDITOR'S ANALYSIS:** The court in this case was particularly dismayed by the attempt by the drafters of the contract to "hide" the disclaiming portion of it by putting it in fine print on the back of the form. The U.C.C., in § 2-316(2), requires that exclusions and modification of warranties "must be conspicuous." According to the Official Comment, it is also required that the disclaimer of an implied warranty of merchantability mention merchantability in its language.

## DORMAN v. INTERNATIONAL HARVESTER CO.

46 Cal. App. 3d 11, 120 Cal. Rptr. 516 (1975).

**NATURE OF CASE: Appeal from judgment n.o.v. upon award of damages for breach of warranty.**

**FACT SUMMARY: Dorman (P) contended that Harvester (D) had given insufficient notice of a disclaimer of the implied warranties of merchantability and fitness for a particular purpose because it was not set out in bold type.**

**CONCISE RULE OF LAW: In order to have a valid disclaimer provision, it must be in clear and distinct language, and prominently set forth in large, bold print in such position as to compel notice.**

**FACTS:** On October 31, 1968, Dorman (P) entered into a Retail Installment Conditional Sales Contract with Harvester (D) to purchase a new tractor and backhoe. Dorman (P) took delivery on November 4, 1968, and experienced problems with the tractor from the day he took delivery. The contract which Dorman (P) signed contained an italicized provision at the bottom of the page stating that "no other warranties, express or implied, including without limitation, the implied warranties of merchantability and fitness for a particular purpose shall apply." Dorman (P) filed suit against Harvester (D), alleging breach of warranty, and Harvester (D) cross-claimed for the return of the equipment. The jury returned verdicts for Dorman (P) on both claims, but the trial judge granted Harvester's (D) motion for judgment notwithstanding the verdicts. Dorman (P) then brought this appeal, contending that the disclaimer had been insufficient as a matter of law because it was not set forth noticeably.

**ISSUE:** In order to have a valid disclaimer provision, must it be in clear and distinct language, and prominently set forth in large, bold print in such position as to compel notice?

**HOLDING AND DECISION:** (Stephens, J.) Yes. In order to have a valid disclaimer provision, it must be in clear and distinct language and prominently set forth in large, bold print in such position as to compel notice. An exclusion of the implied warranty of merchantability in case of a writing must be conspicuous and an exclusion of the implied warranty of fitness for particular purpose must be by a writing and conspicuous. Conspicuous is defined as meaning so written that a reasonable person against whom it is to operate ought to have noticed it. A printed heading in capital letters is conspicuous. Language in the body of a form is conspicuous if it is in larger print or of a contrasting type or color. The test of conspicuousness is whether attention can reasonably be expected to be called to the disclaimer provision. Here, the disclaimer provision appeared in close proximity to where Dorman (P) signed the contract, and the implied warranties, wording, "merchantability and fitness for particular purpose shall apply," was italicized. Although the disclaimer provision was printed in a slightly larger typeface than was the preceding paragraph of the contract, it was not in boldface type and it was not sufficiently conspicuous to have negated the implied warranties, particularly where no standard printed warranty was in fact given to Dorman (P) at the time of execution of the contract. Thus, the disclaimer was insufficiently conspicuous to inform a reasonable buyer that he was waiving his right to have a quality product. Reversed.

**EDITOR'S ANALYSIS:** The official comment to the pertinent U.C.C. provision states that: "This section is designed principally to deal with those frequent clauses in sales contracts which seek to exclude all warranties, express or implied. It seeks to protect a buyer from unexpected and unbargained language of disclaimer by denying effect to such language when inconsistent with language of express warranty and permitting the exclusion of implied warranties only by conspicuous language or other circumstances which protect the buyer from surprise." Official Comment to U.C.C. § 2-316.

**NOTES:**

## McCARTY v. E.J. KORVETTES, INC.

28 Md. App. 421, 347 A.2d 253 (1975).

**NATURE OF CASE: Appeal from denial of damages for breach of warranty.**

**FACT SUMMARY: McCarty (P) contended that a clause in Korvettes's (D) tire guarantee, purporting to avoid liability for consequential damages, was unconscionable as a matter of law.**

**CONCISE RULE OF LAW: Reasonable agreements which limit or modify remedies will he given effect, but the parties are not free to shape their remedies in an unreasonable or unconscionable way.**

**FACTS:** McCarty (P), who had purchased tires from Korvettes (D), brought suit claiming breach of express tire warranty. McCarty (P) had been injured and his car damaged in an accident caused by the blowout of a tire under warranty. The warranty, labeled "Korvettes Tire Centers All-Road-Hazards Tire Guarantee," provided that the tires were guaranteed against all road hazards including stone bruises, impact bruises, blowout tread separation, "glass cuts and fabric breaks, only when used in normal noncommercial passenger car service." The guarantee further stated that "neither the manufacturer nor Korvettes Tire Centers shall be liable for any consequential damage and our liability is limited solely to replacement of the product." At the conclusion of McCarty's (P) case, the trial court granted Korvettes's (D) motion for a directed verdict. McCarty (P) then brought this appeal, claiming that the limitation of liability contained in the guarantee was unconscionable as a matter of law.

**ISSUE:** Will reasonable agreements which limit or modify remedies be given effect if the parties do not attempt to shape their remedies in an unreasonable or unconscionable way?

**HOLDING AND DECISION:** Yes. Reasonable agreements which limit or modify remedies will be given effect, but the parties are not free to shape their remedies in an unreasonable or unconscionable way. Limitation of consequential damages for injury to the person in the case of consumer goods is prima facie unconscionable. After a finding of unconscionability, the court, in its discretion, may refuse to enforce the contract as a whole if it is permeated by the unconscionability, or may strike any single clause or group of clauses which are so tainted or which are contrary to the essential purpose of the agreement, or may simply limit unconscionable clauses so as to avoid unconscionable results. Here, the clause purporting to limit the consumers' remedy solely to replacement of the tire purports to exclude liability for both personal injury and property damage. To the extent that the clause purports to limit consequential damages for personal injury, it is unconscionable as a matter of law. Reversed.

**EDITOR'S ANALYSIS:** The section of the Uniform Commercial Code dealing with contractual modifications or limitations of remedies states that: "Consequential damages may be limited or excluded unless the limitation or exclusion is unconscionable. Limitation of consequential damages for injury to the person in the case of consumer goods is prima facie unconscionable but limitation of damages where the loss is commercial is not." U.C.C. § 2-719(3). The present case is in accordance with this general rule.

**NOTES:**

## FORD MOTOR CO. v. MOULTON

511 S.W.2d 690, cert. denied
419 U.S. 870, 95 S. Ct. 129, 42 L.. Ed. 2d 109 (1974).

**NATURE OF CASE: Appeal from reversal of dismissal of action for breach of warranty.**

**FACT SUMMARY: Moulton (P) contended that Ford's (D) contract, disclaiming all implied warranties, was unconscionable.**

**CONCISE RULE OF LAW: Implied warranties of merchantability and fitness may be disciaImed if the disclaimer is conspicuous and mentions merchantability.**

**FACTS:** Moulton (P) and his wife filed a complaint alleging that he had purchased a Ford (D) LTD automobile and had been seriously injured while driving the car when it suddenly veered to the right, jumped the guard rail, and fell twenty-six feet to the street below. Moulton (P) alleged in his complaint that the loss of control was due to a defect in the steering mechanism of the car. Both the automobile dealer and Ford (D) had disclaimer clauses in their contracts with Moulton (P), which purportedly disclaimed all implied warranties. In addition, the contract contained a one-year or 12,000-mile limitation on the express warranty. The one-year period had elapsed by the time of the incident. Moulton (P) contended that both the disclaimer and the limitation of warranty were unconscionable. The court of appeals reversed the trial judge's dismissal of Moulton's (P) tort claims as barred by the statute of limitations, and the warranty claims for failure to state a cause of action. Ford (D) then brought this appeal of that reversal.

**ISSUE:** May implied warranties of merchantability and fitness be disclaimed if the disclaimer is conspicuous and mentions merchantability?

**HOLDING AND DECISION:** (Chattin, J.) Yes. Implied warranties of merchantability and fitness may be disclaimed if the disclaimer is conspicuous and mentions merchantability, and if it is in writing with reference to the fitness warranty. U.C.C. § 2-719(3) recognizes the validity of clauses limiting or excluding consequential damages but makes clear that they may not operate in an unconscionable manner. Such terms are merely an allocation of unknown or undeterminable risks. Here, the disclaimer clauses were proper and enforceable. The one-year or 12,000-mile limitation was, in effect, a limitation of the time within which a claim must be asserted under the warranty. The warranty actually provided for repair or replacement of such parts found to be defective within the limited period, and if such discovery was made, presumably a further reasonable period of time would have been allowed for giving notice. Here, however, no such discovery within the limited period was made. Thus, Moulton (P) has no valid claim of breach of express of implied warranty. Affirmed.

**EDITOR'S ANALYSIS:** The U.C.C. holds that "it is of the very essence of a sales contract that at least minimum adequate remedies be available." In this case, the court concluded that those minimum remedies were in fact available, despite the disclaimer of implied warranties. The time limitation on the express warranties involved a fairly standard time period for automobile warranties.

**NOTES:**

# CHAPTER 5
# STRICT LIABILITY IN TORT

## QUICK REFERENCE RULES OF LAW

1. **Development.** A plaintiff who demonstrates that an injury or damages sustained would probably not have occurred in the absence of a legal wrong by the defendant may invoke the doctrine of res ipsa loquitur. (Escola v. Coca Cola Bottling Co. of Fresno)

2. **Development.** A plaintiff may recover for breach of an implied warranty of merchantability despite the absence of privity and the presence of a disclaimer. (Henningsen v. Bloomfield Motors, Inc.)

3. **Development.** A manufacturer is strictly liable in tort when an article he places on the market, knowing it will not be inspected for defects, proves to have a defect that causes injury to a human being. (Greenman v. Yuba Power Products, Inc.)

4. **Development.** In order to prove a cause of action for strict liability, the plaintiff need not prove any specific act of negligence on the part of the seller. (Phipps v. General Motors Corp.)

5. **Rationales.** The imposition of strict liability causes manufacturers to make safer products. (First National Bank v. Nor-Am Agricultural Products, Inc.)

## ESCOLA v. COCA-COLA BOTTLING CO. OF FRESNO

24 Cal. 2d 453, 150 P.2d 436 (1944).

**NATURE OF CASE: Appeal from award of damages for personal injuries.**

**FACT SUMMARY: Escola (P), a restaurant waitress, was transferring a bottle of Coca-Cola (D) from its case to a refrigerator when it exploded and injured her hand.**

**CONCISE RULE OF LAW: A plaintiff who demonstrates that an injury or damages sustained would probably not have occurred in the absence of a legal wrong by the defendant may invoke the doctrine of res ipsa loquitur.**

**FACTS:** Escola (P) was a waitress in a restaurant. While working, she picked up a bottle of Coca-Cola (D) from its case to place it into a refrigerator. The bottle exploded, injuring her hand. Escola (P) brought this action relying on the doctrine of res ipsa loquitur and alleging that either excessive pressure in the bottle or a defect in the glass bottle caused the explosion. A witness testified that Escola (P) did not cause or permit any impact between the bottle and any other object. The jury brought in a verdict for Escola (P), and Coca-Cola (D) appealed.

**ISSUE:** May a plaintiff who demonstrates that an injury or damages sustained would probably not have occurred in the absence of a legal wrong by the defendant invoke the doctrine of res ipsa loquitur?

**HOLDING AND DECISION:** (Gibson, J.) Yes. Sound and properly prepared bottles of carbonated liquids do not ordinarily explode when carefully handled. Thus, since no other force damaged the bottle after delivery, it follows that the bottle was defective when it left the manufacturer's control. A plaintiff who demonstrates that an injury or damages sustained would probably not have occurred in the absence of a legal wrong by the defendant may invoke the doctrine of res ipsa loquitur. If due care had been used, neither excessive pressure nor defective glass would have caused the accident. Res ipsa loquitur may thus, in this case, supply the inference of Coca-Coca's (D) negligence. Affirmed.

**CONCURRENCE:** (Traynor, J.) Negligence should no longer be recognized as a basis of a plaintiff's right to recover in cases like this. Rather, a manufacturer should be held to incur absolute liability when injury is caused by an article he has placed on the market without proper inspection. It is in the public interest to place the responsibility upon the manufacturer even if he is not negligent. This theory is applicable in the case of defective foodstuffs, and for the same reasons should apply here.

**EDITOR'S ANALYSIS:** The traditional elements of the doctrine of res ipsa loquitur are: (1) the event would probably not have happened without negligence; (2) the defendant had exclusive control of the instrumentality causing the injury or damage; and (3) the plaintiff was in no way contributorily negligent. It is generally thought that in cases where res ipsa loquitur applies, the defendant has greater access to the evidence and the plaintiff has a ready insurmountable task in establishing an act of negligence.

**NOTES:**

## HENNINGSEN v. BLOOMFIELD MOTORS, INC.

N.J. Sup. Ct., 32 N.J. 358, 161 A.2d 69 (1960).

**NATURE OF CASE: Appeal from award of damages for breach of implied warranty of merchantability.**

**FACT SUMMARY: The Henningsens (P) sued Chrysler (D), contending it should be held strictly liable for a defective automobile that caused Mrs. Henningsen (P) to be injured when its steering malfunctioned.**

**CONCISE RULE OF LAW: A plaintiff may recover for breach of an implied warranty of merchantability despite the absence of privity and the presence of a disclaimer.**

**FACTS:** Mr. Henningsen (P) purchased a car manufactured by Chrysler from Bloomfield Motors (D), a dealership. Two fine-print paragraphs on the purchase order contained a disclaimer of liability by Bloomfield Motors (D) and a limitation on remedies. Mrs. Henningsen (P) was injured in a car accident when the steering mechanism malfunctioned ten days after the Henningsens (P) took delivery of the car. They sued for damages, claiming breach of an implied warranty of merchantability. The jury returned a verdict for the Henningsens (P). Chrysler (D) and Bloomfield Motors (D) appealed, arguing that lack of privity and the disclaimer of liability shielded them from liability.

**ISSUE:** May a plaintiff recover for breach of an implied warranty of merchantability despite the absence of privity and the presence of a disclaimer?

**HOLDING AND DECISION:** (Francis, J.) Yes. A plaintiff may recover for breach of an implied warranty of merchantability despite the absence of privity and the presence of a disclaimer. First of all, there is no rational basis for the privity bar in warranty cases involving defective automobiles. Warranties run directly to the purchaser, despite the absence of privity of contract. Secondly, the legislature has imposed an implied warranty of merchantability on the sale of any product that is recognizably dangerous. The judicial process has recognized a right to recover damages for personal injuries arising from a breach of that warranty. The disclaimer of an implied warranty is violative of public policy and is therefore void. Affirmed.

**EDITOR'S ANALYSIS:** Unlike negligence liability, the defendant in a strict products liability case, who is otherwise without fault, may be held liable for merely selling a defective product. In the above case, for example, Mrs. Henningsen (P) was able to establish liability by testifying that she heard a loud noise, something cracked, and then the steering wheel spun in her hands, sending the car out of control. This was sufficient for the jury to infer that the car was defective, and that the defect occurred during the manufacturing process, although it was insufficient to infer negligence.

## GREENMAN v. YUBA POWER PRODUCTS, INC.

59 Cal. 2d 57, 27 Cal. Rptr. 697, 377 P.2d 897 (1963).

**NATURE OF CASE: Appeal from award of damages for breach of implied warranty.**

**FACT SUMMARY: Greenman (P) was seriously injured when a tool manufactured by Yuba (D) malfunctioned by sending pieces of wood flying out at Greeman's (P) forehead.**

**CONCISE RULE OF LAW: A manufacturer is strictly liable in tort when an article he places on the market, knowing it will not be inspected for defects, proves to have a defect that causes injury to a human being.**

**FACTS:** Greenman's (P) wife gave him a Shopsmith powertool manufactured by Yuba (D) as a Christmas gift. The tool could be used as a power saw, a drill, or a lathe, depending upon the attachments used. Greenman (P) purchased the proper attachments to use the tool as a lathe and began to use it, at different times, to make a chalice out of a piece of wood. One time while using the tool, the piece of wood flew out of the machine, struck Greenman (P) in the forehead, and caused him serious injuries. After trial of Greenman's action for damages based upon breach of express and implied warranties and upon negligence, the jury awarded him $65,000. Both Greenman (P) and Yuba (D) appealed, Greenman (P) seeking a reversal of the part of the judgment in favor of the retailer who sold the tool.

**ISSUE:** Is a manufacturer strictly liable in tort when an article he places on the market, knowing it will not be inspected for defects, proves to have a defect that causes injury to a human being?

**HOLDING AND DECISION:** (Traynor, J.) Yes. The recognition that the liability in these kinds of cases is not assumed by agreement but imposed by law, and the refusal to permit manufacturers to define the scope of their liability for defective products, make it clear that the liability is governed by strict liability in tort rather than by contract law. Thus, even in the absence of proof regarding express warranties or negligence of Yuba (D), it was sufficient that Greenman (P) showed that he used the Shopsmith in its intended fashion and that an undiscovered defect making the tool unsafe caused the injury. A manufacturer is strictly liable in tort when an article he places on the market, knowing it will not be inspected for defects, proves to have a defect that causes injury to a human being. There was no error in rendering judgment upon the jury's verdict. Affirmed.

**EDITOR'S ANALYSIS:** An imperfection in a product is not necessarily a defect. What constitutes a defect is a matter of reasonable consumer expectation. Furthermore, if a defect or a danger is very obvious, the product may be regarded as nondefective or, in appropriate cases, the manufacturer will be held only to a duty to warn of possible danger.

## PHIPPS v. GENERAL MOTORS CORP.

278 Md. 337, 363 A.2d 955 (1976).

**NATURE OF CASE: Motion to dismiss action for negligence and strict liability.**

**FACT SUMMARY: General Motors (D) moved to dismiss an action in strict liability, on the grounds that the Maryland courts had not adopted this rule of law.**

**CONCISE RULE OF LAW: In order to prove a cause of action for strict liability, the plaintiff need not prove any specific act of negligence on the part of the seller.**

**FACTS:** Phipps (P) was injured while driving a car manufactured by General Motors (D) when without warning the accelerator suddenly stuck. The car accelerated out of control and crashed into a tree. Phipps (P) brought suit against General Motors (D) in federal district court on grounds of negligence, warranty, and strict liability in tort. General Motors (D) moved to dismiss the strict tort count, arguing that the doctrine had not been adopted by the Maryland courts. The federal court certified this question to the Maryland court of appeals.

**ISSUE:** Does a plaintiff have to prove any specific act of negligence on the part of the seller in order to prove a cause of action for strict liability?

**HOLDING AND DECISION:** (Eldridge, J.) No. The plaintiff need not prove any specific act of negligence on the part of the seller in order to prove a cause of action for strict liability. For recovery, it must be established that the product was in a defective condition at the time that it left the possession or control of the seller, that it was unreasonably dangerous to the user or consumer, that the defect was a cause of the injuries, and that the product was expected to and did reach the consumer without substantial change in its condition. However, the seller is not liable where injury results from abnormal handling or use of the product, where mishandling or alteration after delivery of the product renders it unsafe, or if warnings or instructions supplied with the product are disregarded by the consumer where, if used in accordance with these warnings, the product would be safe. Additionally, where the plaintiff unreasonably proceeds to use a product despite a known risk or danger, the defense of assumption of the risk is still available. Here, there is no reason why a party injured by a defective and unreasonably dangerous product, which when placed on the market is impliedly represented as safe, should bear the loss of that injury when the seller of that product is in a better position to take precautions and protect against the defect. Accordingly, the Maryland courts adopt the theory of strict liability.

**EDITOR'S ANALYSIS:** The reasoning of the court in adopting the rule of strict liability was that proof of a defect in a product at the time it left the control of the seller implies fault on the part of the seller sufficient to justify imposing liability for injuries caused by the product. Where the seller supplies a defective and unreasonably dangerous product, the seller or someone employed by him is held to have been at fault in designing or constructing the product.

## FIRST NATIONAL BANK v. NOR-AM AGRICULTURAL PRODUCTS, INC.

N.M. Ct. of App., 88 N.M. 74, 537 P. 2d 682 (1975).

**NATURE OF CASE: Appeal from summary judgment dismissing products liability claim.**

**FACT SUMMARY: The Huckley family (P) suffered injuries after eating a pig that had been fed mercury-laced grain supplied by Nor-Am (D).**

**CONCISE RULE OF LAW: The imposition of strict liability causes manufacturers to make safer products.**

**FACTS:** The Huckleby's (P) fed a pig grain supplied by Nor-Am Agricultural Products, Inc. (D). Unbeknownst to them, the grain had been treated with a mercury-containing disinfectant. As a result of mercury poisoning, the Huckleby's (P) children suffered blindness and paralysis. They sued Nor-Am (D) for strict liability for their failure to warn of the danger. A trial court granted summary judgment dismissing the action, and an appeal was taken.

**ISSUE:** Does the imposition of strict liability make products safer?

**HOLDING AND DECISION:** (Sutin, J.) Yes. The imposition of strict liability causes manufacterers to make safer products. If plaintiffs are not forced to prove negligence, manufacturers will have to take cautionary steps to prevent dangerous defective products. The public interest in safety requires that the law give consumers maximum protection against dangerous products. Accordingly, strict liability must be available to plaintiffs. Reversed.

**EDITOR'S ANALYSIS:** Products liability law has become something of a political battleground in recent years. Supporters of the status quo point to increased product safety. Supporters of reform note that products liability laws have greatly increased costs of doing business and have hurt some industries.

**NOTES:**

# CHAPTER 6
# TESTS OF DEFECTIVENESS

## QUICK REFERENCE RULES OF LAW

1. **Consumer Expectations.** Whether a product contains an unreasonably dangerous defect depends upon the reasonable expectations of the ordinary consumer concerning the characteristics of this type of product. (Vincer v. Esther Williams All-Aluminum Swimming Pool Co.)

2. **Risk-Utility.** A product whose danger falls within the consumer's reasonable expectation may still be unreasonably dangerous. (Nichols v. Union Underwear Co.)

3. **Risk Utility.** Courts should apply a risk-utility analysis to determine product defectiveness rather than a consumer expectations analysis. (Sperry-New Holland v. Prestage)

4. **Alternative Tests of "Defect."** Where a plaintiff establishes that a product contained a defect which proximately caused his injuries, he need not show that the product was furthermore unreasonably dangerous to the user or consumer. (Cronin v. J.B.E. Olson Corp.)

5. **Alternative Tests of "Defect."** Products are considered defectively designed if they fail to perform as safely as an ordinary consumer would expect if used in a reasonably foreseeable manner. (Barker v. Lull Engineering Co.)

6. **Alternative Tests of "Defect."** Consumer expectations are not an appropriate defectiveness standard for complex products. (Soule v. General Motors Corp.)

7. **Alternative Tests of "Defect."** Products is defectively designed if the dangers of the design outweigh the benefits of the design, even if the danger is obvious. (Todd v. Société BIC (Todd I))

8. **Alternative Tests of "Defect."** Not stated casebook opinion. (Todd v. Société BIC (Todd II))

9. **Alternative Tests of "Defect."** The risk-utility test of design defectiveness should not be applied to a simple but obviously dangerous product. (Todd v. Société BIC (Todd III))

10. **Defect-Specific Tests.** To prove a manufacturing defect, one need not prove that the product deviated from its design specifications. (Magnuson v. Kelsey-Hayes Co.)

11. **Warnings and Instructions Defects.** Jury instructions regarding a failure-to-warn claim for damages must be submitted under a theory of negligence rather than a theory of strict liability. (Olson v. Prosoco, Inc.)

## VINCER v. ESTHER WILLIAMS ALL-ALUMINUM SWIMMING POOL CO.

69 Wis. 2d 326, 230 N.W.2d 794 (1975).

**NATURE OF CASE: Appeal from demurrer for action for strict liability.**

**FACT SUMMARY: Vincer (P), a child, was injured when he climbed the ladder of a swimming pool, fell into the waiter, and suffered brain damage.**

**CONCISE RULE OF LAW: Whether a product contains an unreasonably dangerous defect depends upon the reasonable expectations of the ordinary consumer concerning the characteristics of this type of product.**

**FACTS:** Vincer (P), who was two years old at the time of the incident, fell into a swimming pool in the back yard of the home of his grandparents, who he was visiting. The complaint alleged that a retractable ladder to the pool had been left in the down position, that the pool was unsupervised, and that Vincer (P) climbed the ladder, fell into the water and remained there for an extended period of time, resulting in severe brain damage causing permanent and total disablement. The strict tort count alleged that the swimming pool was defective and unreasonably dangerous because Williams (D) failed to take the reasonable precaution of building the swimming pool so that the fencing extended across the deck at the top of the ladder opening, with a self-closing, self-latching gate on the deck of the swimming pool, so as to prevent access to the swimming pool area by children of young age. Williams (D) demurred to the complaint, the trial court sustained the demurrer, and Vincer (P) brought this appeal.

**ISSUE:** Does the issue of whether a product contains an unreasonably dangerous defect depend upon the reasonable expectations of the ordinary consumer concerning the characteristics of the type of product?

**HOLDING AND DECISION:** (Hansen, J.) Yes. Whether a product contains an unreasonably dangerous defect depends upon the reasonable expectations of the ordinary consumer concerning the characteristics of this type of product. If the average consumer would reasonably anticipate the dangerous condition of the product and fully appreciate the attendant risk of injury, it would not be unreasonably dangerous and defective. In order to be liable for strict liability, the article sold must be dangerous to an extent beyond that which would be contemplated by the ordinary consumer who purchases it, with the ordinary knowledge common to the community as to its characteristics. Here, the lack of a self-latching gate certainly falls within the category of an obvious rather than a latent condition. The average consumer would be completely aware of the risk of harm to small children due to this condition, when the retractable ladder is left in a down position and the children are left unsupervised. Affirmed.

**EDITOR'S ANALYSIS:** This case illustrates the role that the reasonable expectations of the average consumer have in determining strict liability in tort. As one of the most famous legal scholars has noted: "In civilized society men must be able to assume that those with whom they deal in the general intercourse of society will act in good faith and hence will make good reasonable expectations which their promises or other conduct reasonably create; (and) will carry out their undertakings according to the expectations which the moral sentiment of the community attaches thereto." R. Pound, Social Control through Law 114 (1942, 1968 reprint).

**NOTES:**

## NICHOLS v. UNION UNDERWEAR CO., INC.

Ky. Sup. Ct., 602 S.W.2d 429 (1980).

**NATURE OF CASE: Appeal from denial of damages for products liability.**

**FACT SUMMARY: The trial court instructed the jury that Union's (D) product was unreasonably dangerous only if its danger went beyond that expected by a reasonable consumer.**

**CONCISE RULE OF LAW: A product whose danger falls within the consumer's reasonable expectation may still be unreasonably dangerous.**

**FACTS:** Nichols (P), a child, was severely burned when his T-shirt caught fire. He sued Union (D), the manufacturer, for strict liability based on a design defect rendering the shirt unreasonably dangerous. The trial court instructed the jury that the product was unreasonably dangerous only if its danger exceeded that expected by a reasonable consumer. Nichols (P) objected, contending unreasonable danger went beyond consumer expectation. Nichols (P) appealed from a verdict for Union (D).

**ISSUE:** May a product whose danger falls within that expected by a reasonable consumer still be found to be unreasonably dangerous?

**HOLDING AND DECISION:** (Stephens, J.) Yes. A product whose danger falls within the consumer's reasonable expectation may still be found to be unreasonably dangerous. Consumer expectation is merely one factor in determining whether a product is unreasonably dangerous. A product does not become insulated from liability merely because its danger is patent rather than latent. By instructing the jury only on consumer expectation, the court prejudiced the jury by isolating one among many factors. Thus, the instruction was error. Reversed and remanded.

**CONCURRENCE:** (Lukowsky, J.) Whether a product contains a design defect must be determined using a social utility test, that is, whether the costs of a safer design are outweighed by the benefit of the increased safety.

**EDITOR'S ANALYSIS:** This majority opinion and the concurrence point out a significant issue in product design cases. This is the applicability of the social interest test. Several jurisdictions have adopted this balancing test as the definitive statement of liability. The consumer expectation test can be viewed as a restriction on liability while the social utility test takes a broader view.

**NOTES:**

## SPERRY-NEW HOLLAND v. PRESTAGE

Miss. Sup. Ct., 617 So. 2d 248 (1993).

**NATURE OF CASE: Appeal from jury verdict for plaintiff in an action for damages for negligence and strict liability in tort.**

**FACT SUMMARY: Prestage (P), who was injured by Sperry-New Holland's (D) combine, contended that Mississippi courts had replaced the consumer expectations analysis with a risk-utility test when evaluating products liability.**

**CONCISE RULE OF LAW: Courts should apply a risk-utility analysis to determine product defectiveness rather than a consumer expectations analysis.**

**FACTS:** Prestage (P) was using a combine manufactured by Sperry-New Holland (D) when his untucked shirt became stuck in the machine, injuring him. He sued Sperry (D) for defective design, alleging negligence and strict liability in tort. At trial, the judge instructed the jury to apply a "risk-utility" theory of recovery, i.e., to balance the utility and danger-in-fact of the combine when determining whether the combine was unreasonably dangerous. The jury returned a verdict in favor of Prestage (P), and Sperry (D) appealed, contending that the court should have applied a consumer expectations test instead, permitting Prestage (P) to recover only if an ordinary consumer would not expect the combine to be dangerous.

**ISSUE:** When determine product defectiveness, should courts apply a risk-utility analysis rather than a consumer expectations analysis?

**HOLDING AND DECISION:** (Prather, J.) Yes. When determining product defectiveness, courts should apply a risk-utility analysis rather than a consumer expectations analysis. In a risk-utility analysis, a product is unreasonably dangerous, and therefore defective, if a reasonable person would conclude that the danger-in-fact, whether foreseeable or not, outweighs the utility of the product. Whether a plaintiff appreciates the danger of a product is irrelevant to this analysis. Older cases may have applied a consumer expectations analysis, but the national trend now is to focus upon the utility and safety of a product in view of its intended function. A risk-utility analysis best protects both the manufacturer and the consumer. It requires the manufacturer to make its product reasonably safe regardless of whether the consumer is aware of the product's dangerousness, while at the same time taking into account an ordinary person's ability to avoid the danger. Affirmed.

**EDITOR'S ANALYSIS:** A risk-utility approach involves balancing the probability and seriousness of harm against the costs of taking precautions. It therefore provides an incentive to manufacturers to design their hazardous products in such a way as to minimize harm to their users. Factors to be considered when employing a risk-utility test include the availability of alternative designs, the cost and feasibility of adopting alternative designs, and the frequency or infrequency of injury resulting from the design.

## CRONIN v. J.B.E. OLSON CORP.

8 Cal. 3d 121, 104 Cal. Rptr. 433, 501 P.2d 1153 (1972).

**NATURE OF CASE: Appeal from award of damages for personal injury.**

**FACT SUMMARY: Cronin (P), who was driving a bread truck when it collided with another vehicle, causing a metal hasp holding the trays in place to break, was seriously injured when the trays came forward and propelled him through the windshield.**

**CONCISE RULE OF LAW: Where a plaintiff establishes that a product contained a defect which proximately caused his injuries, he need not show that the product was furthermore unreasonably dangerous to the user or consumer.**

**FACTS:** Cronin (P) was driving a bread delivery truck in the course of his employment when he attempted to pass a pickup truck. The two collided, and Cronin's (P) truck ran into a ditch. The metal hasp that was holding the bread trays in place gave way, allowing the trays to fly forward upon impact. The trays propelled Cronin (P) through the windshield, and he sustained serious personal injuries. At the close of evidence, the trial court refused to instruct the jury that Cronin (P) had to show that the metal hasp was unreasonably dangerous to the user or consumer in addition to proving that it was defective and that the defect proximately caused his injuries. Olson (D) appealed.

**ISSUE:** Where a plaintiff establishes that a product contained a defect which proximately caused his injuries, must he also show that the product was unreasonably dangerous to the user or consumer?

**HOLDING AND DECISION:** (Sullivan, J.) No. This court recently held that a manufacturer is strictly liable in tort when an article he places on the market, knowing that it is to be used without inspection for defects, proves to have a defect that causes injury to a human being. This holding intertwines with the Restatement (Second) of Torts § 402A, which imposes liability for selling products in a defective condition unreasonably dangerous to the user or consumer. Rejected is the notion that a plaintiff must prove first, the defect and second, unreasonable dangerousness. Where a plaintiff establishes that a product contained a defect which proximately caused his injuries, he need not also show that the product was unreasonably dangerous to the consumer or user. A seller should be liable for all injuries proximately caused by any of its products that are adjudged "defective." Affirmed.

**EDITOR'S ANALYSIS:** Most cases and commentators are not in accord with the Cronin approach to strict liability. The term "defect" is viewed as vague in the absence of a determination of whether it is unreasonably dangerous. The reason the law attaches liability to the seller is that it has subjected an unsuspecting member of the public to potential injury, and the term "defect" does not make this plain by itself.

## BARKER v. LULL ENGINEERING CO.

Cal. Sup. Ct., 20 Cal. 3d 413 (1978).

**NATURE OF CASE: Appeal from defense verdict in personal injury action.**

**FACT SUMMARY: Barker (P) contended that a forklift had been defectively designed.**

**CONCISE RULE OF LAW: Products are considered defectively designed if they fail to perform as safely as an ordinary consumer would expect if used in a reasonably foreseeable manner.**

**FACTS:** Barker (P) was injured while using a forklift made by Lull Engineering Co. (D). He sued, contending a design defect. The trial court instructed the jury that liability could be found if the forklift had been "unreasonably dangerous." The jury returned a verdict in favor of Lull (D), and the court of appeal affirmed. Barker (P) appealed.

**ISSUE:** Are products considered defectively designed if they fail to perform as safely as an ordinary consumer would expect if used in a reasonably foreseeable manner?

**HOLDING AND DECISION:** (Tobriner, J.) Yes. Products are considered defectively designed if they fail to perform as safely as an ordinary consumer would expect if used in a reasonably foreseeable manner. Plaintiffs cannot be expected to identify the precise nature of a design defect. The consumer expectation test, largely borrowed from the contract concepts of warranty of merchantability and fitness, steers the correct course between making the manufacturer an insurer of its product and placing insurmountable obstacles in the path of an injured plaintiff. Here, the "unreasonably dangerous" standard articulated by the trial court could have been construed by the jury as demanding an explanation from Barker (P) as to the nature of the defect he alleged, an improper burden. Reversed.

**EDITOR'S ANALYSIS:** Some courts have required that a product be used in an intended manner. The test employed here is somewhat more plaintiff-friendly. Under the standard here, a consumer can misuse a product from a manufacturer's point of view but still recover if the use was foreseeable.

**NOTES:**

## SOULE v. GENERAL MOTORS CORP.

Cal. Sup. Ct., 8 Cal. 4th 548 (1994).

**NATURE OF CASE: Appeal from verdict awarding damages for personal injury.**

**FACT SUMMARY: GM (D) contended that consumer expectations were not an appropriate standard for defectiveness when a complex product was involved.**

**CONCISE RULE OF LAW: Consumer expectations are not an appropriate defectiveness standard for complex products.**

**FACTS:** Soule (P) was injured when she was involved in an accident driving an automobile, that was made by General Motors Corp. (D). The trial court instructed the jury that the car could be considered defective if: (1) it failed to meet reasonable consumer expectations; or (2) the utility of its design was not outweighed by the risk of harm. The jury returned a verdict awarding damages. The court of appeals affirmed, and the California Supreme Court granted review.

**ISSUE:** Is consumer expectations an appropriate standard for determining the defectivenes of complex products?

**HOLDING AND DECISION:** (Baxter, J.) No. Consumer expectations are not an appropriate defectiveness standard for complex products. Two distinct tests exist for gauging design defectiveness: (1) whether the product fails to perform as safely as a reasonable consumer would expect when using the product in a reasonably foreseeable way; or (2) whether the dangers created by the product outweigh the benefits of the challenged design. In a complex product, it is difficult to envision what a reasonable consumer could expect in terms of safety, as the product's complexity forecloses a layman from having ordinary expectations. The second test, which requires expert testimony regarding the risks and benefits of the products, is much more appropriate in cases involving complex products. Therefore, the consumer expectation test should not be used in cases involving complex products, such as the automobile at issue here. In the instant case, the jury appears to have employed the risk-utility test. Therefore, the verdict is affirmed.

**EDITOR'S ANALYSIS:** The analysis of the court here is generally accepted in those jurisdictions having ruled on the issue. Consumers cannot have expectations outside of their common experience. Technical products are usually not part of most people's common experience.

## TODD v. SOCIÉTÉ BIC (TODD I)

U.S. Ct. of App., 991 F. 2d 1334 (7th Cir. 1993).

**NATURE OF CASE: Appeal from summary judgment dismissing wrongful death lawsuit.**

**FACT SUMMARY: Todd (P) contended that a cigarette lighter made by BIC (D) was defective because its dangers outweighed its design benefits.**

**CONCISE RULE OF LAW: Products is defectively designed if the dangers of the design outweigh the benefits of the design, even if the danger is obvious.**

**FACTS:** Todd's (P) decedent, a young child, was killed when another child started a fire with a cigarette lighter manufactured by BIC (D). Todd (P) filed a wrongful death action based on alleged defective design for lacking child resistant features and adequate warnings. The district court held that the fire danger of a cigarette lighter was obvious, so the lighter had lived up to consumer expectations, and the court granted BIC's (D) motion for summary judgment.

**ISSUE:** Is a product defectively designed if the dangers of the design outweigh the benefits of the design, even if the danger is obvious?

**HOLDING AND DECISION:** (Kaufman, J.) Yes. A product is defectively designed if the dangers of the design outweigh the benefits of the design, even if the danger is obvious. Two tests exist for a design defect, the "consumer expectation" test and the "risk-utility" test. Under this test, if the product's design legally causes injury, it will be held defective if the design's risks are not outweighed by the benefits of the design. Where the dangers of a product are obvious and the mechanism is simple, the consumer expectations test may not be proper. Here, evidence was submitted of potentially safer designs of the BIC lighter, indicating that the risk-utility test should have been employed. Reversed.

**DISSENT:** (Manion, J.) The dangers here were sufficiently obvious that the consumer contemplation test should have been used.

**EDITOR'S ANALYSIS:** This decision was just the beginning of the case's appellate journey. The casebook includes the subsequent history. Deciding which test to use is not the end of the inquiry in design defect analysis. Some courts limit the "consumer" to a purchaser. Others include foreseeable users, a broader category.

**NOTES:**

## TODD v. SOCIÉTÉ BIC (TODD II)

U.S. Ct. of App. 9 F. 3d 1216 (7th Cir. en banc).

**NATURE OF CASE: Appeal from reversal of summary judgment dismissing personal injury action.**

**NOTES:**

**FACT SUMMARY: Not stated in casebook opinion.**

**CONCISE RULE OF LAW: Not stated casebook opinion.**

**FACTS:** Not stated in the casebook opinion.

**ISSUE:** Not stated in the casebook opinion.

**HOLDING AND DECISION:** (Easterbrook, J.) [The Seventh Circuit, sitting en banc, reviewed the opinion of a three-judge panel regarding the proper test to be used in a design defect action. Not satisfied with the panel's opinion, the court certified to the Illinois Supreme Court two questions of law (as this was a diversity federal action, state substantive law applied): (1) whether a "consumer" of a product included nonpurchasers; and (2) whether the risk-utility test applies to consumer products whose dangers can be appreciated by their intended users.]

**EDITOR'S ANALYSIS:** Federal courts, constrained by Article III's cases and controversies requirements, cannot issue advisory opinions. This is not true for state courts. State courts can and do issue such opinions, and its is not uncommon for federal courts to request them.

## TODD v. SOCIÉTÉ BIC (TODD III)

21 F.3d 1402 (7th Cir. 1994).

**NATURE OF CASE: En banc rehearing of order reversing summary judgment dismissing wrongful death action.**

**FACT SUMMARY: Société Bic (D) contended that the "risk-utility" test should not be used to estimate the costs and benefits of manufacturing a child-resistant lighter.**

**CONCISE RULE OF LAW: The risk-utility test of design defectiveness should not be applied to a simple but obviously dangerous product.**

**FACTS:** Todd's (P) decedent, a child, died in a fire caused by another child playing with a cigarette lighter. Todd (P) sued Société Bic (D), the lighter's manufacturer. The district court granted summary judgment dismissing the action, concluding that the lighter had met consumer expectations. A panel of the Seventh Circuit reversed, holding that a triable issue of fact existed as to whether the risks of the lighter's design outweighed its utility. After the Illinois Supreme Court refused to answer two certified questions of law posed by the Seventh Circuit sitting en banc, the court ordered an en banc rehearing.

**ISSUE:** Should the risk-utility test of design defectiveness be applied to a simple but obviously dangerous product?

**HOLDING AND DECISION:** (Marion, J.) No. The risk-utility test of design defectiveness should not be applied to a simple but obviously dangerous product. The classic and still preferable test for a design defect is the consumer contemplation test: In this case, what does an ordinary consumer expect when he buys a lighter? A second test has been articulated for products too complex for an ordinary consumer to have a reasonable expectation of performance. As to these products, the utility of the design is weighed against its risks. However, when a product is simple enough that a consumer can have a reasonable expectation of performance, the risk-utility test should not be used. Here, a cigarette lighter is a simple product that performs a simple function. Bic's (D) lighter did what any reasonable adult consumer would have expected it to do, light a fire. A lighter is obviously, but not unreasonably, dangerous. Based on this, the lighter was not defective. District court affirmed.

**DISSENT:** (Cudahy, J.) Social policy dictates that when children are involved the threshold for liability should be very low. The societal costs of inevitable injuries to children should be borne by the manufacturer and passed on to society as a whole, not borne by individual victims.

**DISSENT:** (Flaum, J.) Illinois law required the district court to apply the risk-utility doctrine in this product liability case.

**DISSENT:** (Ripple, J.) En banc review was inappropriate here.

**EDITOR'S ANALYSIS:** Products liability law is, to a large extent, a societal insurance policy. It is a court-imposed system of risk spreading, where society pays a premium for compensating accident victims. The Seventh Circuit, long dominated by judges with laissez-faire economic views, not unexpectedly looked askance at this system.

**NOTES:**

## MAGNUSON v. KELSEY-HAYES CO.

Mo. Ct. of App., 844 S.W.2d 448 (1992).

**NATURE OF CASE: Appeal from grant of defense motion for a new trial following award damages in personal injury action alleging negligence and strict liability.**

**FACT SUMMARY: At trial, Magnuson (P) proved that the wheel that broke loose from a truck and struck him was defectively manufactured, but Kelsey-Hayes Co. (D) contended that he must also prove that the wheel did not conform to design specifications.**

**CONCISE RULE OF LAW: To prove a manufacturing defect, one need not prove that the product deviated from its design specifications.**

**FACTS:** Magnuson (P) was seriously injured when a wheel came off a Chrysler pick-up truck and struck him. Magnuson (P) sued Kelsey-Hayes Co. (D) and Chrysler (D), alleging strict liability on design and manufacturing defects. After Chrysler (D), which had designed but not manufactured the wheel, was dismissed from the case, Magnuson (P) abandoned his design defect claim. At trial, Magnuson's (P) expert gave testimony that tended to prove both a manufacturing and a design defect. A jury awarded $4,750,000. The court, however, granted a new trial ruling that Magnuson's (P) abandonment of the design defect claim precluded Kelsey-Hayes (D) from impleading Chrysler (D). Magnuson (P) appealed.

**ISSUE:** Must one, to prove a manufacturing defect, prove that the product deviated from its design specifications?

**HOLDING AND DECISION:** (Breckinridge, J.) No. One need not, to prove a manufacturing defect, prove that the product deviated from its design specifications. A manufacturing defect is proven by showing (1) that a defendant manufactured a product; (2) that it was in a defective condition when put to a reasonably anticipated use; (3) that the product was put to such a use; and (4) that injury was proximately caused by such use. A showing that the product did not conform to design specifications is not necessary. Here, proof of the above elements was put forth at trial by Magnuson (P) against Kelsey-Hayes (D), so he proved a manufacturing defect. This is sufficient to sustain the jury verdict. Reversed.

**EDITOR'S ANALYSIS:** The rule here is not universally, or even generally, followed. Many courts do make a clearer analytical distinction between manufacturing defects and design departure-from-defects than did the court here, and do require a showing of deviation. Some states have even enacted the deviation-from-specifications test into law.

## OLSON v. PROSOCO, INC.

Sup. Ct. Iowa, 522 N.W.2d 284 (1984).

**NATURE OF CASE: Appeal from verdict awarding damages in a personal injury action.**

**FACT SUMMARY: In Olson's (P) personal injury action based on an alleged failure to warn, the judge instructed the jury on both negligence and strict liability.**

**CONCISE RULE OF LAW: Jury instructions regarding a failure-to-warn claim for damages must be submitted under a theory of negligence rather than a theory of strict liability.**

**FACTS:** Olson (P) was injured when, while moving a drum of mortar cleaner, the bung popped up, splashing acidic liquid in his eyes. He brought a lawsuit against the manufacturer, Prosoco, Inc. (D), alleging a failure to warn of the product's dangers. The court submitted the matter to the jury on both negligence and strict liability theories. The jury returned a verdict for Olson (P), and Prosoco (D) appealed.

**ISSUE:** Must jury instructions regarding a failure-to-warn claim for damages be submitted under a theory of negligence rather than a theory of strict liability?

**HOLDING AND DECISION:** (Snell, J.) Yes. Jury instructions regarding a failure-to-warn claim for damages must be submitted under a theory of negligence rather than a theory of strict liability. Whether or not to place a warning, and what kind of warning to place, inevitably involves an inquiry into the reasonableness of the manufacturer's conduct in designing and selling the product as it did. This is different from strict liability, which focuses not on a defendant's conduct, but rather on the condition of the product itself. Therefore, instructing the jury on strict liability in a failure-to-warn case presents a serious prospect of juror confusion. However, although the instruction was error, it was not reversible error. Affirmed.

**EDITOR'S ANALYSIS:** If the negligence-only doctrine is employed, establishing liability in a failure-to-warn case requires a showing that the manufacturer knew or should have known of the danger, in light of prevailing best scientific knowledge, yet did not provide adequate warning to users or consumers. The manufacturer is held to the standard of care of an expert in its field. The new Restatement of Torts, on the other hand, defines a product as "defective" (thereby rendering its manufacturer strictly liable) when the foreseeable risks of harm posed by a product could have been avoided by a warning and omission of the warning makes the product not reasonably safe. See § 2(c).

**NOTES:**

# CHAPTER 7
# TYPES OF DEFECT

## QUICK REFERENCE RULES OF LAW

1. **Defective Manufacture.** A jury may infer manufacturer negligence from circumstantial evidence where there is direct evidence in the record of an actual defect in the product. (Pouncey v. Ford Motors Co.)

2. **Defective Manufacture.** A malfunction by a product establishes a prima facie case of product defect. (Ducko v. Chrysler Motors Corp.)

3. **Food and Drink.** A manufactured food product may be considered defective if it contains an unexpected natural substance. (Jackson v. Nestle-Beich, Inc.)

4. **Food and Drink.** When a plaintiff produces evidence that his injury was caused by a defect in a product which was present at the time the product left the hands of the manufacturer, it is up to the manufacturer to offer evidence of tampering with the product. (Shoshone Coca-Cola Bottling Co. v. Dolinski)

5. **Defective Design.** Where a product's design conceals an inherently dangerous mechanism, the product's design should incorporate a protective housing for the mechanism. (Matthews v. Lawnlite Co.)

6. **Defective Design.** A manufacturer will be liable for reasonable reliance on instructions warranting safety features. (McCormack v. Hankscraft Co.)

7. **Defective Design.** In a products liability case based upon defective design, the plaintiff has the burden of proving the availability of a cost-effective, alternative design for the product. (Knitz v. Minster Machine Co.)

8. **Delegation.** A manufacturer may be liable for injuries caused by the failure to install a feasible safety device. (Bexiga v. Havir Manufacturing Corp.)

9. **Delegation.** Where a finished product is the result of substantial work by more than one party, the determination of responsibility for the absence of a safety device is made by balancing the relevant factors. (Verge v. Ford Motor Co.)

10. **Expert Testimony.** Expert testimony regarding human behavior is admissible to prove a defect in a product. (Carroll v. Otis Elevator Co.)

11. **Expert Testimony.** Expert testimony about design defects is admissible only if it is scientifically based. (Pestel v. Vermeer Manufacturing Co.)

12. **Defective Marketing: Warnings and Instructions.** The adequacy of the warning given by a manufacturer in a negligence action presents an issue of fact for the jury. (Michael v. Warner/Chilcott)

13. **Defective Marketing: Warnings and Instructions.** To support a finding of a failure to warn, expert testimony regarding alternative warnings must establish feasibility, adequacy, and effectiveness. (Meyerhoff v. Michelin Tire Corp.)

14. **Delegation.** There is no duty on product suppliers to warn ultimate users of product-related hazards in products supplied in bulk to a knowledgeable user. (Higgins v. E.I. DuPont de Nemours & Co.)

# Notes

**POUNCEY v. FORD MOTOR CO.**

464 F.2d 957 (5th Cir. 1972).

**NATURE OF CASE: Appeal from award of damages for products liability.**

**FACT SUMMARY: Ford (D) contended that the evidence was insufficient to support the jury's verdict for Pouncey (P) because Pouncey's (P) expert testimony did not make any one cause of the source of the injury more probable than another.**

**CONCISE RULE OF LAW: A jury may infer manufacturer negligence from circumstantial evidence where there is direct evidence in the record of an actual defect in the product.**

**FACTS:** Pouncey (P) was injured while putting antifreeze in his 1966 Ford (D) automobile. While he was accelerating the engine with the hood open, a blade broke off the radiator fan, cut through the water hose, and struck him in the face causing permanent facial disfigurement. The car had been driven approximately 62,000 miles at the time of the accident. Pouncey (P) brought this action against Ford (D), seeking damages for the injury on a products liability theory. The main thrust of Pouncey's (P) case was that the fan blade failure occurred because of a fatigue fracture in the metal fan blade. It was Pouncey's (P) theory that the premature fatigue failure was caused by an excessive number of impurities in the metal of the blade, which weakened the metal. Pouncey's (P) expert witness testified unequivocally that enormous impurities in the metal had caused premature fatigue failure. The case was tried to a jury which returned a verdict in favor of Pouncey (P). Ford (D) then brought this appeal, contending that the evidence was insufficient because Pouncey's (P) expert testimony, viewed in its best light, did not make any one cause of the blade separation more probable than another.

**ISSUE:** May a jury infer manufacturer negligence from circumstantial evidence where there is direct evidence in the record of an actual defect in the product?

**HOLDING AND DECISION:** (Morgan, J.) Yes. A manufacturer's liability for a defective product is predicated upon negligence in the manufacture or design of the product. However, a jury is freely permitted to infer manufacturer negligence from circumstantial evidence where there is direct evidence in the record of an actual defect in the product. Here, there was direct evidence that Ford's (D) supplier manufactured the blades with "dirty" spring steel. There was also testimony by Pouncey's (P) expert that Ford (D) and its supplier could reasonably expect a premature fatigue failure from steel with that level of impurity. Finally, Ford (D) itself offered no evidence as to the quality control procedures actually employed with regard to the radiator fans produced in 1966. Thus, the trial court committed no error in permitting the jury to infer negligence from this evidence on the part of Ford (D) in placing on the market a defective radiator fan which could reasonably have been expected to produce injury or damage. Affirmed.

**EDITOR'S ANALYSIS:** "The determination of defect and its unreasonable danger is, in one sense, subjective because each product must be viewed in the particular context of its function and use. The use of the same product in two different environments, domestic and industrial, for example, may lead to different conclusions regarding its defectiveness and unreasonable danger." Weinstein, Twerski, Piehler, Donarher, Product Liability: An Interaction of Law and Technology, 12 Duquesne L. Rev. 425, 430-433 (1974).

**NOTES:**

## DUCKO v. CHRYSLER MOTORS CORP.

Pa. Super. Ct., 433 Pa. Super. 47, 639 A.2d 1204 (1994).

**NATURE OF CASE: Appeal from summary judgment dismissing strict product liability action.**

**FACT SUMMARY: Ducko (P) was unable to explain the mechanics of an alleged malfunction in her auto, but claimed that a malfunction by a product establishes a prima facie case of product defect.**

**CONCISE RULE OF LAW: A malfunction by a product establishes a prima facie case of product defect.**

**FACTS:** Ducko (P) was injured when her brand-new car suddenly veered off the road. She could not point to a specific defect, but claimed that both the steering and brakes had malfunctioned simultaneously. Chrysler Motors (D), the manufacturer, moved for summary judgment. The trial court granted the motion, and Ducko (P) appealed, contending that the "malfunction theory" of products liability permitted her to use circumstantial evidence to establish that the car was defective.

**ISSUE:** Does a malfunction in a product establish a prima facie case of product defect?

**HOLDING AND DECISION:** (Wieand, J.) Yes. A malfunction in a product establishes a prima facie case of product defect. When a plaintiff alleges a manufacturing defect and can eliminate misuse of the product as a cause, proof of the malfunction creates a presumption of defect, which the defendant must rebut. Here, Ducko (P) gave evidence of a malfunction, and also adduced evidence of proper use. This was sufficient to allow the matter to go to a jury, so summary judgment was inappropriate. Reversed.

**EDITOR'S ANALYSIS:** While not citing it, the court here essentially recast the rule from Barker v. Lull, 20 Cal. 3d 913 (1978). Barker held that a product was defective if it proved dangerous when used in a reasonably foreseeable manner. Note that when the alleged malfunction occurs shortly after the product is purchased, the inference that the defect originated with the manufacturer is stronger.

**NOTES:**

## JACKSON v. NESTLE-BEICH, INC.

Ill. Sup. Ct., 147 Ill. 2d 408, 589 N.E.2d 547 (1992).

**NATURE OF CASE: Review of order reversing summary judgment for the defense in products liability action.**

**FACT SUMMARY: Since Jackson (P) was injured while eating a Nestle (D) pecan candy by biting on a pecan shell, Nestle (D) argued it should not be liable because the shell naturally occurred in the product.**

**CONCISE RULE OF LAW: A manufactured food product may be considered defective if it contains an unexpected natural substance.**

**FACTS:** Jackson (P) broke a tooth while eating a pecan candy which contained a piece of a pecan shell. She sued Nestle (D), the candy's manufacturer, for breach of implied warranty and strict products liability. The trial court granted Nestle's (D) motion for summary judgment, holding that since the shell naturally occurred in pecan products, the candy could not be considered a defective product. The court of appeals reversed, and the state supreme court granted review.

**ISSUE:** May a manufactured food product be considered defective if it contains an unexpected natural substance?

**HOLDING AND DECISION:** (Freeman, J.) Yes. A manufactured food product may be considered defective if it contains an unexpected natural substance. Older cases have held that a food product containing an unnatural contaminant could be considered defective, but when the contaminant was a byproduct of the food used in making the food product, products liability was held inapplicable. This was always an artificial distinction and certainly does not comport with the realities of modern-day food consumption, where the consumer usually purchases a processed food product with a reasonable expectation that it will be free of potentially injurious substances, be they natural or otherwise. Therefore, a better test for defectiveness of a food product is: Would a reasonable consumer expect that a given product might contain the substance causing a particular injury? Since the trial court used the inappropriate "foreign/natural" distinction, the court of appeals properly reversed it. Affirmed.

**DISSENT:** (Heiple, J.) A consumer should reasonably expect that a food product might contain a naturally occurring byproduct.

**EDITOR'S ANALYSIS:** One of the main rationales behind products liability law involves the relative positions of manufacturers and consumers. As the manufacturer is in a better position to minimize a product's risk, it should bear the consequences of that risk. The foreign-natural doctrine rejected by the court in the above case is at odds with that policy and is therefore falling out of favor.

## SHOSHONE COCA-COLA BOTTLING CO. v. DOLINSKI

82 Nev. 439, 420 P.2d 855 (1966).

**NATURE OF CASE: Appeal from award of damages for product liability.**

**FACT SUMMARY: Dolinski (P) drank part of a bottle of "Squirt" before discovering the decomposed remains of a mouse in it.**

**CONCISE RULE OF LAW: When a plaintiff produces evidence that his injury was caused by a defect in a product which was present at the time the product left the hands of the manufacturer, it is up to the manufacturer to offer evidence of tampering with the product.**

**FACTS:** Dolinski (P) drank part of a bottle of "Squirt" before discovering the decomposed remains of a mouse in it. Dolinski's (P) expert testified that the mouse had been dead for some time and that the dark stains on the bottom of the bottle were mouse feces and had been there before the liquid was added. Shoshone's (D) manager testified that the processes preceding the filling of the bottles would have eradicated the mouse and that the mouse got into the bottle after it left Shoshone's (D) possession. The jury awarded Dolinski (P) $2,500 after trial, and Shoshone (D) appealed.

**ISSUE:** When a plaintiff introduces evidence that his injury was caused by a defect in a product which was present at the time the product left the hands of the manufacturer, is it up to the manufacturer to offer evidence of tampering with the product?

**HOLDING AND DECISION:** (Thompson, J.) Yes. Shoshone (D) urged that the burden was cast upon Dolinski (P) to prove that there was no reasonable opportunity for someone to tamper with the bottle after it left the plant. This is really a matter of causation. Once it is decided that enough evidence is present to trace cause to a defendant, that same evidence may be used by the jury to find an absence of tampering. Any notion that there is a burden of proof as to tampering does not make sense. When a plaintiff introduces evidence that his injury was caused by a defect in a product which was present at the time the product left the hands of the manufacturer, it is up to the manufacturer to offer evidence of tampering with the product. Having shown delivery and dispensing to be in the ordinary course of business, Dolinski (P) had no need to show tampering did not exist. Shoshone's (D) contention that Dolinski (P) failed to show that Shoshone (D) manufactured and sold the bottle was without merit. Affirmed.

**EDITOR'S ANALYSIS:** In most cases, as in this one, direct evidence of tampering or the absence of tampering is not available. The jury must infer that tampering did or did not occur based on the evidence that is available. Foreign matter is more likely to have found its way into a sealed container before leaving the factory than after as a rule, and the defendant's task of showing tampering is not an easy one.

## MATTHEWS v. LAWNLITE CO.

88 So. 2d 299 (1956).

**NATURE OF CASE: Appeal from decision granting motion to dismiss complaint.**

**FACT SUMMARY: Matthews (P) appealed from a decision granting Lawnlite Co.'s (D) motion to dismiss his complaint, arguing the moving parts of the lounge chair he was examining, which severed his finger, should have been protected by a housing.**

**CONCISE RULE OF LAW: Where a product's design conceals an inherently dangerous mechanism, the product's design should incorporate a protective housing for the mechanism.**

**FACTS:** Matthews (P) was examining a lounge chair manufactured by Lawnlite Co. (D). The moving parts of the chair were constructed entirely of aluminium, were essential to the chair's operation, and were completely concealed from the user. While Matthews (P) was examining the chair, those moving parts severed his finger. He brought suit against Lawnlite Co. (D), contending the chair was defectively designed. The trial court granted Lawnlite's (D) motion to dismiss, and from that order, Matthews (P) appealed.

**ISSUE:** Where a product's design conceals an inherently dangerous mechanism, should the product's design incorporate a protective housing for the mechanism?

**HOLDING AND DECISION:** (Terrell, J.) Yes. Where a product's design conceals an inherently dangerous mechanism, the product's design should incorporate a protective housing for the mechanism. In the present case, there was nothing about the lounge chair to suggest to Matthews (P) that he could be injured in that manner. The chair was designed, constructed, and delivered to the public with these inherently dangerous moving parts in place. These parts were completely concealed from Matthews, and if such a mechanism was required by the chair, it should have been protected by a housing. Reversed and remanded.

**EDITOR'S ANALYSIS:** The court's analysis does not discuss the feasibility of an adequate warning, although it is noted that there is no notice of the dangerous mechanism. It is unlikely that any warning would suffice, unless it is demonstrated that the mechanism was essential to the product and the incorporation of a protective housing would destroy the utility of the product.

**NOTES:**

**McCORMACK v. HANKCRAFT CO.**

278 Minn. 322 (1967).

**NATURE OF CASE: Action for breach of express and implied warranties.**

**NOTES:**

**FACT SUMMARY: Hankcraft (D) stated in its instructions that its vaporizer was safe, could be left unattended, and was spill-proof.**

**CONCISE RULE OF LAW: A manufacturer will be liable for reasonable reliance on instructions warranting safety features.**

**FACTS:** McCormack (P) purchased a Hankcraft (D) vaporizer. McCormack (P) read the directions which indicated that the unit was safe, tip-proof, and could be left unattended with complete safety. McCormack (P) failed to discover that the reserve water became scalding hot, because she followed directions which requested use of a mitt or glove when emptying to avoid steam. No notice of the potential danger was included in the instructions. McCormack's (P) daughter (P) tipped over the vaporizer and was severely scalded. A design expert stated that the potential problem could have been avoided by inexpensively securing the top of the unit so that the water would not come out if tipped over. The jury found for McCormack (P) on her counts for breach of express and implied warranties. The court granted a judgment n.o.v. McCormack (P) appealed, alleging that she reasonably relied on the assurances of safety contained in the directions.

**ISSUE:** May a buyer reasonably rely on assurances by the manufacturer that its product was designed to safely operate in normal circumstances?

**HOLDING AND DECISION:** (Rogosheske, J.) Yes. A manufacturer may be held liable for a design defect when it advertises that its product is safe without disclosing the existence of a dangerous condition which is not readily discoverable by the user. Where the defect can be easily remedied and the danger from normal use is readily foreseeable, the design must be deemed defective. A user is entitled to rely on the representations of safety and the instructions and this may cause an otherwise adequate design to be deemed defective. Reversed.

**EDITOR'S ANALYSIS:** Many cases in this area are resolved on a theory of misrepresentation or on a theory that the instructions or representations create a trap for the unwary. Even obvious dangers may be deemed latent defects if instructions are calculated to have or have the effect of masking or unduly minimizing them. Even if the defect could not be guarded against, failure to adequately warn of the danger or to instruct in the proper use will render the design unnecessarily dangerous.

## KNITZ v. MINSTER MACHINE CO.

1987 WL 6486 (Westlaw, 1987).

**NATURE OF CASE: Appeal from award of damages for products liability.**

**FACT SUMMARY: Minster Machine Co. (D) appealed from an award in favor of Knitz (P) in her products liability action, arguing that the trial court erred in placing the burden of proving the availability of a cost-effective alternative design for the punch press of Minster (D).**

**CONCISE RULE OF LAW: In a products liability case based upon defective design, the plaintiff has the burden of proving the availability of a cost-effective, alternative design for the product.**

**FACTS:** Knitz (P) was injured while operating a sixty-ton OBI press manufactured by Minster (D). As originally ordered, the press had a two-hand button tripping device, which required both hands to activate the press. TDM, Knitz's (P) employer, also ordered the optional foot pedal tripping device sold and manufactured by Minster (D), which allowed the press to be operated by foot. TDM installed a pullback safeguard with the foot pedal which would physically pull the operator's wrists out of the die area when the ram of the press was activated. Knitz (P), without safeguards attached, attempted one day to reposition the foot pedal with her foot. The ram was activated and her fingers were severed. Her initial suit against Minster (D) based upon the defective design of the press was dismissed. After that decision was reversed and remanded, the jury returned an award for Knitz (P). Minster (D) appealed, arguing in part that the trial court erred in placing the burden of proving the unavailability of cost-effective, alternative design on Minster (D).

**ISSUE:** In a products liability case based upon defective design, does the plaintiff have the burden of proving the availability of a cost-effective, alternative design for the product?

**HOLDING AND DECISION:** (Per curiam) Yes. In a products liability action based upon defective design, the plaintiff has the burden of proving the availability of a cost-effective, alternative design for the product. (The court discussed in great detail the expert testimony on the foot pedal tripping device and the wrist pullback safeguards, as well as alternative designs to these features on the press.) This jurisdiction, in adopting the risk-benefit analysis test, has not adopted the shift in this burden to the manufacturer. To do so in the present case places Minster (D) in the unenviable position of arguing that the costs of any safety device outweigh human well-being. Regardless of its efforts in the development and design of a product, the manufacturer will be placed in a difficult, if not impossible, situation. To instruct the jury that Minster (D) had this burden was reversible error. (The court also found the trial court erred in excluding evidence of government and industry standards as a factor to be employed in the risk-benefit analysis.) Reversed and remanded.

**EDITOR'S ANALYSIS:** In determining the availability of a feasible alternative design, the trier of fact must focus not only on the cost of the alternative design, but also on the new design's impact on the overall operation and utility of the product. On the evidentiary issue raised by the court, it is clear that compliance with applicable standards is not conclusive on the issues of tort liability.

**NOTES:**

## BEXIGA v. HAVIR MANUFACTURING CORP.

60 N.J. 402, 290 A.2d 281 (1972).

**NATURE OF CASE: Appeal from dismissal of action for personal injuries.**

**FACT SUMMARY: Havir (D) contended that it should not be held liable for failure to install safety device, because the buyer would normally install such a device.**

**CONCISE RULE OF LAW: A manufacturer may be liable for injuries caused by the failure to install a feasible safety device.**

**FACTS:** Bexiga (P), a minor, was operating a power punch press for his employer, Regina Corporation (D), when his right hand was crushed by the ram of the machine, resulting in the loss of fingers and deformity of his hand. The machine that caused the injuries was a ten-ton punch press. With the exception of a guard over the flywheel, there were no safety devices of any kind on the machine when it was shipped. Bexiga (P) brought suit against Havir (D), the manufacturer, for negligence, breach of warranty, and strict liability in tort. His theory was that the punch press was so dangerous in design that Havir (D) was under a duty to equip it with some form of safety device to protect the user while the machine was being operated. Bexiga's (P) expert witness conceded at trial that the custom of the trade was to leave the selection and installation of safety devices to the ultimate user. He was of the opinion, however, that the custom was improper in that the machine was defectively designed for safety, and purchasers "almost never" provided safety devices. After Bexiga's (P) action was dismissed by the trial court, and the dismissal was affirmed by the court of appeals, Bexiga (P) brought this appeal.

**ISSUE:** May a manufacturer be liable for injuries caused by the failure to install a feasible safety device?

**HOLDING AND DECISION:** (Proctor, J.) Yes. Where a manufacturer places into the channels of trade a finished product which can be put to use and which should be provided with safety devices because without such it creates an unreasonable risk of harm, and where such safety devices can feasibly be installed by the manufacturer, the fact that he expects that someone else will install such devices should not immunize him. The only way to be certain that such devices will be installed on all machines, which clearly the public interest requires, is to place the duty on the manufacturer where it is feasible for him to do so. Where there is an unreasonable risk of harm to the user of a machine that has no protective safety device, as here, the jury may infer that the machine was defective in design unless it finds that the incorporation by the manufacturer of a safety device would render the machine unusable for its intended purposes. Here, while Havir (D) may have thought that Regina (D) would have taken adequate precautions to protect its employees or that it would be required to do so by statute, Havir (D) did not have a right as a matter of law to assume such devices would be provided. Reversed and remanded for a new trial.

**EDITOR'S ANALYSIS:** In a leading California case, Justice Traynor wrote that: "A manufacturer is strictly liable in tort when an article he places on the market, knowing that it is to be used without inspection for defects, proves to have a defect that causes injury to a human being. Since the liability is strict, it encompasses defects regardless of their source, and therefore a manufacturer of a completed product cannot escape liability by tracing the defect to a component part supplied by another." Vandermark v. Ford Motor Co., 61 Cal. 2d 256, 37 Cal. Rptr. 896, 391 P.2d 168 (1964).

**NOTES:**

## VERGE v. FORD MOTOR CO.

581 F.2d 384 (3rd Cir. 1978).

**NATURE OF CASE: Appeal from award of damages for personal injury.**

**FACT SUMMARY: Ford (D) contended that it should not be held liable in a products liability action because it was not responsible for the installation of a safety device.**

**CONCISE RULE OF LAW: Where a finished product is the result of substantial work by more than one party, the determination of responsibility for the absence of a safety device is made by balancing the relevant factors.**

**FACTS:** Verge (P) was an employee of the Government of the Virgin Island's Department of Public Works Sanitation Division. He worked on a garbage collection crew in St. Croix. On February 23, 1973, while he was standing at the rear of a garbage truck, the driver, without checking behind him, placed the truck into reverse gear, pinning Verge (P) between the truck and a garbage can. As a result, Verge (P) suffered a broken leg. Verge (P) then filed a complaint against Ford (D), Elgin-Leach Corp. (D), and Leach Co. (D), the final assembler of the truck, alleging that the defendants were negligent in failing to equip the truck with mirrors or other devices by which the operator of the truck would be able to ascertain the presence of individuals to its rear, prior to reversing the vehicle. The jury returned a verdict against Ford (D) after the other two defendants settled. The trial court then denied Ford's (D) motion for judgment notwithstanding the verdict, and Ford (D) brought this appeal, contending that it should not be held liable for negligence because Leach Co. (D) was responsible for the installation of safety devices on the trucks.

**ISSUE:** Where a finished product is the result of substantial work by more than one party, is the determination of responsibility for the absence of a safety device made by balancing the relevant factors?

**HOLDING AND DECISION:** (Higginbotham, J.) Yes. Where a finished product is the result of substantial work by more than one party, the determination of responsibility for the absence of a safety device is made by looking primarily to at least three factors: trade custom, relative expertise, and practicality. Here, there was inadequate testimony at trial to determine the trade custom in this matter. However, the evidence relating to comparative expertise indicated that Leach (D) is more expert than Ford (D) in the design of refuse collection vehicles. Leach (D) testified that his company does install warning devices. There was no testimony relating to Ford's (D) expertise in the design of garbage collection vehicles. There is no evidence that Ford (D) ever installed a warning device of the type in question. Finally, it is clear from the record that it is considerably more practical for warning devices to be installed by Leach (D) rather than Ford (D). The Ford (D) cab and chassis was a multipurpose vehicle, which could be modified for a number of uses that would require no backup buzzer. Accordingly, Ford (D) was not responsible for including a backup device or other safety device on the cab and chassis here, and is not liable for injuries caused by the absence of such a device. Reversed with instructions to grant judgment n.o.v. in favor of Ford (D).

**EDITOR'S ANALYSIS:** The Arizona state legislature adopted a statute to deal with many situations of the type illustrated by this case. Ariz. Rev. Stat § 12-684(C) provides in relevant part that a manufacturer may be indemnified for judgments rendered against it by the seller "if the seller provided the plans or specifications for the manufacture of preparation of the product and such plans or specifications were a substantial cause of the product's alleged defect.."

**NOTES:**

## CARROLL v. OTIS ELEVATOR CO.

896 F.2d 310 (7th Cir. 1990).

**NATURE OF CASE: Appeal from judgment awarding damages in a personal injury action.**

**FACT SUMMARY: Carroll (P), in a products liability action, introduced expert testimony regarding a child's propensity to push a "stop" button on an escalator.**

**CONCISE RULE OF LAW: Expert testimony regarding human behavior is admissible to prove a defect in a product.**

**FACTS:** Carroll (P) was injured when an escalator on which she was riding suddenly stopped, causing her to fall. She sued Otis Elevator Co. (D), the manufacturer, claiming strict liability for defective design. Carroll (P) contended that the emergency stop button had been pushed by a child. At trial, she introduced a psychologist who testified that the red stop button was displayed in a such a manner that it was attractive to children and, since it was uncovered and situated low, was likely to be pushed by one. The jury awarded her $43,000. Otis (D) appealed, contending that the trial court abused its discretion in qualifying the psychologist as an expert on elevator design.

**ISSUE:** Is expert testimony regarding human behavior admissible to prove a defect in product?

**HOLDING AND DECISION:** (Eschback, J.) Yes. Expert testimony regarding human behavior is admissible to prove a defect in a product. Federal Rule of Evidence 702 gives broad discretion to district courts to admit, as expert testimony, opinions by a person having knowledge superior to a layman about a matter relevant to the case. When human behavior is relevant to the use or misuse of a product, testimony regarding such behavior may be admitted. Here, as the allegation was that a child tripped the escalator's emergency stop button, testimony by an expert in the study of human perception regarding child behavior was appropriate. Affirmed.

**CONCURRENCE:** (Easterbrook, J.) The present case is an excellent example of all that is wrong with products liability law. Products liability has become a very expensive and inefficient form of social insurance having little to do with traditional tort principles. However, federal courts sitting in diversity are in no position to begin reforming the system; state courts must take the lead, which they have been doing to some extent over the last decade.

**EDITOR'S ANALYSIS:** Judge Easterbrook's position as articulated in his concurrence has many supporters. The detractors of products liability law compare it to social insurance programs in "social democracies" such as Western European nations. These countries created social insurance directly, but it has been imported through the back door by U.S. courts, as political consensus for such policies never existed in the United States.

## PESTEL v. VERMEER MANUFACTURING CO.

64 F.3d 382 (8th Cir. 1995).

**NATURE OF CASE: Appeal from directed verdict for the defense in product liability action.**

**FACT SUMMARY: Pestel (P) sought to have expert testimony admitted regarding an alternative design for a stump cutter safety guard, although it had not been fully tested.**

**CONCISE RULE OF LAW: Expert testimony about design defects is admissible only if it is scientifically based.**

**FACTS:** Pestel (P) stepped in front of a Vermeer (D) stump cutter to check on the operator's work and slipped. His right foot slid into the cutter wheel and was injured. Pestel (P) brought a products liability action against Vermeer (D). Pestel (P) hired Vidal, a mechanical engineer, to determine whether a safety-bar guard could have been made for the stump cutter that would have prevented the injury. Vidal developed a design for a guard but did not perform a patent search or consult any actual operators to determine how his design would work in the field. Vidal also did not test his guard design. The trial court excluded Vidal's expert testimony and directed a verdict for Vermeer (D). Pestel (P) appealed.

**ISSUE:** Is expert testimony about design defects always admissible?

**HOLDING AND DECISION:** (Arnold, J.) No. Expert testimony about design defects is admissible only if it is scientifically based. The admissibility of expert testimony is governed by Federal Rule of Evidence 702 and the Supreme Court's decision in Daubert v. Merrell Dow Pharmaceuticals, Inc., 113 S.Ct. 2786 (1993). That decision holds that a trial court should consider the following factors when assessing the reliability of expert testimony: 1) whether the concept has been tested; 2) whether the concept was subjected to peer review; and 3) whether the concept has been generally accepted. In this case, Pestel's (P) expert Vidal had not tested his guard design. Vidal had not submitted his design to any manufacturers or other experts. Vidal did not perform any patent searches so it was not possible to determine whether there was general acceptance of stump cutter guards. Therefore, the trial court's exclusion of Vidal's testimony was proper. Affirmed.

**EDITOR'S ANALYSIS:** The Daubert case involved the admission of expert testimony in toxic substance litigation. Complex scientific questions regarding causation were at issue. The instant case shows that the Daubert decision is now being used to exclude testimony in simpler cases.

**NOTES:**

## MICHAEL v. WARNER/CHILCOTT

91 N.M. 651, 579 P.2d 183 (1978).

**NATURE OF CASE: Appeal from denial of motion for summary judgment.**

**FACT SUMMARY: Skaggs (D) and other defendants contended that, as a matter of law, a warning that "medication may damage the kidneys when used in large amounts or for a long period of time" was adequate notice of the dangers of Skaggs's (D) products.**

**CONCISE RULE OF LAW: The adequacy of the warning given by a manufacturer in a negligence action presents an issue of fact for the jury.**

**FACTS:** Michael (P) suffered with sinus congestion symptoms since about 1952. Around 1965, his physician prescribed "Sinutab" in writing to be ingested four per day on a daily basis. Michael (P) purchased this over-the-counter drug at Skaggs Drug Center (D). In 1970, Michael (P) went to Skaggs (D) to make another purchase of "Sinutab" and was informed by the cashier that Skaggs (D) had its own house brand called "Sinus Congestion Tablets." Michael (P) bought this product, which contained a warning on its side that "This medication may damage the kidneys when used in large amounts or for a long period of time." Michael (P) read the label and continued ingestion of this over-the-counter drug, four per day, on a regular daily basis until April 1973, when his kidney failure was first diagnosed. After the various defendants moved for summary judgement, the trial court found that it could not conclude as a matter of law that the warnings furnished by Skaggs (D) on its tablets did constitute adequate notice as a matter of law. Skaggs (D) and its other defendants then brought this appeal.

**ISSUE:** Does the adequacy of the warning given by a manufacturer in a negligence action present an issue of fact for the jury?

**HOLDING AND DECISION:** (Sutin, J.) Yes. The adequacy of the warning given by a manufacturer in a negligence action presents an issue of fact for the jury. The warning must adequately indicate the scope of the danger. The warning must reasonably communicate the extent or seriousness of harm that could result from the danger. The physical aspects of the warning's conspicuousness, prominence, relative size of print, etc., must be adequate to alert the reasonably prudent person. Here, the warning did not apprise the consumer of the fact that it would damage the kidneys. The warning did not define the term "large amounts." Accordingly, a genuine issue of material fact exists on the adequacy of the warning. Affirmed.

**EDITOR'S ANALYSIS:** Most cases involving the adequacy of warnings given regarding product use usually fall into one of two categories. The first category involves cases raising the issue of the adequacy of information provided on the hazards of normal use of the product. The second category of cases involving the adequacy of warnings usually concerns the sufficiency of the information provided on misuse of the particular product.

## MEYERHOFF v. MICHELIN TIRE CORP.

852 F.Supp. 933 (D. Kan. 1994).

**NATURE OF CASE: Defense motion for judgment after trial jury award of damages for failure to warn.**

**FACT SUMMARY: Michelin (D) contended that Meyerhoff's (P) expert testimony was inadequate to prove an inadequate warning.**

**CONCISE RULE OF LAW: To support a finding of a failure to warn, expert testimony regarding alternative warnings must establish feasibility, adequacy, and effectiveness.**

**FACTS:** Meyerhoff's (P) decedent was killed when a Michelin (D) tire he was attempting to repair exploded because it had been driven upon while underinflated. A suit was brought by Meyerhoff's next-of-kin (P) against Michelin (D) for failure to provide an adequate warning on the tire of this danger. Wells, Meyerhoff's (P) expert, testified that a contrasting color warning should have been placed on the tire's sidewall. However, there was no testimony regarding the feasibility or potential effectiveness of this warning. The jury ascribed some fault to Michelin (D), which then moved for judgment after trial.

**ISSUE:** Must expert testimony regarding alternative warnings establish feasibility, adequacy, and effectiveness?

**HOLDING AND DECISION:** (Belot, J.) Yes. To support a finding of failure to warn, expert testimony regarding alternative warnings must establish feasibility, adequacy, and effectiveness. The Supreme Court's decision in Daubert v. Merrell Dow Pharmaceuticals, Inc., 509 U.S. 579 (1993), held that the subject of expert testimony must be scientific knowledge. This implies that there must be a grounding in methods and procedures of science, not mere subjective belief or speculation. Meyerhoff's (P) experts never established the feasibility of placing a colored warning on a tire, nor was there any evidence that the warning would have been adequate. Furthermore, the warning devised by Meyerhoff (P) addressed only the danger which killed Meyerhoff (P). There was no attempt to describe all of the possible hidden dangers that may have been needed on a warning. Accordingly, there was not sufficient evidence for the jury to ascribe fault to Michelin (D) for failure to warn. Michelin (D) is entitled to post-trial judgment. Motion granted.

**EDITOR'S ANALYSIS:** Other issues regarding the adequacy of warnings include the conspicuousness and location of the warning. Warnings must be of a sufficient size and color. They should also be included on the product itself, if feasible, and use signal words such as "Warning" or "Danger."

**NOTES:**

## HIGGINS v. E.I. DUPONT DE NEMOURS

671 F. Supp. 1055 (Md. 1987).

**NATURE OF CASE: Motion for summary judgment in product liability action.**

**FACT SUMMARY: Eastern (D) and Union Carbide (D) moved for summary judgment in the products liability action brought by Higgins (P), who represented a class of firefighters, arguing they had no duty, as bulk suppliers of commodity chemicals, to warn Higgins (P) of possible effects of the chemicals or the product in which they were incorporated.**

**CONCISE RULE OF LAW: There is no duty on product suppliers to warn ultimate users of product-related hazards in products supplied in bulk to a knowledgeable user.**

**FACTS:** Eastern (D) and Union Carbide (D) produced chemical ingredients which were shipped in bulk to E.I. DuPont de Nemours & Co., Inc. (D), which in turn incorporated these chemicals in a paint called Imron. This was sold to fire departments, which used it to paint fire-fighting equipment. Certain firefighters who used the paint, including Higgins (P), sued Eastern (D), Union Carbide (D), and DuPont (D), claiming the teratogenic effects of the chemicals in Imron interfered with fetal development of their children, who died at birth. The evidence indicated that DuPont (D), in particular, was aware of the effects of these chemicals. Eastern (D) and Union Carbide (D) moved for summary judgment, contending that as bulk chemical suppliers of DuPont (D), they had no duty to warn Higgins (P) of the effects of the chemicals. Higgins (P) opposed, arguing in part that their strict liability claims were unaffected by the defense.

**ISSUE:** Is there a duty on product suppliers to warn ultimate users of products of product-related hazards in products supplied in bulk to a knowledgeable user?

**HOLDING AND DECISION:** (Smalkin, J.) No. There is no duty on product suppliers to warn ultimate users of product-related hazards in products supplied in bulk to a knowledgeable user. This defense has already been recognized with respect to employees of knowledgeable industrial purchasers. Whether the action is one of negligent failure to warn or strict liability failure to warn, the question is whether the supplier has acted reasonably in relying on the purchaser to promulgate an adequate warning. DuPont (D) qualifies as a knowledgeable purchaser of bulk chemicals in general and of these chemicals in particular. DuPont (D) was in a much better position to communicate an effective warning to its customers, including Higgins (P). There is no material issue of fact as to whether Eastern (D) and Union Carbide (D), as suppliers, reasonably relied on DuPont (D) to warn its customers. Motions for summary judgment granted.

**EDITOR'S ANALYSIS:** Not all courts adopt the reasoning in the present case. Some courts find that a supplier's obligations to provide warnings to the ultimate user is a question of fact, with the risk posed by the product balanced against the feasibility of the warning. Higgins (P), in the present case, could have argued that no steps were taken to ensure that DuPont (D) was promulgating an effective warning, undercutting the "reasonable" nature of moving parties' reliance.

**NOTES:**

# CHAPTER 8
# REGULATING DEFECTIVENESS

## QUICK REFERENCE RULES OF LAW

1. **Direct Agency Regulation.** The Consumer Products Safety Act (CPSA) requires that safety standards of the CPSC (D) be supported by substantial evidence such that a reasonable mind might accept as adequate to support the conclusion reached in the standard. (Southland Mower Co. v. Consumer Product Safety Commission)

2. **Preemption.** (1) The 1965 Federal Smoking Act does not preempt state law damages actions. (2) The 1969 Federal Smoking Act preempts failure to warn claims against tobacco manufacturers based on advertising after 1969. (Cipollone v. Liggett Group, Inc.)

3. **Preemption.** FIFRA preempts state tort claims based on alleged failure to provide adequate warnings on a product's label. (King v. E.I. Dupont De Nemours & Co.)

4. **Preemption.** The Medical Device Amendments of 1976 do not preempt state common law claims. (Kennedy v. Collagen Corp.)

## SOUTHLAND MOWER CO. v. CONSUMER PRODUCT SAFETY COMMISSION

619 F.2d 499 (5th Cir. 1980).

**NATURE OF CASE: Petition for review of order of the Consumer Product Safety Commission (CPSC).**

**FACT SUMMARY: Southland (P), represented by the Outdoor Power Equipment Institute (OPEI) (P), contended safety standards promulgated by the CPSC (D) were not supported by substantial evidence and were thus invalid.**

**CONCISE RULE OF LAW: The Consumer Products Safety Act (CPSA) requires that safety standards of the CPSC (D) be supported by substantial evidence such that a reasonable mind might accept as adequate to support the conclusion reached in the standard.**

**FACTS:** The CPSC (D), after receiving testimony and documentary evidence on the incidence of accidents caused by the use of power lawn mowers, promulgated safety standards for the manufacture of such machines. It required a foot probe test to avoid injuries from the insertion of the feet in the discharge chute; it required a blade control system; and it required adequate labeling of the product concerning the potential risk of injury. The OPEI (P), a manufacturers group, petitioned for review of the standard on the basis it was not supported by substantial evidence that such was needed. It challenged the specific requirements and the standard as a whole. The CPSC (D) relied on evidence showing a small number of accidents involving the discharge chute; that the blade control system would eliminate numerous injuries if the blade stopped three seconds after the operator's hands leave the operating position; and on evidence that pictorial labeling would dissuade the insertion of extremities into the blade area.

**ISSUE:** Must CPSC (D) standards be supported by sufficient evidence of their connection to alleviating the possibility of injury?

**HOLDING AND DECISION:** (Gee, J.) Yes. The CPSA requires that CPSC (D) standards be supported by substantial evidence such that a reasonable mind might accept as adequate to support the conclusion reached in the standard. The evidence supporting the foot probe was not sufficient. The evidence showed few if any foot injuries resulted from insertion in the discharge chute. Thus, this standard is invalid. The blade control system was shown to remedy a significant number of injuries by cutting off the blade. Also, the labeling requirement was sufficiently shown to deter the insertion of extremities in the blade area. The standard as a whole was properly supported by the wealth of documented injuries and the social utility in implementing this standard. Affirmed in part; vacated in part.

**EDITOR'S ANALYSIS:** The practical effect of this type of standard is that it places a floor on acceptable safety precautions. A failure to abide by the precaution can preclude the sale of the product or can establish a defect as a matter of law. It must of course be shown that this failure was the proximate cause of the injury involved. Manufacturers are often moved to establish their own safety standards to avoid having harsher standards imposed upon them by a governmental agency.

**NOTES:**

## CIPOLLONE v. LIGGETT GROUP, INC.

505 U.S. 504 (1992).

**NATURE OF CASE: Appeal from a denial of relief based on preemptive grounds.**

**FACT SUMMARY: Liggett (D) contended that the Federal Smoking Acts of 1965 and 1969 preempted state law damages actions relating to smoking and health that challenge either the adequacy of the warning on cigarette packages or the propriety of a party's actions with respect to advertising and promotion of cigarettes.**

**CONCISE RULES OF LAW: (1) The 1965 Federal Smoking Act does not preempt state law damages actions. (2) The 1969 Federal Smoking Act preempts failure to warn claims against tobacco manufacturers based on advertising after 1969.**

**FACTS:** Cipollone's (P) mother was a heavy smoker and died of lung cancer in 1984. He claimed that Liggett (D) was responsible for his mother's death because it breached express warranties contained in its advertising, which failed to warn consumers about the hazards of smoking, and because it fraudulently misrepresented those hazards to consumers. Liggett (D) claimed that the Federal Smoking Acts of 1965 and 1969 protected it from liability. The district court, in a pretrial ruling, held that the federal statutes were intended to establish a uniform warning but that the statutes did not preempt common law actions. The court of appeals reversed, rejecting Liggett's (D) contention that the federal acts expressly preempted common law actions but accepting its contention that such actions would conflict with federal law. Cipollone (P) appealed. The U.S. Supreme Court granted certiorari to consider the preemptive effect of the federal statute.

**ISSUES:** (1) Does the 1965 Federal Smoking Act preempt state law damages actions. (2) Does the 1969 Federal Smoking Act preempt failure to warn claims against tobacco manufacturers based on advertising after 1969?

**HOLDING AND DECISION:** (Stevens, J.) (1) No. The 1965 Federal Smoking Act does not preempt state law damages actions. On its face, the 1965 preemption provision regarding advertising merely prohibited state and federal rulemaking bodies from mandating particular cautionary statements on cigarette labels or in cigarette advertisements. The 1965 Act's statement of purpose expressed an intent to avoid diverse, nonuniform, and confusing labeling and advertising regulations with respect to any relationship between smoking and health. The Act only preempted state and federal rulemaking bodies from mandating particular cautionary statements and did not preempt state law damages actions. (2) Yes. The 1969 Federal Smoking Act preempts failure to warn claims against tobacco manufacturers based on advertising after 1969. The language of the 1969 Act is much broader in that the 1969 Act does not simply bar statements but rather requirements or prohibitions under state law. Also, the 1969 Act reaches beyond statements in the advertising to obligations with respect to the advertising or promotion of cigarettes. Cipollone's (P) claims are preempted to the extent that they rely on a state law requirement or prohibition with respect to advertising or promotion. Insofar as Cipollone's (P) failure to warn theory requires a showing that Liggett's (D) post-1969 advertising or promotions should have included additional or more clearly stated warnings, those claims are preempted. The 1969 Act does not preempt Cipollone's (P) claims based on express warranty, intentional fraud and misrepresentation, or conspiracy. Reversed in part; affirmed in part.

**CONCURRENCE AND DISSENT:** (Blackmun, J.) By finding federal preemption of certain state common law damages claims, the Court eliminates a critical component of the state's traditional ability to protect the health and safety of its citizens. Yet, such a radical readjustment of federal-state relations is warranted under this Court's precedents only if there is clear evidence that Congress intended that result. Neither version of the Federal Cigarette Labeling and Advertising Act evidences such a clear congressional intent to preempt state common law actions.

**EDITOR'S ANALYSIS:** After complying with the court of appeal's mandate, the district court held that Cipollone's (P) failure to warn, express warranty, fraud, and conspiracy claims were barred to the extent they relied on Liggett's (D) advertising activities. The design defect claims were barred on other grounds. At trial, the jury awarded no damages to Cipollone's (P) estate because she was 80% responsible for her injuries but awarded damages to compensate her husband for his losses.

**NOTES:**

## KING v. E.I. DUPONT DE NEMOURS & CO.

996 F.2d 1346 (1st Cir. 1993).

**NATURE OF CASE: Appeal from summary judgment for the defense in a product liability action.**

**FACT SUMMARY: Dupont (D) contended that it could not be sued on the basis of inadequate warnings on its insecticides when the labels complied with the Federal Insecticide, Fungicide, and Rodenticide Act (FIFRA).**

**CONCISE RULE OF LAW: FIFRA preempts state tort claims based on alleged failure to provide adequate warnings on a product's label.**

**FACTS:** King (P) and others were injured when they were exposed to significant amounts of chemicals manufactured by Dupont (D) and sprayed on crops. King (P) alleged that Dupont (D) was liable in tort for its failure to provide adequate warnings on the dangers of exposure to the chemicals. The labels had been approved by the Environmental Protection Agency as required by the Federal Insecticide, Fungicide and Rodenticide Act (FIFRA). The district court granted Dupont's (D) motion for summary judgment on the grounds that state tort law damages were inconsistent with the labeling requirements of FIFRA. King (P) appealed.

**ISSUE:** Does FIFRA preempt state tort claims based on alleged failure to provide adequate warnings on a product's label?

**HOLDING AND DECISION:** (Friedman, J.) Yes. FIFRA preempts state tort claims based on alleged failure to provide adequate warnings on the product's label. FIFRA provides a detailed scheme for regulating the content of insecticide and herbicide labels. It contains comprehensive labeling requirements governing the scope, content, wording and format of the labeling. FIFRA expressly states that no individual states may impose any requirements in addition to, or different from, the FIFRA mandates. If King (P) could recover on state tort law claims for failure to provide adequate warnings, these additional warnings would be inconsistent with FIFRA. Accordingly, such claims are preempted by federal law. This interpretation is consistent with the Supreme Court's decision in Cipollone v. Liggett Group, Inc., 505 U.S. 504 (1992), where a similar issue was addressed in terms of cigarette warnings. Therefore, the district court was correct in granting Dupont's (D) motion for summary judgment. Affirmed.

**EDITOR'S ANALYSIS:** This decision is in accord with three other circuits who have also faced the FIFRA preemption question. The Seventh, Tenth and Eleventh Circuits all agreed that FIFRA preempts state claims based on failure to warn through product labels. King (P) had relied on a D.C. Circuit decision that arose before Cipollone was decided and thus probably is no longer good law.

## KENNEDY v. COLLAGEN CORP.

67 F.3d 1453 (9th Cir. 1995).

**NATURE OF CASE: Appeal from summary judgment for the defense in a product liability action.**

**FACT SUMMARY: Collagen (D) contended that the Medical Device Amendments of 1976 (MDA) preempted Kennedy's (P) state tort claims arising out of her use of Zyderm.**

**CONCISE RULE OF LAW: The Medical Device Amendments of 1976 do not preempt state common law claims.**

**FACTS:** Kennedy (P) used Zyderm, a prescription medical product produced by Collagen (D), for treatment of a skin defect. Zyderm is a Class III medical device under the MDA, meaning it is implanted in the body and poses a potentially unreasonable risk of injury. Class III devices must be approved by the Federal Drug Administration (FDA) prior to their commercial use. Kennedy (P) contracted an autoimmune disorder and brought suit against Collagen (D) for strict products liability and negligence. The district court granted summary judgment in favor of Collagen (D) on the grounds that the MDA preempted state tort claims. Kennedy (P) appealed.

**ISSUE:** Do the Medical Device Amendments preempt state common law claims?

**HOLDING AND DECISION:** (Ferguson, J.) No. The Medical Device Amendments of 1976 do not preempt state common law claims. There is a strong presumption against federal preemption of state law. The federal law in question must have the clear and manifest purpose of preemption. The MDA provides that states shall not impose requirements that are different from, or in addition to, the requirements of the MDA. FDA regulations interpret this provision to mean that state or local requirements are preempted only when the FDA has established specific requirements applicable to a particular device. Laws of general applicability are not preempted, according to FDA regulations. Clearly, state common law tort actions are not specific regulations, but rather laws of general applicability. State common law imposes only indirect effects on manufacturers and serves different purposes than state regulations. Accordingly, there is no basis for finding that the MDA preempts state tort claims. Thus, Kennedy's (P) suit must be allowed to proceed. Reversed.

**EDITOR'S ANALYSIS:** The Ninth Circuit openly addressed the fact that most other courts have found that the MDA preempts state tort claims dealing with safety or effectiveness. It should be noted that this decision came after the Supreme Court's ruling in Cipollone v. Liggett Group, Inc., 505 U.S. 504 (1992), which held that federal cigarette labeling statutes preempted state common law lack-of-warning claims. It is very difficult to reconcile these two cases.

# CHAPTER 9
# LIMITING DEFECTIVENESS: USER CHOICE

## QUICK REFERENCE RULES OF LAW

1. **Obvious Dangers.** A manufacturer has no duty to fabricate a completely safe machine as long as the danger is obvious to all users. (Campo v. Scofield)

2. **Obvious Dangers.** A product manufacturer is not shielded from liability for negligent design merely because the risk of injury is open and obvious. (Micallef v. Miehle Co.)

3. **Obvious Dangers.** There is no liability for failing to warn of obvious dangers. (Belling v. Haugh's Pools, Ltd.)

4. **Obvious Dangers.** The patency of a danger in the use of a product is a question of fact. (Laaperi v. Sears, Roebuck & Co.)

5. **General Risks: Product Category Liability.** Personal safety devices are not defective merely because they do not provide the maximum protection. (Linegar v. Armour of America, Inc.)

6. **General Risks: Product Category Liability.** Products with obvious and inherent dangers are not unreasonably dangerous for lack of warnings. (Jordon v. K-Mart Corp.)

7. **General Risks: Product Category Liability.** A product is not unreasonably dangerous if its dangers are generally known and recognized. (Fraust v. Swift & Co.)

8. **General Risks: Product Category Liability.** Plaintiffs are not required to prove the existence of safer alternative designs in order to have the jury consider the risk-utility of an alleged defective product. (O'Brien v. Muskin Corp.)

9. **Misuse.** Where it is "reasonably foreseeable" that a product will be used in a certain manner, such use is not a misuse of the product. (Ellsworth v. Sherne Lingerie, Inc.)

10. **Misuse.** A manufacturer's warranty of product fitness for ordinary use does not extend any guarantee that the product will withstand, in a reasonably safe manner, misuse not incident to or arising out of the product's intended use. (Venezia v. Miller Brewing Co.)

11. **Misuse.** The duty of a manufacturer to warn of latent dangers inherent in its product extends to all uses which are reasonably foreseeable. (Moran v. Faberge, Inc.)

# Notes

## CAMPO v. SCOFIELD

N.Y. Ct. App., 301 N.Y. 408, 95 N.E.2d 802 (1950).

**NATURE OF CASE: Appeal from denial of damages for products liability.**

**FACT SUMMARY: Campo (P) contended Scofield (D) was liable for his injuries even though the injury suffered resulted from a patent risk of such injury.**

**CONCISE RULE OF LAW: A manufacturer has no duty to fabricate a completely safe machine as long as the danger is obvious to all users.**

**FACTS:** Campo (P) was injured when his hands were caught in the revolving rollers of an onion-topping machine manufactured by Scofield (D). Scofield (D) unsuccessfully moved to dismiss the complaint on the basis that the risk of Campo's (P) injury was obvious from the nature of the machine, thus precluding liability. Scofield (D) appealed, and the appellate court reversed. Campo (P) appealed.

**ISSUE:** Does a machine manufacturer have a duty to make a machine which is completely free from risk of injury?

**HOLDING AND DECISION:** (Fuld, J.) No. A machine manufacturer has no duty to fabricate a completely safe machine as long as the danger of use is obvious to all users. The danger in this case was inherent in the type of machine involved. The danger was thus patent, or known to all users. As a result, no liability could attach for this type of injury. Affirmed.

**EDITOR'S ANALYSIS:** The rationale behind this case is a variation on the theory of assumption of a known risk. The manufacturer of a hand saw is not responsible for injuries caused by placing the user's hand between the blade and the wood being cut. This risk is assumed by the user. However, any latent or unknown risk may involve liability. This case is used for historical perspective and does not display the current state of the law in several jurisdictions including New York where it was decided.

**NOTES:**

## MICALLEF v. MIEHLE CO.

N.Y. Ct. App., 39 N.Y. 2d 376, 384 N.Y.S. 2d. 115, 348 N.E. 2d 571 (1976).

**NATURE OF CASE: Appeal from denial of damages for products liability.**

**FACT SUMMARY: Miehle (D) contended it had no liability for negligent design of its printing machine because the risk of injury suffered by Micallef (P) was open and obvious.**

**CONCISE RULE OF LAW: A product manufacturer is not shielded from liability for negligent design merely because the risk of injury is open and obvious.**

**FACTS:** Micallef (P) was injured on a printing machine manufactured by Miehle (D). The accident occurred when Micallef (P) attempted to remedy an imperfection in the printing plate in a manner customary in the printing industry. The method used was known to Miehle (D), and the risk of injury was known to Micallef (P). The jury returned a verdict for Micallef (P), which was reversed by the appellate court. It held that no liability could attach because the risk of injury was open and obvious. Micallef (P) appealed.

**ISSUE:** Is a product manufacturer shielded from liability for negligent design merely because the risk of injury is open and obvious?

**HOLDING AND DECISION:** (Cooke, J.) No. A product manufacturer is not shielded from liability for negligent design merely because the risk of injury is open and obvious. The manufacturer must still meet basic standards of safety in placing the product in commerce. While prior cases have recognized such a shield, such cannot be perpetuated in an increasingly technologically based world. Reversed.

**EDITOR'S ANALYSIS:** This case directly overruled the case of Campo v. Scofield, 95 N.E.2d 802 (1950), which recognized the shield of patent danger. This case does not render moot the distinction between latent and patent danger. Rather, it serves to eliminate an absolute bar from recovery. If the danger is known, the question becomes one of contributory or comparative negligence.

**NOTES:**

## BELLING v. HAUGH'S POOLS, LTD.

126 A.D.2d 958, 511 N.Y.S. 732 (1987).

**NATURE OF CASE: Appeal from order denying motions for summary judgment.**

**FACT SUMMARY: Belling (P) brought suit for injuries he sustained when he jumped into an above-ground swimming pool, contending the manufacturer and retailer (collectively Haugh's Pools, Ltd.) (D) failed to provide adequate warnings of the dangers inherent in diving in the pool.**

**CONCISE RULE OF LAW: There is no liability for failing to warn of obvious dangers.**

**FACTS:** Belling (P) was injured when he dived through an innertube in a friend's four-foot, above-ground swimming pool. Belling (P) is six fee elven inches tall, weighs 215 lbs., and was an experienced swimmer. He had helped install the pool. He sued Haugh's Pools, Ltd. (D), claiming it failed to give him adequate warnings of the dangers inherent in diving into the pool. Haugh's Pools, Ltd. (D), moved for summary judgment, arguing the dangers Belling (P) claimed he was not warned of were obvious, and therefore there was no liability for failure to warn. The motion was denied, and Haugh's Pools, Ltd. (D), appealed.

**ISSUE:** Can there be liability for failing to warn one of obvious dangers?

**HOLDING AND DECISION:** (Memorandum) No. There is no liability for failing to warn of obvious dangers. Belling (P) must establish that the failure to warn was a proximate cause of his injuries. When a danger is obvious, however, a warning has no additional effect, as users are aware of the danger. A warning that has no effect cannot be the proximate cause of injury, and the proximate cause issue can be decided as a matter of law. Reversed; motions for summary judgment granted.

**DISSENT:** (Green, J.) The obviousness of a danger does not militate against a duty to warn but rather is a factor to take into account in assessing comparative fault.

**EDITOR'S ANALYSIS:** In Corbin v. Coleco Industries, 748 F.2d 411 (7th Cir. 1984), the plaintiff successfully opposed a summary judgment in a factually similar case. It was argued that although it was generally dangerous for a six-foot man to jump into a four-foot pool, a belief generally held that there was a safe way to make a flat shallow dive raised a question of fact as to whether the failure to provide a conspicuous prohibition against all diving was a proximate cause of the injury.

## LAAPERI v. SEARS, ROEBUCK & CO., INC.

787 F.2d 726 (1st Cir. 1986).

**NATURE OF CASE: Appeal from award of damages for products liability.**

**NOTES:**

**FACT SUMMARY: Sears (D) contended it owed no duty to warn Laaperi (P) that the smoke detector he purchased would not function if the electrical current was cut off because such was obvious.**

**CONCISE RULE OF LAW: The patency of a danger in the use of a product is a question of fact.**

**FACTS:** Laaperi (P) purchased a smoke detector from Sears (D). Laaperi (P), an electrical handyman, installed the device which was powered by the ac current in the house. A short circuit started a fire, terminating power to the alarm. Laaperi's (P) sons were killed. He sued, contending Sears' (D) negligent failure to warn him that a short circuit would render the alarm useless was the proximate cause of the deaths. He testified he never considered such an accident would occur and that if he had been adequately warned, he would have used a battery-operated alarm. The jury returned a verdict for Laaperi (P). Sears (D) moved for judgment n.o.v. on the basis the risk of such an occurrence, that the device would not work without electricity, was obvious, especially to someone familiar with electrical devices. The trial court denied the motion, and Sears (D) appealed.

**ISSUE:** Is the patency of danger in the use of products a question of fact?

**HOLDING AND DECISION:** (Campbell, J.) Yes. The patency of the danger in the use of the product is a question of fact. The evidence presented indicated Laaperi (P) never considered the consequences of a power surge or short circuit. Whether a failure to warn that such would incapacitate the alarm was necessary was question of fact. It cannot be said as a matter law that such danger was so obvious so as to preclude a duty to warn. As a result, the motion was properly denied. Affirmed.

**EDITOR'S ANALYSIS:** The Court pointed out that the fact the plaintiff was an electrical handyman did not alter the issue concerning the failure to warn. This would of course go to the issue of comparative negligence which goes to the measure of damages.

## LINEGAR v. ARMOUR OF AMERICA, INC.

909 F.2d 1150 (8th Cir. 1990).

**NATURE OF CASE: Appeal from an award of damages in a products liability action.**

**FACT SUMMARY: Linegar's (P) husband, a police officer, was shot and killed although he wore a bulletproof vest made by Armour (D).**

**CONCISE RULE OF LAW: Personal safety devices are not defective merely because they do not provide the maximum protection.**

**FACTS:** Linegar, a state trooper, was killed in the line of duty while wearing a bulletproof vest made by Armour (D). Linegar was shot eleven times. Five bullets hit the vest and were stopped but six missed the vest and hit Linegar. The vest, selected by the highway patrol, was a contour style that provided some protection to the sides of the body but not as much as a wrap-around style. Linegar's family (P) brought suit against Armour (D), claiming that the vest was defectively designed. The jury awarded $1.5 million and Armour (D) appealed.

**ISSUE:** Are personal safety devices defective merely because they do not provide the maximum protection?

**HOLDING AND DECISION:** (Bowman, J.) No. Personal safety devices are not defective merely because they do not provide the maximum protection. The core concern of tort liability is to ensure safe products for consumers. However, manufacturers are not required to produce only the safest design possible. The bulletproof vest at issue in this case permitted the wearer more flexibility and mobility than a wrap-around vest. It was also less expensive. The Armour (D) vest was designed to prevent the penetration of bullets where there was coverage, and Linegar's vest performed this function. To allow the jury verdict to stand would have an adverse effect on the development of equipment designed to help police officers and would cast Armour (D) in the role of insurer. Reversed.

**EDITOR'S ANALYSIS:** The court was swayed in part by testimony that officers often chose not to wear vests that were too bulky. Some officers also testified that they chose to wear the contour vest even when they owned both. This case is a good example of how public policy concerns play a central role in products liability.

## JORDON v. K-MART CORP.

Pa. Super. Ct., 611 A.2d 1328 (1992).

**NATURE OF CASE: Appeal from summary judgment for the defense in a product liability action.**

**FACT SUMMARY: Jordon (P), a ten-year-old boy, was injured when he lost control of a sled bought at K-Mart (D).**

**CONCISE RULE OF LAW: Products with obvious and inherent dangers are not unreasonably dangerous for lack of warnings.**

**FACTS:** Jordon's (P) parents bought him a sled from K-Mart. The sled was plastic and had molded runners that made it unsteerable. The sled also had no braking mechanisms. These features were obvious to persons who bought the sled. Jordon (P) was injured when his sled crashed into a tree, and suit was brought against K-Mart (D) for the lack of warnings and an alleged defective design. The trial court granted summary judgment for K-Mart (D), and Jordon (P) appealed.

**ISSUE:** Are products with obvious and inherent dangers unreasonably dangerous for lack of warnings?

**HOLDING AND DECISION:** (Rowley, J.) No. Products with obvious and inherent dangers are not unreasonably dangerous for lack of warnings. Dangers that are not latent need not be explained by instructions or warnings. The fact that sleds are difficult to steer and stop is obvious, even to an ordinary ten-year-old. The record shows that Jordon (P) recognized and appreciated the risk of sledding. Accordingly, the lack of warning on the K-Mart (D) sled did not make it unreasonably dangerous. Similarly, a design requiring brakes and/or steering would not remove the inherent risks of sledding. Therefore, the K-Mart (D) sled's design did not make it defective. Affirmed.

**EDITOR'S ANALYSIS:** Other courts have agreed with this type of analysis in slightly different contexts. The manufacturer of a jungle gym was also held not responsible in Cozzi v. North Palos Elementary School District, 597 N.E.2d 683 (Ill. App. Ct. 1992). That court found that the lack of warning on a recreational device with obvious dangers did not make it defective.

**NOTES:**

## FRAUST v. SWIFT & CO.

610 F. Supp. 711 (W.D.Pa. 1985).

**NATURE OF CASE: Motion for summary judgment in a product liability action.**

**NOTES:**

**FACT SUMMARY: Fraust (P), a sixteen-month-old child, choked on peanut butter.**

**CONCISE RULE OF LAW: A product is not unreasonably dangerous if its dangers are generally known and recognized.**

**FACTS:** Fraust (P), a sixteen-month-old child, ate Peter Pan Creamy Peanut Butter spread on bread and choked. He suffered severe brain damage, and his family brought an action against the manufacturer of the peanut butter for failure to warn that peanut butter should not be fed to children under four. Swift (D) brought a motion for summary judgment on the basis that its peanut butter was unavoidably unsafe but not defective.

**ISSUE:** Is a product unreasonably dangerous if its dangers are generally known and recognized?

**HOLDING AND DECISION:** (Teitelbaum, J.) No. A product is not unreasonably dangerous if its dangers are generally known and recognized. Section 402A of the Restatement of (Second) Torts differentiates those products that are by their very nature unsafe but not defective from those that are truly defective. For example, good whiskey is not unreasonably dangerous merely because it makes people drunk. Swift (D) argues that good peanut butter is not unreasonably dangerous merely because a young child could choke on it. However, the reason that some products are unavoidably unsafe but not defective is that they present known dangers needing no warning. The danger of a sixteen-month-old child choking on peanut butter is not so generally known that it should be ruled on as a matter of law. Fraust (P) must have a chance to present the issue to a jury. Summary judgment motion denied.

**EDITOR'S ANALYSIS:** This case is in accord with the decision in Emery v. Federated Foods, Inc., 863 P.2d 426 (Mont. 1993). In that case, a two-and-a-half-year-old choked on a marshmallow. The majority ruled that summary judgment for the defense was improper and remanded for trial on the issue of defectiveness for failure to warn. The dissenters claimed that the ruling meant that any food item eaten by a young child could be ruled defective and that it is a matter of common knowledge to all adults that children might choke while eating.

## O'BRIEN v. MUSKIN CORP.

N.J. Sup. Ct., 463 A.2d 298 (1983).

**NATURE OF CASE: Appeal from reversal of jury verdict in a products liability action.**

**FACT SUMMARY: O'Brien (P), injured when he dove into an above-ground pool, claimed that the design of the pool was defective.**

**CONCISE RULE OF LAW: Plaintiffs are not required to prove the existence of safer alternative designs in order to have the jury consider the risk-utility of an alleged defective product.**

**FACTS:** O'Brien (P) dived into an above-ground swimming pool with his outstretched hands in front of him. His hands hit the bottom of the vinyl-lined pool, slid apart, and he struck his head on the bottom, sustaining serious injuries. A one-half-inch high decal on the outside of the pool stated "DO NOT DIVE." O'Brien (P) sued Muskin (D), the manufacturer of the pool, alleging that the pool was defective in design and that the warning was inadequate. O'Brien's (P) expert testified that vinyl should not be used in above-ground pools but admitted that no alternative material was available. The trial court did not allow the jury to consider the design defect claim, and O'Brien (P) appealed this ruling. The appellate court reversed and remanded, and Muskin (D) appealed.

**ISSUE:** Are plaintiffs required to prove the existence of safer alternative designs in order to have the jury consider the risk-utility of an alleged defective product?

**HOLDING AND DECISION:** (Pollock, J.) No. Plaintiffs are not required to prove the existence of safer alternative designs in order to have the jury consider the risk-utility of an alleged defective product. Proof that a product is defective requires more than a mere showing that the product caused an injury. In order to show a defect, a comparison of the utility of the product with the risk of injury that the product poses is required. This comparison focuses on the reasonableness of placing the product on the marketplace. Of course, risk-utility analysis must be done on a case-by-case basis, looking at the specific facts of a case. The risk side of the equation involves looking at the risks that were known or should have been known and the warnings given. The utility side includes an appraisal of the need for the product and the availability of alternative designs. There is no requirement that the plaintiff demonstrate alternative designs, but a jury may consider the other utility factors. In the present case, the jury should have been able to look at the need for pools and the adequacy of the warnings in appraising the utility of the Muskin (D) pool. Therefore, the trial court's decision to exclude the design defect claim was in error. Remanded.

**CONCURRENCE AND DISSENT:** (Schreiber, J.) The majority decision allows the jury to find a defect even though the duty to warn was satisfied and the manufacturer could not possibly have designed the item in a safer manner, simply because it might decide that the risk outweighs the product's usefulness. This essentially makes the manufacturer absolutely liable for all injuries.

**EDITOR'S ANALYSIS:** The dissent was certainly correct in pointing out that although O'Brien (P) carried the burden of proving a defect through risk-utility analysis, much key information was missing. The utility of a product can be difficult to assess. For instance, how much weight should a jury put on the recreational benefits of swimming pools? Subsequent New Jersey law permits defendants to raise a defense to design defect claims if there are no practical design alternatives.

**NOTES:**

## ELLSWORTH v. SHERNE LINGERIE, INC.

303 Md. 581, 495 A.2d 348 (1985).

**NATURE OF CASE: Appeal from affirmation of defense verdict in products liability action.**

**FACT SUMMARY: Ellsworth (P) appealed from the affirmation of a jury verdict for Sherne Lingerie, Inc. (D), and Cone Mills (D), arguing that the trial court improperly instructed the jury on the concept of misuse.**

**CONCISE RULE OF LAW: Where it is "reasonably foreseeable" that a product will be used in a certain manner, such use is not a misuse of the product.**

**FACTS:** Ellsworth's (P) nightgown was designed and manufactured by Sherne Lingerie, Inc. (Sherne) (D), out of material manufactured by Cone Mills (Cone) (D). While wearing the gown inside out, the pocket edge came into contact with the burner on her stove, and she was seriously burned. She sued Sherne (D) and Cone (D) alleging negligence and strict liability in tort related to the flammability of the gown. Sherne (D) and Cone (D) argued that she had misused the gown by wearing it inside out, and the jury was instructed on the doctrine of misuse. The jury returned a verdict for Cone (D) and Sherne (D) which was affirmed on appeal. From this affirmation, Ellsworth (P) appealed.

**ISSUE:** Where it is "reasonably foreseeable" that a product will be used in a certain manner, is such use a misuse of the product?

**HOLDING AND DECISION:** (McAuliffe, J.) No. Where it is "reasonably foreseeable" that a product will be used in a certain manner, such use is not a misuse of the product. In strict liability cases, there has been some dispute over the meaning of the word "misuse." Utilizing the "reasonably foreseeable" standard, the evidence was insufficient to submit the misuse issue to the jury. While wearing the gown inside out may have been careless, it was reasonably foreseeable, and a use within the intended use of the product. Contact between the loose-fitting gown and the flame is also reasonably foreseeable. The circumstances of this case do not indicate misuse of the gown. Reversed and remanded.

**EDITOR'S ANALYSIS:** The standard that appears to be emerging is that if the use of a product is unusual or abnormal, and not related to the actual, designed purpose of the product, it will be considered misuse. Note, however, that if a product is continually misused in a dangerous, unintended manner, the use is probably reasonably foreseeable. See Gootee v. Colt Industries, Inc., 712 F.2d 1057 (6th Cir. 1983).

**NOTES:**

## VENEZIA v. MILLER BREWING CO.

626 F.2d 188 (1st Cir. 1980).

**NATURE OF CASE: Appeal from dismissal of warranty and negligence action.**

**FACT SUMMARY: Venezia (P) appealed from the dismissal of his suit alleging warranty and negligence claims against Miller Brewing Company (D), contending that his injury resulted from an "ordinary" use of a beer bottle and was foreseeable.**

**CONCISE RULE OF LAW: A manufacturer's warranty of product fitness for ordinary use does not extend any guarantee that the product will withstand, in a reasonably safe manner, misuse not incident to or arising out of the product's intended use.**

**FACTS:** Venezia (P), an eight-year-old boy, found a discarded Miller (D) beer bottle and shattered it against a telephone pole. He was injured when particles of glass entered his eyes. He brought suit against Miller (D), asserting warranty and negligence claims. Venezia (P) essentially argued that Miller (D) should have been aware of the dangers inherent in the thin-walled bottle, and should have designed it so that it would safely withstand misuse by children, which he contended was foreseeable. The trial court dismissed Venezia's (P) action for failure to state a claim, and he appealed.

**ISSUE:** Does a manufacturer's warranty of product fitness for ordinary use extend a guarantee that the product will withstand, in a reasonably safe manner, misuse not incident to or arising out of the product's intended use?

**HOLDING AND DECISION:** (Campbell, J.) No. A manufacturer's warranty of product fitness for ordinary use does not extend any guarantee that the product will withstand, in a reasonably safe manner, misuse not incident to or arising out of the product's intended use. Venezia (P) tries to convince the court that his shattering of the bottle was an "ordinary use" of the bottle. It would be stretching too far to hold that the definition of ordinary purpose includes misuse totally unrelated to the bottle's function. Reasonable consumer expectations, apparently those of Venezia (P), would dictate that the bottle, when smashed against the pole, would shatter. (The court went on to state that the bottle was not defective merely because it is foreseeable that it might cause injury if misused, noting that the manufacturer is not an insurer.) To find Miller (D) liable for Venezia's (P) misuse would make every discarded bottle a potential source of litigation. Affirmed.

**EDITOR'S ANALYSIS:** Although the courts are split as to whether this is an affirmative defense, the modern trend is to consider misuse as part of the plaintiff's case. In those jurisdictions where the plaintiff has this burden of proof, it is a factor pertaining to the issues of defectiveness and proximate cause.

## MORAN v. FABERGE, INC.

273 Md. 538, 332 A.2d 11 (1975).

**NATURE OF CASE: Appeal from judgment n.o.v. denying damages for personal injury.**

**FACT SUMMARY: Faberge (D) contended that it was not reasonably foreseeable that its Tigress cologne would be exposed to a lit candle and explode.**

**CONCISE RULE OF LAW: The duty of a manufacturer to warn of latent dangers inherent in its product extends to all uses which are reasonably foreseeable.**

**FACTS:** Moran (P), who was seventeen years old at the time of the accident in question, was injured when her friend Randy Williams poured the contents of a bottle of Faberge's (D) Tigress cologne onto the lower portion of a lit candle in an attempt to give scent to the candle. As the cologne was poured onto the candle, a burst of fire sprang out and burned Moran's (P) neck and breasts as she stood nearby watching but not fully aware of what her friend was doing. Moran (P) then brought this suit for damages for the personal injuries sustained when the bottle of cologne caught fire. At trial, Moran (P) evoked testimony from Faberge (D) representatives that Faberge (D) was aware that its cologne was highly flammable, and also that Faberge (D) foresaw that its product might well be dangerous when placed near flame. The thrust of Moran's (P) case was that Faberge (D) had been negligent in failing to warn against its product's latent flammability characteristic. The jury returned a verdict for Moran (P), but the trial court entered a judgment notwithstanding the verdict for Faberge (D). Moran (P) then brought this appeal.

**ISSUE:** Does the duty of a manufacturer to warn of latent dangers inherent in its product extend to all uses which are reasonably foreseeable?

**HOLDING AND DECISION:** (Digges, J.) Yes. The duty of a manufacturer to warn of latent dangers inherent in its product goes beyond the precise use contemplated by the producer and extends to all those which are reasonably foreseeable. A duty to warn is imposed on a manufacturer if the item it produces has an inherent and hidden danger about which the producer knows, or should know, could be a substantial factor in bringing injury to an individual or his property when the manufacturer's product comes near to, or in contact with, the elements which are normally present in the environment where the product can reasonably be expected to be brought or used. Once the product is used in this general field of danger, if the manufacturer's conduct is a significant factor in causing harm to another, the fact that the manufacturer neither foresaw nor should have foreseen the severity of the harm or the exact manner in which it occurred does not prevent it from being liable. Here, it was only necessary that the evidence be sufficient to support the conclusion that Faberge (D), knowing or deemed to know that its Tigress cologne was a potentially dangerous flammable product, could reasonably foresee that in the environment of its use, this cologne might come close enough to a flame to cause an explosion of sufficient intensity to burn property or injure bystanders. Reversed and remanded for entry of judgment on verdict for Moran (P).

**DISSENT:** (O'Donnell, J.) A manufacturer should not be held liable for a palpably unanticipated and unforeseeable misuse of its product.

**EDITOR'S ANALYSIS:** The comments to the restatement, in discussing manufacturer liability for unanticipated uses, states that: "The manufacturer may. . . reasonably anticipate other uses than the one for which the chattel is primarily intended. The maker of a chair, for example, may reasonably expect that someone will stand on it; and the maker of an inflammable cocktail robe may expect that it will be worn in the kitchen in close proximity to a fire." Restatement (Second) of Torts, § 395, Comment K.

**NOTES:**

# CHAPTER 10
# LIMITING DEFECTIVENESS: PASSAGE OF TIME

## QUICK REFERENCE RULES OF LAW

1. **Deterioration.** A manufacturer has no duty to create a product that does not wear out. (Savage v. Jacobsen Manufacturing Co.)

2. **Disposal and Destruction.** (1) Strict liability does not apply under Restatement (Second) of Torts § 402A for injuries that occur in dismantling an item. (2) A manufacturer has a duty to warn of dangerous contents in its product which could damage or injure, even when the product is not used for its intended purpose. (High v. Westinghouse Electric Corp.)

3. **State of the Art.** It is not negligence to sell an old-model machine not equipped with a safety device found in later models. (Pontifex v. Sears, Roebuck & Co.)

4. **State of the Art.** State of the art evidence is relevant to a strict liability claim. (Bruce v. Martin-Marietta Corp.)

5. **State of the Art.** Evidence regarding state of the art may be introduced in a products liability action based on defective design. (Boatland of Houston, Inc. v. Bailey)

6. **State of the Art.** Defendants in a products liability case based on strict liability for failure to warn may not raise a "state of the art" defense. (Beshada v. Johns-Manville Products Corp.)

7. **State of the Art.** Strict liability will be applied to drug manufacturers. (Feldman v. Lederle Laboratories)

8. **State of the Art.** Strict liability based on defective design does not apply to prescription drugs. (Brown v. Superior Court)

9. **State of the Art.** In a strict products liability action for lack of adequate warnings, the defendant may show that the particular risk was not knowable at the time of the manufacture and distribution of the product. (Anderson v. Owens-Corning Fiberglas Corp.)

10. **Intergenerational Harm.** Ohio does not recognize a cause of action on behalf of a child born with severe birth defects, even if it can be established that such injuries were proximately caused by his mother's DES-induced injuries. (Grover v. Eli Lilly Co.)

11. **Post Sale Duties.** A manufacturer has no duty to notify previous purchasers of its products about later-developed safety devices or to retrofit these products. (Romero v. International Harvester Co.)

12. **Statutory Repose.** That a product has outlived its useful life is not an absolute defense to a personal injury action. (Hodder v. Goodyear Tire & Rubber Co.)

## SAVAGE v. JACOBSEN MANUFACTURING CO.

396 So. 2d 731 (Fla. 1981).

**NATURE OF CASE: Appeal from denial of damages for products liability.**

**NOTES:**

**FACT SUMMARY: Savage (P) contended Jacobsen (D), the manufacturer of the mowing tractor, was liable even though the tractor's original nonskid surface had deteriorated, leading to her fall.**

**CONCISE RULE OF LAW: A manufacturer has no duty to create a product that does not wear out.**

**FACTS:** Savage (P) was injured when she slipped on a lawn mower tractor's platform. The skid-resistant paint originally on the tractor had worn off due to time and use. Her employer and the owner of the machine were aware of this condition. Savage (P) sued Jacobsen (D), the manufacturer of the tractor, contending the absence of skid-resistant paint constituted a defect. Jacobsen (D) successfully moved for summary judgment on the basis that deterioration did not give rise to liability. Savage (P) appealed.

**ISSUE:** Does a manufacturer have a duty to create a product that does not wear out?

**HOLDING AND DECISION:** (Per curiam) No. A manufacturer has no duty to create a product that does not wear out. The condition of this machine which caused this accident was created by normal wear and tear. A manufacturer is not held to produce a nondeteriorating product. A defect is shown only where this deterioration exceeds the reasonable consumer's expectations. As a result, no duty is placed on Jacobsen (D), and the summary judgment was properly entered. Affirmed.

**EDITOR'S ANALYSIS:** Some jurisdictions analyze this situation from a different perspective. Instead of denying the existence of duty, they focus on the lack of probable cause for the accident. In this context, it is a question of fact rather than a question of law. Viewing the problem as a cause inquiry gives rise to more uncertainty because it is an ad hoc inquiry.

## HIGH v. WESTINGHOUSE ELECTRIC CORPORATION

610 So. 2d 1259 (1992).

**NATURE OF CASE: Appeal from grant of summary judgment.**

**FACT SUMMARY: High (P) contended that Westinghouse (D) was strictly liable and negligent for injuries he sustained from a hazardous fluid that was released from dismantled electrical transformers.**

**CONCISE RULES OF LAW: (1) Strict liability does not apply under Restatement (Second) of Torts § 402A for injuries that occur in dismantling an item. (2) A manufacturer has a duty to warn of dangerous contents in its product which could damage or injure, even when the product is not used for its intended purpose.**

**FACTS:** Westinghouse (D) manufactured electrical transformers and sold them to Florida Power and Light Company (FPL), which, from 1967–1983, sold its electrical transformers to Pepper's, a scrap metal salvage business. As early as 1972, Westinghouse (D) acknowledged the potential existence of PCBs, a toxic agent, in its oil-filled transformers. High (P), a truck driver for Pepper's from 1965 to 1983, came into contact with the PCB-contaminated transformer oil. High (P), who believed that his physical and mental problems were attributable to this exposure, brought an action under strict liability and negligence theories. The trial court granted Westinghouse's (D) summary judgment motion, holding that the manufacturer of electrical transformers is not liable to an employee of a scrap metal salvage business for injuries allegedly sustained from a hazardous fluid that was released in dismantling transformers in the scrapping process. The court of appeals affirmed. High (P) appealed.

**ISSUES:** (1) Does strict liability apply under Restatement (Second) of Torts § 402A for injuries that occur in dismantling an item? (2) Does a manufacturer have a duty to warn of dangerous contents in its product which could damage or injure, even when the product is not used for its intended purpose?

**HOLDING AND DECISION:** (Overton, J.) (1) No. Strict liability does not apply under Restatement (Second) of Torts § 402A for injuries that occur in dismantling an item. Section 402A does not apply because of the substantial alteration of the product when High (P) came into contact with the contaminated oil. Section 402A applies to intended uses of products for which they were produced. When an injury occurs under those circumstances, the manufacturer is strictly liable. Under the present circumstances, dismantling a product is not an intended use as prescribed by § 402A. Therefore, strict liability does not apply. Affirmed. (2) Yes. A manufacturer has a duty to warn of dangerous contents in its product which could damage or injure, even when the product is not used for its intended purpose. Although Westinghouse's (D) letter to FPL was adequate notice, Westinghouse (D) had a duty to notify FPL in a timely fashion so that FPL could timely notify Pepper's of the possible danger that could occur in dismantling the transformers. If this notice was not timely, then the next question is whether the lack of timely notice by Westinghouse (D) was the proximate cause of High's (P) injuries. These are issues of fact not proper for summary judgment. Reversed and remanded.

**EDITOR'S ANALYSIS:** The Florida Supreme Court, agreeing with the court of appeals on the strict liability issue, found that the transformers were destroyed prior to High's (P) alleged injuries. While the transformers were sealed and intact, there was no harm. Westinghouse's (D) product as it had originally sold to FPL, for practical purposes, had ceased to exist at the time the alleged injuries occurred.

**NOTES:**

## PONTIFEX v. SEARS, ROEBUCK & CO.

226 F.2d 909 (4th Cir. 1955).

**NATURE OF CASE: Appeal from denial of damages from personal injury.**

**NOTES:**

**FACT SUMMARY: Sears (D) contended that it was not negligent in selling a lawn mower which did not have the safety features found in later models.**

**CONCISE RULE OF LAW: It is not negligence to sell an old-model machine not equipped with a safety device found in later models.**

**FACTS:** Pontifex (P) was injured when she was struck in the eye by a rope pulled to start the gasoline engine of a lawn mower. Pontifex (P) contended that there was negligence in the design of the lawn mower in that the rope was not permanently attached to a spring recoil mechanism, such as was found in the latest models of similar machines, and that no warning was given of the danger of using it. After judgment was given on a directed verdict for Sears (D), Pontifex (D) brought this appeal.

**ISSUE:** Is it negligence to sell an old-model machine not equipped with a safety device found in later models?

**HOLDING AND DECISION:** (Per curiam) No. It is not negligence to sell an old-model machine not equipped with a safety device found in later models. Here, there was no evidence of negligence in the design or construction of the machine or of any need for warning or of any other negligence upon which a verdict for Pontifex (P) could have been based. Affirmed.

**EDITOR'S ANALYSIS:** This case illustrates the problems involved in defining what state of the art means, and how it should be applied in products liability cases. To many defense counsel, this term refers to the customary practice in the industry, while some attorneys prefer to define it to mean the ultimate in existing technology.

## BRUCE v. MARTIN-MARIETTA CORP.

544 F.2d 442 (10th Cir. 1976).

**NATURE OF CASE: Appeal from denial of damages for personal injury and wrongful death.**

**FACT SUMMARY: Bruce (P) contended that state of the art evidence was not relevant to its claim for wrongful death based upon allegedly defective products contained in an airplane.**

**CONCISE RULE OF LAW: State of the art evidence is relevant to a strict liability claim.**

**FACTS:** Bruce (P) and the other plaintiffs were persons injured, or representatives of persons killed, in the crash of an airplane manufactured by Martin (D). The airplane, a Martin 404, was chartered to carry the Wichita State University team and some of its supporters to a football game in Logan, Utah. On October 2, 1970, the plane crashed into a mountain west of Silver Plume, Colorado. The plane first struck trees at an altitude of approximately 10,800 feet, and then traveled 425 feet before coming to rest. Seats in the passenger cabin broke loose from their floor attachments, were thrown forward against the bulkhead of the plane, and blocked exit. A fire then developed and thirty-two of the forty passengers in the plane died. In their complaint, the plaintiffs alleged that the seat fastenings were inadequate, and there was inadequate protection against fire. Martin (D) offered evidence showing that the plane was designed to meet or exceed all applicable standards existing at the time of its manufacture. The plaintiffs stated that state of the art evidence was not material when a claim, such as theirs, was based upon strict liability. They argued that a showing of a design defective in 1970 established that the plane was defective in 1952, the time of the original sale. The district court granted summary judgment for Martin (D), and Bruce (P) appealed.

**ISSUE:** Is state of the art evidence relevant to a strict liability claim?

**HOLDING AND DECISION:** (Breitenstein, J.) Yes. State of the art evidence is relevant to a strict liability claim. There is general agreement that to prove strict liability, a plaintiff must show that the product was dangerous beyond the expectation of the ordinary customer. State of the art evidence helps to determine the expectation of the ordinary consumer. A consumer would not expect a Model T to have the safety features that are incorporated in automobiles made today. The same expectation applies to airplanes. Here, the plaintiffs have not shown that the ordinary consumer would expect a plane made in 1952 to have the safety features of one made in 1970. Affirmed.

**EDITOR'S ANALYSIS:** This case seems to represent the majority view on the issue of whether state of the art evidence is admissible in a case based upon a claim in strict liability. The intermediate appellate courts in Illinois have taken a contrary position, and have held that state of the art evidence is not relevant to a strict liability claim. This view is based upon the principles of the restatement that a seller may be liable in strict liability even though "the seller has exercised all possible care in the preparation and sale of his product." See Restatement (Second) of Torts, § 402(A)(1)(a).

**NOTES:**

## BOATLAND OF HOUSTON v. BAILEY

Tex. Sup. Ct., 609 S.W.2d 743 (1980).

**NATURE OF CASE: Appeal of reversal of denial of damages in action for wrongful death.**

**FACT SUMMARY: Boatland of Houston (D) was permitted to introduce evidence that certain safety technologies were not within the state of the art when its allegedly offending boat was manufactured.**

**CONCISE RULE OF LAW: Evidence regarding state of the art may be introduced in a products liability action based on defective design.**

**FACTS:** Bailey was killed when he fell out of a boat, manufactured by Boatland of Houston (D), which circled back and ran over him. Bailey's heirs (P) brought a wrongful death action. The heirs (P) introduced evidence that certain safety features would have "killed" the engine upon Bailey's ejection had these features been present in the boat. Boatland (D) responded with evidence that the safety features were not available in 1973, when the boat was built. A jury found the boat not defectively designed, and the court rendered a defense verdict. The court of appeals reversed, holding that the evidence presented by Boatland (D) had been improperly admitted. Boatland (D) appealed.

**ISSUE:** May evidence regarding state of the art be introduced in a products liability action based on defective design?

**HOLDING AND DECISION:** (McGee, J.) Yes. Evidence regarding state of the art may be introduced in a products liability action based on defective design. When a plaintiff brings into issue possible alternative designs that should have been incorporated into a particular product, the defendant is entitled to rebut this with evidence that the technology was not available. Here, Bailey's heirs (P) introduced evidence of a certain safety feature. Boatland (D) rebutted this with evidence that the technology for the feature was not available when the boat was built. This was proper. Reversed.

**DISSENT:** (Campbell, J.) "State of the art" means industry knowledge, not industry practice. Boatland's (D) evidence proved that the safety feature in question wasn't being used in 1973. It did not prove that it wasn't available.

**EDITOR'S ANALYSIS:** The major issue in "state of the art" analysis is exactly what the phase refers to. In a narrow sense, it can mean industry custom. This is usually the defendant's argument. In a broader sense, it can encompass the availability of all of modern technology. Jurisdictions vary as to which approach is correct.

**NOTES:**

## BESHADA v. JOHNS-MANVILLE PROD. CORP.

N.J. Sup. Ct., 90 N.J. 191, 44 A.2d 539 (1982).

**NATURE OF CASE: Appeal from denial of plaintiffs' motion to strike a defense in consolidated personal injury and wrongful death actions.**

**FACT SUMMARY: Johns-Manville (D) raised a "state-of the-art defense" to failure-to-warn claims filed by Beshada (P) and others, arguing that the dangers of asbestos were undiscovered at the time its products were marketed.**

**CONCISE RULE OF LAW: Defendants in a products liability case based on strict liability for failure to warn may not raise a "state of the art" defense.**

**FACTS:** Beshada (P) and other workers (P) sued Johns-Manville (D) and other manufacturers (D) of asbestos products for injuries and deaths resulting from asbestos-related illnesses. Beshada (P) based their products liability cases on strict liability for failure to warn of the dangers resulting from asbestos exposure. Johns-Manville (D) asserted that this danger was undiscovered and undiscoverable given the state of scientific knowledge when its products were marketed. Beshada (P) moved to strike Johns-Manville's (D) state-of-the-art defense. The trial court denied the motion, and Beshada (P) appealed.

**ISSUE:** May defendants in a products liability case based on strict liability for failure to warn raise a "state of the art" defense?

**HOLDING AND DECISION:** (Pashman, J.) No. Defendants in a products liability case based on strict liability for failure to warn may not raise a "state of the art" defense. When a plaintiff sues under strict liability, there is no need to prove that the manufacturer knew or should have known of any dangerous propensities of its product—such knowledge is imputed to the manufacturer. A state-of-the-art defense would contravene that by requiring plaintiffs to prove at least that knowledge of the dangers was scientifically available at the time of manufacture. State-of-the-art is a negligence defense only. That a product was unsafe because of the state of technology does not change the fact that the manufacturer should compensate its victims for the misfortune that it inflicted on them. Furthermore, denial of the defense will achieve the various policies underlying strict liability, including risk spreading, accident avoidance, and prevention of jury confusion. Motion to strike the defense is granted.

**EDITOR'S ANALYSIS:** The Beshada court was careful to circumscribe its holding by limiting it to failure-to-warn cases only. It specifically declined to decide whether a state-of-the-art defense would be appropriate in safety device cases. Nevertheless, it noted that there were strong conceptual similarities between warning and safety device cases, especially since, in both types of cases, the defendant's knowledge of the danger was irrelevant.

## FELDMAN v. LEDERLE LABORATORIES

N.J. Sup. Ct., 97 N.J. 429, 479 A.2d 374 (1984).

**NATURE OF CASE: Appeal from denial of damages in a products liability action.**

**FACT SUMMARY: Feldman (P), given a drug made by Lederle (D) as a child, developed tooth discoloration as a side effect.**

**CONCISE RULE OF LAW: Strict liability will be applied to drug manufacturers.**

**FACTS:** Feldman (P) was given tetracycline as a child, specifically declomycin, which was manufactured by Lederle (D). The use of the drug led to tooth discoloration. Evidence showed that, for at least a portion of the period in which Feldman (P) was using declomycin, there was strong evidence of this potential side effect. Lederle (D) eventually adopted a warning of the danger to be placed on containers of the drug. Feldman (P) contended at trial that the drug should have contained a warning about tooth discoloration. Lederle (D) contended it did not have knowledge of the danger at the time of Feldman's (P) use of the drug. The trial resulted in the favor of Lederle (D), and this was affirmed. Feldman (P) appealed.

**ISSUE:** Will strict liability be applied to drug manufacturers?

**HOLDING AND DECISION:** (Schreiber, J.) Yes. Strict liability will be applied to drug manufacturers. While some sorts of health-related activities are exempt from strict liability rules based on public policy concerns, the manufacture and distribution of drugs is more like the standard product distribution system. It also cannot be said that strict liability should not be applied because drugs are unavoidably dangerous. Some drugs may be, but not all are. Here, the product defect consisted of an improper warning. Unlike manufacturing defects, a claim not made here, a factfinder must look to the conduct of the manufacturer; it must find out whether the manufacturer should have known of the dangerous condition. The manufacturer is not under a duty to warn of unknowable dangers, but it will be held to an expert's level of competency, and must disprove that it should have known of the danger, something it did not have to do at the trial. Reversed.

**EDITOR'S ANALYSIS:** It appears that strict liability is something of a misnomer in describing a defective warning cause of action. Strict liability supposedly has no concern for a manufacturer's conduct, and this is the case for manufacturing defects. Design defects and defective warnings do focus on the level of care by a defendant. This is not strict liability at all, but rather negligence analysis. Prosser has noted this (Prosser, Law of Torts 4th 659 n. 72).

## BROWN v. SUPERIOR COURT

Cal. Sup. Ct., 44 Cal .3d 1049 (1988).

**NATURE OF CASE: Review of partial dismissal of action for damages for personal injuries.**

**FACT SUMMARY: Various plaintiffs contended that the drug D.E.S. was defectively designed.**

**CONCISE RULE OF LAW: Strict liability based on defective design does not apply to prescription drugs.**

**FACTS:** Various plaintiffs filed actions against the manufacturer of the drug D.E.S., claiming they were injured in utero when their mothers ingested it. They alleged various causes of action, including a cause of action based on defective design. The trial court held that strict liability based on defective design would not be applied to prescription drugs. The court of appeals denied the petition of a writ of mandate ordering the trial court to reverse itself. The California Supreme Court granted a hearing.

**ISSUE:** Does strict liability based on defective design apply to prescription drugs?

**HOLDING AND DECISION:** (Mosk, J.) No. Strict liability based on defective design does not apply to prescription drugs. Part of the reason for the application of this doctrine is that products should behave per consumer expectations. With drugs, the consumer is not the plaintiff, but rather the physician, so this rationale is inapplicable. More importantly, there is a vital difference between drugs and other types of products. Most products exist to make life easier; drugs often make life possible. To deter manufacturers of most products has minimal social or human costs. To deter manufacturers of drugs from marketing their products can have grave consequences, and therefore public policy militates against extending liability. It is urged that the rule here only be applied to "unavoidably dangerous" drugs. However, this rule would still impose substantial costs upon manufacturers, which is contrary to the public interest. Affirmed.

**EDITOR'S ANALYSIS:** It was also urged upon the court that a "failure to warn" liability be imposed upon manufacturers, even if the danger were unknown or unknowable. The court, for the same reasons as described in the design defect analysis, refused to do so. Liability was to remain based on negligence only.

**NOTES:**

## ANDERSON v. OWENS-CORNING FIBERGLAS CORP.

Cal. Sup. Ct., 53 Cal. 3d. 987, 810 P.2d 549 (1991).

**NATURE OF CASE: Appeal from jury verdict for the defense in a products liability action.**

**FACT SUMMARY: Owens-Corning (D), an asbestos manufacturer, contended that it must be allowed to show that it could not have warned of risks that the best scientific knowledge at the time was not aware of.**

**CONCISE RULE OF LAW: In a strict products liability action for lack of adequate warnings, the defendant may show that the particular risk was not knowable at the time of the manufacture and distribution of the product.**

**FACTS:** Anderson (P) was exposed to asbestos while working in a shipyard from 1941 to 1976 and contracted asbestosis. Anderson (P) filed suit against the manufacturers of asbestos, including Owens-Corning (D). Anderson (P) alleged that Owens-Corning (D) failed to warn users of the risks of asbestos exposure. Owens-Corning (D) responded that the best scientific knowledge at the time did not show these risks. Anderson (P) contended that a requirement of knowability improperly infused a negligence standard into a strict products liability action. The trial court eventually struck Anderson's (P) failure-to-warn theory and the jury ruled for Owens-Corning (D). Anderson (P) appealed.

**ISSUE:** May a defendant show that a particular risk was not knowable at the time of the manufacture and distribution in a strict products liability action for lack of adequate warnings?

**HOLDING AND DECISION:** (Panelli, J.) Yes. In a strict products liability action for lack of adequate warnings, the defendant may show that the particular risk was not knowable at the time of the manufacture and distribution of the product. Strict liability was never intended to make manufacturers and distributors the insurer of their products. It is not absolute liability. Previously, in Brown v. Superior Court, 751 P.2d 470 (1988), this court determined that strict liability does not extend to failure to warn of risks that were unknowable at the time of distribution of prescription drugs. That standard should apply to all strict liability actions for failure to warn. The warning defect theory is rooted more firmly in negligence than in manufacturing and design defect theories. Accordingly, it is appropriate to use some negligence concepts such as knowability. Since strict liability remains unconcerned with the reasonableness of the manufacturer's conduct, plaintiffs need only show that it failed to warn of risks that were known or knowable at the time. This rule best satisfies the public policy reasons for keeping strict liability from becoming absolute liability. Affirmed.

**CONCURRENCE:** (Broussard, J.) The decision should be read as being restricted to cases in which the absence of a warning is used to show a defect. If a plaintiff relies solely on a consumer expectations theory, state-of-the-art evidence should not be relevant or admissible.

**DISSENT:** (Mosk, J.) Failure-to-warn actions should lie solely in negligence. The blending of negligence and strict liability only serves to breed confusion and bad law.

**EDITOR'S ANALYSIS:** This decision is in accord with the majority of jurisdictions who have ruled on the issue. Prior to the 1990s, many cases came to the opposite conclusion. For example, see Johnson v. Raybestos-Manhattan, Inc. 740 P.2d 548 (Haw. 1987).

**NOTES:**

## GROVER v. ELI LILLY & CO.

63 Ohio St. 3d 756, 591 N.E.2d 696 (1992).

**NATURE OF CASE: Answering of a certified question.**

**FACT SUMMARY: Grover (P) contended that his birth defects were proximately caused by his grandmother's ingesting DES during her pregnancy with his mother and that his cause of action should be recognized.**

**CONCISE RULE OF LAW: Ohio does not recognize a cause of action on behalf of a child born with severe birth defects, even if it can be established that such injuries were proximately caused by his mother's DES-induced injuries.**

**FACTS:** Grover (P), who was born premature with severe birth defects, contended that those defects were proximately caused by his grandmother's ingesting a defective drug, known as DES, during her pregnancy with Grover's (P) mother. The United States District Court for the Northern District of Ohio certified the issue in this case to the Ohio Supreme Court.

**ISSUE:** Does Ohio recognize a cause of action on behalf of a child born with severe birth defects, even if it can be established that such injuries were proximately caused by his mother's DES-induced injuries?

**HOLDING AND DECISION:** (Wright, J.) No. Ohio does not recognize a cause of action on behalf of a child born with severe birth defects, even if it can be established that such injuries were proximately caused by his mother's DES-induced injuries. In Enright v. Eli Lilly & Co., 77 N.Y. 2d 377 (1991), the New York Court of Appeals held that a child does not have a cause of action, in negligence or strict liability, against a prescription drug company based on the manufacture of DES if the child was never exposed to the drug in utero. The New York Court of Appeals' holding is persuasive. Even if knowledge of the drug's dangerous propensities is sufficient to create liability to the women exposed to the drug in utero, this same knowledge does not automatically justify the extension of liability to those women's children. When a pharmaceutical company such as Eli Lilly (D) prescribes drugs to a woman, the company, under ordinary circumstances, does not have a duty to her daughter's infant who will be conceived 28 years later. Because of the remoteness in time and causation, Grover (P) does not have an independent cause of action.

**DISSENT:** (Resnick, J.) To hold that Grover's (P) injuries were not foreseeable is to ignore an entire body of scientific information which was available or could have easily become available with a measure of care concerning the effects of DES on subsequent generations.

**EDITOR'S ANALYSIS:** In Crislip v. TCH Liquidating Co., 52 Ohio St. 3d 251 (1990), the Ohio Court of Appeals discussed the confusion that existed when deciding causation on the issue at bar. The court argued that many justices confuse the issue by characterizing the question as whether the pharmaceutical companies should have known that DES could cause reproductive abnormalities in a developing fetus. The issue is not whether the pharmaceutical companies knew of some dangers from the use of DES but whether the drug companies should have known, at the time it was prescribed, that DES could cause a birth defect that would result in the delivery of a premature child 20 or 30 years later.

**NOTES:**

## ROMERO v. INTERNATIONAL HARVESTER CO.

979 F.2d 1444 (10th Cir. 1992).

**NATURE OF CASE: Appeal from denial of motion for new trial in a products liability action.**

**FACT SUMMARY: Romero's old tractor did not have a roll bar although subsequent models included them.**

**CONCISE RULE OF LAW: A manufacturer has no duty to notify previous purchasers of its products about later-developed safety devices or to retrofit these products.**

**FACTS:** Romero, a farm worker, was killed when he was sitting in an International Harvester (D) tractor that rolled over. Romero's family (P) filed suit against International Harvester (D), alleging that the tractor should have been equipped with a roll bar or a Roll Over Protective Structure (ROPS). They claimed that the tractor should have been retrofitted with a ROPS after it was sold. The tractor was sold to its first owner in 1963 and later acquired by Romero's employer in 1983. In 1963, a ROPS was not required by government standards. A ROPS system was developed in the mid-60s and did not become mandatory for new tractors until years later. At trial, the jury found that although the tractor's design was not defective, International Harvester (D) should have retrofitted the tractor with a roll guard. International Harvester's (D) motion for J.N.O.V. or a new trial was denied.

**ISSUE:** Does a manufacturer have a duty to notify previous purchasers of its products about later-developed safety devices or to retrofit these products?

**HOLDING AND DECISION:** (Anderson, J.) No. A manufacturer has no duty to notify previous purchasers of its products about later-developed safety devices or to retrofit these products. Previous cases involving postsale duties of manufacturers have established that there is a duty to retrofit or to warn previous purchasers only if the product was defective at the time it was distributed. If the product was not defective at the time it was sold, there is no postsale duty to warn the purchasers. This view is consistent with § 402A of the Restatement of Torts (Second). Additionally, this rule extends to both negligence and strict liability claims. The jury in this case determined that the tractor was not defective when it was sold. Therefore, International Harvester (D) had no postsale duties with regard to the tractor and cannot be held liable for Romero's death. Reversed.

**EDITOR'S ANALYSIS:** This decision is in accord with most other jurisdictions. Texas stands as an exception, imposing a broader postsale duty. See Bell Helicopter v. Bradshaw, 549 S.W.2d 519 (1979).

## HODDER v. GOODYEAR TIRE & RUBBER CO.

Minn. Sup. Ct. 426 N.W.2d 826 (1988).

**NATURE OF CASE: Appeal of award of damages for personal injury.**

**FACT SUMMARY: Hodder (P) was seriously injured while changing a tire on a rim which had outlived its useful life.**

**CONCISE RULE OF LAW: That a product has outlived its useful life is not an absolute defense to a personal injury action.**

**FACTS:** Goodyear Tire & Rubber Co. (D) had manufactured a type of tire rim, called the K-rim, since the 1920s. By the late 1950s, Goodyear (D) became aware that the rims, under certain circumstances, could separate. The product was discontinued in 1962, and Goodyear (D) began to produce educational materials as to proper handling of the rim. In 1981, Hodder (P), while mounting a tire on a K-rim, was seriously injured when the rim separated and the tire exploded. The rim had been made in 1955. Hodder (P) sued for personal injuries. The jury found the rim to have outlived its useful life, but nonetheless awarded compensatory and punitive damages. Goodyear (D) appealed.

**ISSUE:** Is it an absolute defense to a personal injury action that a product has outlived its useful life?

**HOLDING AND DECISION:** (Simonett, J.) No. That a product has outlived its useful life is not an absolute defense to a personal injury action. Minnesota statute 604.03(1) provides that it shall be a defense to a products liability action that a product has outlived its useful life. However, the statute does not say whether the defense focuses on a particular item, a particular product line, or a generic product line. Further, it is not clear whether the defense is absolute or conditional. It should be noted that the legislature considered an absolute statute of repose and rejected the concept. From this it may be inferred that the useful-life defense is not an absolute defense, but rather a factor a jury can consider in determining liability. Here, the jury apparently decided that Goodyear's (D) efforts to warn users of the K-rim's faults were inadequate, and this was not insufficient to support the verdict. Affirmed.

**EDITOR'S ANALYSIS:** Statutes of repose differ from statutes of limitation. The latter begin to run from the time of injury. The former are calculated as beginning when the potentially wrongful acts of a defendant occur. Generally speaking, statutes of repose favor defendants more than statutes of limitation.

**NOTES:**

# CHAPTER 11
# CAUSE IN FACT

## QUICK REFERENCE RULES OF LAW

1. **Identifying the Defendant.** In a products liability action, the plaintiff need only prove by a preponderance of the evidence that it was the defendant's product that caused the harm complained of. (Drayton v. Jiffee Chemical Corp.)

2. **Identifying the Defendant.** One who is injured by a defective product, who through no fault of his own cannot identify the manufacturer, may recover proportionately from those manufacturers whose combined production represented a substantial percentage of the market of the product. (Sindell v. Abbott Laboratories.)

3. **Establishing Causation.** A plaintiff may prove causation through circumstantial evidence where an allegedly defective product has destroyed itself. (Henderson v. Sunbeam Corp.)

4. **Establishing Causation.** More possibility of causation is insufficient to establish a cause of action in strict products liability. (Calhoun v. Honda Motors Co.)

5. **The Special Problem of Warnings and Reliance.** Where the presence of a warning could not have prevented an accident, its absence cannot be a cause in fact of that accident. (Greiner v. Volkswagenwerk Aktiengesellschaft)

6. **The Special Problem of Warnings and Reliance.** In cases involving failure to warn, the presumption is that an adequate warning would have been read and heeded; but it may be rebutted by a showing that absence of the warning was not a cause of the accident. (Nissen Trampoline Co. v. Terre Haute First National Bank)

## DRAYTON v. JIFFEE CORP.

395 F. Supp. 1081 (N.D. OH 1978).

**NATURE OF CASE: Action for damages for personal injuries.**

**FACT SUMMARY: After being sued as a result of a chemical burn, Jiffee (D) claimed that its product was not responsible.**

**CONCISE RULE OF LAW: In a products liability action, the plaintiff need only prove by a preponderance of the evidence that it was the defendant's product that caused the harm complained of.**

**FACTS:** Drayton (P) incurred severe facial disfigurement as a result of being doused with liquid drain cleaner. Witnesses testified that the product used was Jiffee's (D) "liquid-plumr," yet the procedures employed by the person using it corresponded more to those appearing on the container of a competing product and did not indicate that the instructions appearing on a "liquid- plumr" container were those being followed. Also, there was evidence that the destruction caused by the cleaner was inconsistent with that which should have been caused by "liquid-plumr." The container of the product used to clear the drain was never recovered and the circumstances of its disposal never ascertained.

**ISSUE:** In a products liability action, need the plaintiff prove only by a preponderance of the evidence that it was the defendant's product that caused the harm complained of?

**HOLDING AND DECISION:** (Battisti, J.) Yes. In a products liability action, the plaintiff need only prove by a preponderance of the evidence that it was the defendant's product that caused the harm complained of. Even though the actions of the person who used the drain cleaner were more consistent with having read the label of a product other than "liquid-plumr," such an inference is not sufficient to offset the uncontroverted testimony of three people that the product was "liquid-plumr," absent a finding that the testimony of all three witnesses was not credible. The fact that sulfuric acid acts much more quickly on human skin than does sodium hydroxide does not mean that sodium hydroxide does not burn the skin, especially when it is noted that the amount of time during which Drayton (P) was exposed to the drain cleaner was not insubstantial. Also, the fact that the shirt of a person holding the injured infant, Drayton (P), on the way to the hospital was eaten through, and that the effect on the shirt was inconsistent with exposure to 30% sodium hydroxide, does not identify the drain cleaner absent precise information about the shirt's fiber and the duration of the chemical contact. Judgment for Drayton (P).

**EDITOR'S ANALYSIS:** An essential element of the plaintiff's case in a products liability action is proving the identity of the defective product, or that the defect complained of is traceable to the defendant. The Drayton case indicates that the plaintiff need demonstrate that it is more likely than not that the defendant's product did the damage. There was evidence indicating that it was unlikely that "liquid-plumr" did the damage, but the court felt that the testimony of three witnesses that it was "liquid-plumr" made it more likely than not that it was.

**NOTES:**

## SINDELL v. ABBOTT LABORATORIES

Cal. Sup. Ct., 26 Cal.3d 588 (1980), cert. denied, 449 U.S. 912 (1980).

**NATURE OF CASE: Appeal from grant of demurrer to action in strict liability.**

**FACT SUMMARY: Sindell (P) and others developed cancer as adults due to side effects of the drug D.E.S. taken by their mothers during pregnancy, but due to the time lapse, they could not identify the specific manufacturer of the particular dosage taken by their mothers.**

**CONCISE RULE OF LAW: One who is injured by a defective product, who through no fault of his own cannot identify the manufacturer, may recover proportionately from those manufacturers whose combined production represented a substantial percentage of the market of the product.**

**FACTS:** Sindell (P) and many other women whose mothers took the drug D.E.S. during pregnancy developed cancer as adults due to side effects of the drug. No warning of dangers was given, and the drug was produced according to a uniform formula used by all manufacturers, none of whom tested the drug for safety, yet all contributed to promoting the drug as safe. Due to the time lapse between use of D.E.S. and the manifestations of cancer, neither Sindell (P) nor the other victims could specifically identify the manufacturer of the drug taken by their respective mothers. Sindell (P) sued various manufacturers on behalf of herself and others similarly situated, seeking to hold them liable on several grounds. Abbott's (D) and other manufacturers' demurrer to the complaint was granted by the trial court. Sindell (P) appealed.

**ISSUE:** May one who is injured by a defective product who through no fault of his own cannot identity the manufacturer recover proportionately from those manufacturers whose combined production represented a substantial percentage of the market of the product?

**HOLDING AND DECISION:** (Mosk, J.) Yes. One who is injured by a defective product who through no fault of his own cannot identify the manufacturer may recover proportionately from those manufacturers whose production represented a substantial percentage of the market of the product. Between an innocent plaintiff and negligent defendants the cost of injury should fall on the negligent. The use of a "market share liability" standard is more likely to place the burden on those actually responsible than the traditional methods used in this situation, such as shifting the burden to the defendant to prove nonresponsibility, or placing liability on the industry as a whole. Where, as in this case, the product was produced from a standard formula, each defendant may be held responsible for the proportion of the judgment represented by its share of the market unless it can prove that it could not have made the product that caused Sindell's (P) harm. If Sindell (P) can prove that the drug manufacturers she joins represent a substantial percentage of the market, she can recover for proximately caused injuries. Reversed.

**EDITOR'S ANALYSIS:** This "market share liability" theory has met with substantial criticism by many courts. Some have found it against public policy to adopt it; others have limited it so as not to apply it in all unknown defendant cases. For example, asbestos injuries may be caused by several products which do not exclusively contain asbestos. In this area the market share liability theory is very difficult to apply because the cause of the injury is not settled.

**NOTES:**

## HENDERSON v. SUNBEAM CORP.

1995 WL 39022, aff'd, 46 F.3d 1151 (10th Cir. 1995).

**NATURE OF CASE: Appeal of award of damages in a products liability action.**

**FACT SUMMARY: Henderson (P) attempted to prove a defect in an electric blanket although the blanket had been destroyed in a fire.**

**CONCISE RULE OF LAW: A plaintiff may prove causation through circumstantial evidence where an allegedly defective product has destroyed itself.**

**FACTS:** A fire began on Henderson's (P) bed due to an electrical source. Henderson (P) claimed that the fire was due to a faulty electric blanket manufactured by Sunbeam (D). Henderson (P) presented two expert witnesses at trial. The first expert, Hallman, faulted the control unit. The second, Croenwett, believed that a broken connection in the heating element caused the fire, which could have been prevented by a simple safety device but could not identify the exact wire. Sunbeam (D) appealed an adverse jury verdict, contending that Henderson (P) had not presented sufficient evidence of causation.

**ISSUE:** May a plaintiff prove causation through circumstantial evidence where an allegedly defective product has destroyed itself?

**HOLDING AND DECISION:** Yes. A plaintiff may prove causation through circumstantial evidence where an allegedly defective product has destroyed itself. If direct evidence of the precise operative defect becomes unavailable, circumstantial evidence presented through expert testimony is sufficient to prove that a product caused an injury. A plaintiff's expert need not agree on a theory of causation in order for the question to be presented to the jury. Therefore, it is clear that Henderson (P) put forth adequate evidence showing that a defect in the Sunbeam (D) blanket caused the fire. Affirmed.

**EDITOR'S ANALYSIS:** Expert testimony on causation is not always required. If the causal connection would be apparent to a layperson, many courts will allow the decision to go to the jury without expert testimony. For example, see Coca Cola Bottling Co. v. Cromwell, 159 S.W.2d 744 (Ark. 1942), in which the plaintiff choked on something in her Coke, which was found to have six spider legs remaining in the bottle.

## CALHOUN v. HONDA MOTOR CO., LTD.

738 F2d 126 (6th Cir. 1984).

**NATURE OF CASE: Appeal of judgment in an action for damages for personal injury.**

**FACT SUMMARY: Calhoun (P) was unable to demonstrate more than a possibility that a defect in his motorcycle caused an accident.**

**CONCISE RULE OF LAW: More possibility of causation is insufficient to establish a cause of action in strict products liability.**

**FACTS:** Calhoun (P) was seriously injured when the motorcycle he was riding collided with a stationary vehicle. He was unable to remember the incident due to his injuries. He sued Honda Motor Company (D), alleging a design defect. A problem existed with the type of motorcycle he had been riding in that the brakes sometimes malfunctioned during rain. It had not been raining, but he had recently had it washed. A jury awarded him $1,250,000, but the court awarded Honda (D) a judgment, concluding that causation had not been proven. Calhoun (P) appealed.

**ISSUE:** Is mere possibility of causation sufficient to establish a cause of action in strict products liability?

**HOLDING AND DECISION:** (Keith, J.) No. Mere possibility of causation is insufficient to establish a cause of action in strict products liability. To recover on a strict liability theory, not only must a defect be shown, but it also must be demonstrated that the defect probably caused the injury of which complaint is made. Mere possibility is insufficient. Here, Calhoun (P) was unable to show more than the possibility that the alleged defect caused the accident; other, equally possible causes could not be ruled out. This being so, Calhoun (P) failed to show causation. Affirmed.

**EDITOR'S ANALYSIS:** Direct proof of causation is not required. Causation may be circumstantially proved by demonstrating a defect and then disproving possible alternative theories as to causation. Calhoun (P) was unable to do this.

**NOTES:**

## GREINER v. VOLKSWAGENWERK AKTIENGESELLSCHAFT

429 F. Supp. 495 (E.D. Penn. 1977).

**NATURE OF CASE: Action for damages for personal injury.**

**FACT SUMMARY: In a case involving injury to a passenger in a Volkswagen that overturned, a judgment for Volkswagenwerk A.G. (D) was vacated because Greiner's (P) theory on failure to warn was withheld from the jury and the case was remanded for further consideration.**

**CONCISE RULE OF LAW: Where the presence of a warning could not have prevented an accident, its absence cannot be a cause in fact of that accident.**

**FACTS:** Greiner (P) was injured when the Volkswagen beetle in which she was riding overturned. The jury found that the vehicle was not defectively designed, and Greiner (P) appealed the withholding from the jury of her contention that failure to warn of the propensity of beetles to turn over was a proximate cause of the accident. Judgment for Volkswagenwerk A.G. (D) was vacated on the ground that the issue of failure to warn should have been presented to the jury, and the case was remanded for further consideration.

**ISSUE:** Where the presence of a warning could not have prevented an accident, can its absence be a cause in fact of the accident?

**HOLDING AND DECISION:** (Lord, J.) No. Where the presence of a warning could not have prevented an accident, its absence cannot be a cause in fact of that accident. Here, before turning to the left and tipping over, the car was heading for a concrete bridge railing approximately ten feet away. It is not within the bounds of reason to suppose that, had there been a warning, the driver would have recalled it, considered it, and then intentionally crashed head-on into a concrete rail. When the car was ten feet from the railing, a serious accident was inevitable, warning or no warning, and Greiner (P) made no showing that one would have been less devastating than the other. The causal connection between the lack of warning and Greiner's (P) injury is too remote to raise a jury question. There have been cases where recovery has been held allowable absent specific evidence of proximate cause. One involved a helicopter crash after a power failure where there was no warning to instantaneously shift to auto rotation in the event of power failure. In each of these cases, the nature of the required warning was specific and easily followed, and it was reasonable to infer from the circumstances that the instructions would have been followed. As to the allegation that the driver would not have bought a Volkswagen had she been warned of its propensity to overturn, there are no proven facts to support such an inference. To recover, the plaintiff must show that an adequate warning would have prevented the harm. Judgment for Volkswagen (D) reinstated.

**EDITOR'S ANALYSIS:** A product may be properly manufactured and well designed, yet be found defective because of lack of an adequate warning. From the facts of the Greiner cases, the most obvious defect would seem to be the Volkswagen's propensity to overturn on sharp steering maneuvers. However, the jury found that the car was not defectively designed. There was no issue raised of defective manufacture. Therefore, in order to prove a defect, Greiner (P) alleged that the warning was inadequate.

**NOTES:**

## NISSEN v. TERRE HAUTE FIRST NATIONAL BANK

Ind. App. Ct., 332 N.E.2d 820 (1975).

**NATURE OF CASE: Appeal from grant of new trial after denial of damages for personal injury.**

**FACT SUMMARY: Garzolini (P) was injured when he caught his boot in a diving contraption manufactured by Nissen (D) which did not provide warning of the danger of a foot getting caught in the contraption.**

**CONCISE RULE OF LAW: In cases involving failure to warn, the presumption is that an adequate warning would have been read and heeded; but it may be rebutted by a showing that absence of the warning was not a cause of the accident.**

**FACTS:** While using an "Aqua Diver," a circular trampoline with a metal frame thirty-six inches in diameter and a bed of approximately sixteen inches in diameter which is part of a diving apparatus, Garzolini (P) caught his foot in the cables connecting the bed to the frame, sustaining injuries which resulted in partial amputation of his leg. Prior to marketing the Aqua Diver, Nissen Trampoline Co. (D) had discovered through testing that it was possible for a user's foot to pass between the elastic cables connecting the bed of the trampoline to the circular frame and thereby cause injury. However, the product was marketed without a warning. Terre Haute First Nat. Bank (D), the guardian of Garzolini's (P) estate, filed suit, alleging that Nissen (D) was liable under the doctrine of strict liability. Although the jury verdict was in Nissen's (D) favor, Terre Haute (P) was granted a new trial, and Nissen (D) appealed.

**ISSUE:** Although in cases involving failure to warn there is a presumption that an adequate warning would have been read and heeded, may it be rebutted by a showing that absence of the warning was not a cause of the accident?

**HOLDING AND DECISION:** (Lynbrook, J.) Yes. In cases involving failure to warn there is a presumption that an adequate warning would have been read and heeded, but it may be rebutted by a showing that absence of the warning was not a cause of the accident. The issue of causation in both negligence and strict liability cases wherein the defect is in design or manufacture differs fundamentally from causation in failure to warn cases. In the former, it is generally required that the plaintiff establish a causal connection in fact by proof that the harm resulted from the defect. In the latter, the law should supply the presumption (that an adequate warning would have been read and heeded) and place the burden of rebutting the presumption of causation on the manufacturer. This presumption is not an abrogation of the issue of causation, but merely shifts the burden of proof in situations where the fact-finder could only speculate as to whether the injury could have been prevented by a warning. Affirmed.

**EDITOR'S ANALYSIS:** Whether or not an injury could have been prevented by a warning must always be speculative. One can speculate that a young man wishing to have fun at the beach is unlikely to be deterred from using a contraption placed there for his use. However, the relatively small area of the trampoline compared to the area of the circle formed by the frame might make the product look dangerous. The appearance, along with the warning, might have deterred Garzolini (P) from using the device.

**NOTES:**

# CHAPTER 12
# PROXIMATE CAUSE

## QUICK REFERENCE RULES OF LAW

1. **Duty and Foreseeability Limitations on Liability.** If the damages are only the imaginary or possible result of the tortious act, or other and contingent circumstances preponderate largely in causing the injurious effect, such damages are too remote to be the basis of recovery against the wrongdoer. (Crankshaw v. Piedmont Driving Club, Inc.)

2. **Duty and Foreseeability Limitations on Liability.** A manufacturer is not liable for injuries resulting from use by a person who is not a reasonably forseeable user of the product causing such injuries. (Winnett v. Winnett)

3. **Duty and Foreseeability Limitations on Liability.** A manufacturer's duty to design a product which is reasonably fit for its intended use encompasses foreseeable ancillary consequences of normal use. (Richelman v. Kewanee Machinery & Conveyor Co.)

4. **Intervening Causes.** The negligence of another may break the chain of causation between a defective product and an injury. (Dugan v. Sears, Roebuck & Co.)

5. **Intervening Causes.** Only intervening acts which are not reasonably foreseeable may be considered a superseding cause. (Anderson v. Dreis & Krump Manufacturing Corp.)

6. **Intervening Causes.** Criminal or tortious third-party conduct only severs the chain of proximate causation when it is not reasonably foreseeable. (Price v. Blaine Kern Artista, Inc.)

7. **Intervening Causes.** An intervening criminal act does not necessarily break the causal connection between the defective product and the injury if that act is probable and foreseeable. (Williams v. RCA Corp.)

## CRANKSHAW v. PIEDMONT DRIVING CLUB, INC.

Ga. Ct. App., 156 S.E.2d 208 (1967).

**NATURE OF CASE: Appeal from demurrer to action for damages for sale of unwholesome food.**

**FACT SUMMARY: Crankshaw (P), who slipped while rushing to aid a companion who became ill after eating shrimp at the Piedmont Driving Club, Inc. (D), appealed the judgment on the demurrer to her complaint.**

**CONCISE RULE OF LAW: If the damages are only the imaginary or possible result of the tortious act, or other and contingent circumstances preponderate largely in causing the injurious effect, such damages are too remote to be the basis of recovery against the wrongdoer.**

**FACTS:** Crankshaw's (P) companion ordered shrimp at the Piedmont Driving Club, Inc. (D). After eating some, she noticed a peculiar odor which caused her to feel ill, and she vomited just inside the restroom. When Crankshaw (P) followed, she slipped entering the restroom when she stepped into the vomit and broke her hip. Judgment was entered on a demurrer to the complaint alleging negligence in selling unwholesome food and Crankshaw (P) appealed, contending that the legal issue is whether or not the negligent serving of the food was the proximate cause of her injury.

**ISSUE:** If the damages are only the imaginary or possible result of the tortious act, or other and contingent circumstances preponderate largely in causing the injurious effect, are such damages too remote to be the basis of recovery against the wrongdoer?

**HOLDING AND DECISION:** (Jordan, J.) Yes. If the damages are only the imaginary or possible result of the tortious act, or other and contingent circumstances preponderate largely in causing the injurious effect, such damages are too remote to be the basis of recovery against the wrongdoer. Damages must flow from the "legal and natural result of the act done." Although the question of proximate cause is one for a jury ordinarily, the facts in this petition make the case indisputable and subject to being ruled upon as a matter of law. A jury could not reasonably conclude that Crankshaw's (P) injury was proximately caused by Piedmont Driving Club's (D) negligence in serving unwholesome food to another person. Affirmed.

**EDITOR'S ANALYSIS:** The rule of the Crankshaw case is simply the statement of the nature of proximate cause as contained in the Georgia statutes. It is but one of numerous statements of that concept. It involves a question not so much of whether or not the defendant's action caused the harm, but rather of whether or not the defendant had a duty to protect the plaintiff from the harm sustained. Piedmont's (D) negligence was the cause in fact of Crankshaw's (P) injury since "but for" the negligence, there would have been no injury. The question then is did Piedmont (D) have a duty to protect Crankshaw (P) from the consequence of its negligence toward her companion? Although it did not apply the term "foreseeability" to the facts, the court seems to think it unforeseeable that one would sustain injury in the way Crankshaw (P) did, and thus Piedmont (D) owed her no duty.

**NOTES:**

## WINNETT v. WINNETT

57 Ill.2d 7, 310 N.E.2d 1 (1974).

**NATURE OF CASE: Appeal from reversal of dismissal of products liability action.**

**NOTES:**

**FACT SUMMARY: Winnett (P), a four-year-old girl, placed her hand on a moving conveyor belt on a forage wagon operating on her grandfather's (Winnett's (D)) farm and suffered injuries.**

**CONCISE RULE OF LAW: A manufacturer is not liable for injuries resulting from use by a person who is not a reasonably forseeable user of the product causing such injuries.**

**FACTS:** Winnett (P), a four-year-old girl, was injured when she placed her hand on the conveyor belt or screen of a forage wagon then being operated on her grandfather's (Winnett's (D)) farm. Winnett (P) settled her suit with Winnett (D) and proceeded against the manufacturer (D) on the ground that it was defective design that caused her injuries. The trial court dismissed the complaint for failure to state a cause of action, but on appeal the dismissal was reversed. The manufacturer (D) appealed.

**ISSUE:** Is a manufacturer liable for injuries resulting from use by a person who is not a reasonably foreseeable user of the product causing such injuries?

**HOLDING AND DECISION:** (Underwood, J.) No. Whether Winnett (P) can here be deemed entitled to the protections afforded by strict tort liability depends upon whether the manufacturer (D) could reasonably foresee that a four-year-old girl would be allowed to place her fingers on the conveyor belt of the forage wagon. To show that a product is unreasonably dangerous, it is necessary to show that the product was operated for its intended purpose by one for whose use it was intended. A manufacturer is not liable for injuries resulting from use by a person who is not a reasonably foreseeable user of the product causing such injuries. The trial court was correct in properly dismissing Winnett's (P) complaint against the manufacturer (D). Appellate court reversed; circuit court affirmed.

**DISSENT:** (Goldenhersh, J.) The question of the foreseeability of Winnett's (P) contact with the forage wagon machine was one for the jury and should not be decided as a matter of law.

**EDITOR'S ANALYSIS:** It cannot be questioned that a product which is reasonably safe for some users is dangerous in the hands of others. An automobile, safe in that it is free from defects endangering a competent adult driver, is unsafe with a child behind the wheel. It is nonetheless not defectively designed, and the manufacturer should not be subjected to liability for injuries resulting from such use of the product.

## RICHELMAN v. KEWANEE MACHINERY & CONVEYOR CO.

Ill. App. Ct., 375 N.E.2d 885 (1978).

**NATURE OF CASE: Appeal from award of damages for strict liability and negligence.**

**FACT SUMMARY: Richelman's (P) leg was amputated when it was caught in a grain auger designed by Kewanee Machinery & Conveyor Co. (D) which appealed the verdict for Richelman (P).**

**CONCISE RULE OF LAW: A manufacturer's duty to design a product which is reasonably fit for its intended use encompasses foreseeable ancillary consequences of normal use.**

**FACTS:** Richelman (P), who was less than three years old, suffered an amputation of his right foot when he became entangled in a grain auger after his father, thinking he was asleep, had stalled the mechanism and then left to feed cattle nearby. The auger, designed by Kewanee Machinery & Conveyor Co. (D), was used, among other things, for the purpose of conveying grain from a hopper located on the ground to a storage silo. It consists of a long tube in which revolves a screw-like mechanism. No one saw how Richelman (P) became entangled in the machinery. In a suit based upon strict liability and negligence, the jury found for Richelman (P) by a verdict founded on both theories. The auger was designed only with the safety of its operators being considered and not that of bystanders, even though the designers knew that augers are generally located in a farmhouse complex where small children often play. Because of the spacing of the bars of the auger guard, anyone whose shoe width was less than 4 inches (12-B shoe width) could have been similarly injured. Kewanee (D) appealed.

**ISSUE:** Does a manufacturer's duty to design a product which is reasonably fit for its intended use encompass foreseeably ancillary consequences of normal use?

**HOLDING AND DECISION:** (Moran, J.) Yes. A manufacturer's duty to design a product which is reasonably fit for its intended use encompasses foreseeably ancillary consequences of normal use. The real question is not so much whether Kewanee (D) could "objectively expect" that Richelman (P) would venture outdoors on the day in question and become entangled in the grain auger, but, rather, whether Kewanee (D) could "objectively expect" that if one with a smaller than 4 -inch shoe width were to trip or fall near the auger he could be injured because of the inadequate safety guard. The cases construing the Winnett case indicate nothing more than a reluctance by the judiciary to hold a manufacturer liable when children are allowed to play with dangerous objects. In this case, however, there is no positive evidence that Richelman (P) was actively playing with or attempting to operate the grain auger. Thus, the jury could have inferred that Richelman (P) inadvertently tripped or fell into the open hopper. While the Winnett court felt that the facts there in issue were such that nonliability could be found as a matter of law, the evidence here presents factual questions upon which reasonable men might differ and thus was properly submitted to the jury. Affirmed.

**DISSENT:** (Jones, J.) The question to be decided does not involve foreseeability of injury in general but whether this particular plaintiff's injury was reasonably foreseeable. The Winnett case held that it was not and should be followed. A safer auger would be less effective in doing what it was designed to do.

**EDITOR'S ANALYSIS:** Both the majority and dissent indicate an almost conscious intention of the designers of the auger not to make it any safer than it was. The question could be phrased as one of policy: should the designer be required to make the machine safe for operators with big feet; for all operators; for bystanders; for children who wander by; for children who want to play with the machine? The majority phrased its answer in terms leaving out only the last category the dissent would perhaps protect only operators with big feet.

**NOTES:**

## DUGAN v. SEARS, ROEBUCK & CO.

Ill. App. Ct., 113 Ill. App. 3d 740 (1983).

**NATURE OF CASE: Appeal of denial of damages in action for personal injury.**

**FACT SUMMARY: A jury found another's negligence to have superseded, from a causation perspective, any defect in the design of a lawn mower sold by Sears, Roebuck & Company (D).**

**CONCISE RULE OF LAW: The negligence of another may break the chain of causation between a defective product and an injury.**

**FACTS:** Favia was mowing a lawn with a lawn mower sold by Sears, Roebuck & Company (D). The lawn mower contained a warning that small objects could be thrown to the side of the mower while it operated and that, therefore, it should not be used near bystanders. Nonetheless, Favia operated the mower near Dugan (P). A small piece of plastic was ejected by the machine, which put out Dugan's (P) right eye. Dugan (P) sued Sears (D) and Roper Corp. (D), alleging a strict products liability cause of action. Sears (D) and Roper (D) contended that Favia's negligence was solely responsible for the incident. A jury returned a defense verdict, and Dugan (P) appealed.

**ISSUE:** May the negligence of another break the chain of causation between a defective product and an injury?

**HOLDING AND DECISION:** (Lorenz, J.) Yes. The negligence of another may break the chain of causation between a defective product and an injury. The concept of superseding cause, in which an act of another, not foreseeable and probable, breaks the legal causation chain between an act and an injury, applies to strict products liability as well as negligence. Here, the jury apparently concluded that the negligence of Favia was the sole proximate cause of the injury superseding the effects of whatever defect may have existed in the mower. This is a factual issue properly decided by a jury, and the decision here was not unsupported by the evidence. Affirmed.

**EDITOR'S ANALYSIS:** Superseding cause is discussed in the Restatement (Second) Torts, §§ 440-42. Various factors are discussed in these sections regarding exactly what can constitute superseding cause. No hard rule can be distilled in this regard. Whether or not superseding cause exists must be seen as an exercise in factor analysis.

**NOTES:**

### ANDERSON v. DREIS & KRUMP MANUFACTURING CORP.

Wash. Ct. App., 48 Wash. App. 432, 739 P.2d 1177 (1987).

**NATURE OF CASE: Appeal from summary judgment dismissing a products liability claim.**

**FACT SUMMARY: Anderson (P) was injured by a Dreis (D) press, but Dreis (D) claimed it was not liable because Anderson's (P) employer had modified the press.**

**CONCISE RULE OF LAW: Only intervening acts which are not reasonably foreseeable may be considered a superseding cause.**

**FACTS:** Anderson (P), an employee of Comet, operated a press manufactured by Dreis (D). Comet used the press for corrugating metal. The press, as designed and sold to Comet, could be activated by either of two means, a two-button control or a foot treadle. The two-button system served as an effective safety device because both of the operator's hands were needed and thus were clear of the press. Comet, despite the instructions included with the press, modified the press by disconnecting the two-button control and installing a single button control at the end of a long flexible cord. Anderson (P) reached into the press to clear debris and his stomach accidentally hit the start button, causing severe injuries to his hand. Dreis (D) moved for summary judgment dismissal of Anderson's (P) subsequent lawsuit, claiming that Comet's modification was the superseding cause of the injury. The trial court agreed and dismissed the action. Anderson (P) appealed.

**ISSUE:** Are intervening acts always considered a superseding cause?

**HOLDING AND DECISION:** (Munson, J.) No. Only intervening acts which are not reasonably foreseeable may be considered a superseding cause. Proximate cause consists of two elements: (1) factual or "but for" causation and (2) legal causation. Factual causation is established where the injury would not have occurred but for the defendant's act. Assuming that Dreis's (D) failure to equip the press with guards was the factual cause of Anderson's (P) injury, legal causation must still be proved. Legal causation hinges on policy considerations as to how far the legal consequences of an act should extend. The doctrine of superseding cause provides that where the act of a third-party intervenes between the original conduct and injury, the defendant may not be held liable. Whether a third party act is considered a superseding cause depends on whether the intervening act was reasonably foreseeable. If the intervening act was foreseeable, it cannot be a legally superseding cause breaking the causation chain. In the present case, Comet's modification of the Dreis (D) press was not unforeseeable as a matter of law. The question should have been presented to a jury. Reversed.

**DISSENT:** (Green, J.) It is clear from the facts that the sole and proximate cause of Anderson's (P) injury was Comet's negligent modification of the activation system. Only if the accident had happened in a different manner should a design defect claim be allowed.

**EDITOR'S ANALYSIS:** The majority noted that Comet's modification did not result in a different type of harm than otherwise would have occurred from a failure to supply guards with the press. The majority disputed the dissent's position, finding that the modification was not independent of the lack of guards. They stated that Anderson's (P) hand would not have been injured if there were guards, no matter how the press was activated.

**NOTES:**

## PRICE v. BLAINE KERN ARTISTA, INC.

Nev. Sup. Ct., 893 P.2d 367 (1995).

**NATURE OF CASE: Appeal from summary judgment dismissing a products liability action.**

**FACT SUMMARY: Price (P) was injured while wearing a BKA (D) caricature mask when he was pushed down.**

**CONCISE RULE OF LAW: Criminal or tortious third-party conduct only severs the chain of proximate causation when it is not reasonably foreseeable.**

**FACTS:** Price (P), an entertainer at Harrah's in Reno, was wearing a large and heavy caricature mask of George Bush. Price (P) was pushed from behind by a patron, fell and was injured. Price (P) alleged that the lack of a safety harness in the mask to support his head and neck caused the injury. BKA (D), the manufacturer of the mask, moved for summary judgment on the grounds that the patron's push was the superseding cause of the injury, absolving BKA (D) of liability. Price (P) appealed the trial court's grant of the motion.

**ISSUE:** Does criminal or tortious third party conduct always sever the chain of proximate causation?

**HOLDING AND DECISION:** (Per curiam) No. Criminal or tortious third-party conduct only severs the chain of proximate causation when it is not reasonably foreseeable. For negligence actions, criminal or tortious third-party conduct ordinarily severs the proximate cause chain. However, this is only true as long as the third-party act was not reasonably foreseeable. In strict liability, the rule is nearly the same, but the focus is on whether the harm is of a kind and degree that is so unforeseeable to the manufacturer that if would be unfair to find liability. In the present case, Price (P) alleged that his injuries were due to the heavy BKA (D) mask rather than to the immediate result of the push. Since it was clearly foreseeable to BKA (D) that persons wearing its masks would fall down for some reason, the alleged injuries suffered by Price (P) are within the realm of risks that should have been considered by BKA (D). Therefore, it was error to find that, as a matter of law, the alleged defect in the mask was not a substantial factor in producing Price's (P) injuries. Reversed.

**EDITOR'S ANALYSIS:** This decision is in general accord with the majority of cases throughout the country. The key question is always how narrowly or broadly to frame the question of foreseeability. See §§ 448 and 449 of the Restatement of (Second) Torts for more information on superseding causes.

**NOTES:**

## WILLIAMS v. RCA CORP.

Ill. App. Ct., 376 N.E.2d 37 (1978).

**NATURE OF CASE: Appeal from dismissal of complaint sounding in strict tort liability.**

**FACT SUMMARY: A security guard was injured when his RCA (D) portable two-way receiver failed to operate when he used it to request assistance in making an arrest, and he was shot by the suspect.**

**CONCISE RULE OF LAW: An intervening criminal act does not necessarily break the causal connection between the defective product and the injury if that act is probable and foreseeable.**

**FACTS:** Williams (P), a security guard, was assigned the duty of watching a certain restaurant and, when a robbery occurred there, he used a portable two-way receiver, manufactured by RCA Corp. (D), to communicate with automobile patrols in the area to converge and assist him in the apprehension of the offender. Unknown to Williams (P) at the time, the receiver did not function so that his request for assistance was not received and, when he attempted to make the arrest by himself, he was shot and wounded by the robber. Williams (P) sued under a theory of strict liability in tort, alleging that the receiver was unreasonably dangerous as a result of defects which existed when it left the control of RCA (D), and that the defective condition of the receiver was the proximate cause of his having been wounded. RCA (D) moved to dismiss, asserting that as a matter of law the shooting was an independent, intervening cause which broke any causal connection between the receiver and Williams's (P) injury. Williams (P) appealed from the order granting the motion to dismiss his complaint, arguing that RCA (D) should have foreseen that a security guard would be imperiled if the receiver failed to function properly.

**ISSUE:** Does an intervening criminal act necessarily break the causal connection between the defective product and the injury if that act is probable and foreseeable?

**HOLDING AND DECISION:** (Sullivan, J.) No. An intervening criminal act does not necessarily break the causal connection between the defective product and the injury if that act is probable and foreseeable. Only one case has been found where a manufacturer was held liable for injuries from use of a product where a criminal act has intervened: Klagas v. General Ordinance Equipment Corp. 367 A.2d 304 involved a mace weapon which failed to function when the plaintiff attempted to use it against a robber and was shot. However, the mace weapon was designed to prevent attack, while the receiver was not. RCA (D) may assume that no one will violate the criminal law and it could not reasonably foresee that Williams (P) would approach the robber alone whether or not he knew of the receiver's malfunction. Affirmed.

**EDITOR'S ANALYSIS:** Since the Williams court knew of only one case where a manufacturer was found liable where a criminal act intervened between the defect and the injury, the Williams facts must be very unusual. Note that the complaint involved strict tort liability, and thus under § 402A of the Restatement (Second) of Torts, in order to prevail the plaintiff must show that the defective condition is unreasonably dangerous, which seems on its face unlikely when the defect simply caused a failure of radio communication rather than a direct injury such as electric shock.

**NOTES:**

# CHAPTER 13
# DEFENSES BASED ON PLAINTIFF'S CONDUCT

## QUICK REFERENCE RULES OF LAW

1. **Contributory and Comparative Negligence.** Contributory negligence will bar recovery in a negligence action. (Reed v. Carlyle & Martin, Inc.)

2. **Contributory and Comparative Negligence.** The defenses of contributory negligence and assumption of the risk may be invoked where the defendant's alleged breach of duty is based on a failure to warn. (Parris v. M.A. Bruder & Sons, Inc.)

3. **Contributory and Comparative Negligence.** Contributory negligence is not an available defense to strict liability actions. (McCown v. International Harvester Co.)

4. **Contributory and Comparative Negligence.** The principles of comparative negligence apply to actions founded on strict products liability. (Daly v. General Motors Corp.)

5. **Contributory and Comparative Negligence.** A consumer will not be comparatively negligent in falling to discover in food a foreign substance which he could not reasonably expect to find. (Coulter v. American Bakeries Co.)

6. **Assumption of Risk.** A plaintiff who knows a product is in a dangerous condition and proceeds in disregard of this known danger may not recover for resulting injuries. (Moran v. Raymond Corp.)

7. **Assumption of Risk.** A person may not recover for an injury received when he voluntarily exposes himself to a known and appreciated danger. (Heil Co. v. Grant)

8. **Assumption of Risk.** In a products liability action, a plaintiff will be barred from recovering if his decision to encounter the risk was unreasonable. (Johnson v. Clark Equipment Co.)

## REED v. CARLYLE & MARTIN, INC.

419 U.S. 859 (1974).

**NATURE OF CASE: Appeal from denial of damages for personal injury.**

**NOTES:**

**FACT SUMMARY: Carlyle (D) contended that Reed (P) could not recover against Carlyle (D) in a personal injury action because he had been guilty of contributory negligence.**

**CONCISE RULE OF LAW: Contributory negligence will bar recovery in a negligence action.**

**FACTS:** On September 29, 1970, Reed (P) was employed as a laborer on a farm, where he had been working in an ensilage wagon purchased by the farm owner from Carlyle (D). The ensilage wagon subsequently developed operating problems, and a repairman was called to the scene, who advised Reed (P) that the wagon would have to be unloaded before he could examine it. While unloading the ensilage, Reed (P) fell into the machine's beaters when the ensilage under his feet gave way, causing severe injuries. Reed (P) then brought this action against Carlyle (D), the manufacturer, and the repair company, to recover damages for the injuries he had sustained. Reed (P) testified that although he had not used this type of wagon before, he had previously worked on a wagon manufactured by the John Deere Company, which was basically the same as the wagon in question. Reed (P) testified that he was fully familiar with that type of wagon, and with the way it operated. The defendants then filed motions for summary judgment, alleging that the testimony showed that Reed (P) was guilty of contributory negligence as a matter of law. The trial court granted the motion, and Reed (P) then brought this appeal.

**ISSUE:** Will contributory negligence bar recovery in a negligence action?

**HOLDING AND DECISION:** (Carrico, J.) Yes. Contributory negligence will bar recovery in a negligence action. The test is not whether the plaintiff actually knew of the danger confronting him, but whether, in the exercise of reasonable care, he should have known he was in a situation of peril. Here, Reed (P) should have known of his peril. Reed (P), an experienced farmer, admitted that he was familiar with the operation of the type of ensilage wagon in which he was working. Moreover, the revolving beaters were exposed to his plain view. The danger posed by the turning, spike-like mechanism was, therefore, open and obvious to Reed (P). In exposing himself to this obvious danger, he failed to exercise reasonable care for his own safety. Affirmed.

**EDITOR'S ANALYSIS:** "(O)ver two-thirds of all injuries related to consumer products have nothing to do with the design or the performance of the product. They relate to the misuse or abuse of the product." John Byington, Chairman, Consumer Product Safety Commission, Trial Magazine 25 (Feb. 1978).

## PARRIS v. M. A. BRUDER & SONS, INC.

261 F. Supp. 406 (E.D. Penn. 1966).

**NATURE OF CASE: Motion for new trial.**

**FACT SUMMARY: Bruder (D) contended that Parris (P), a longtime spray painter, had been contributorily negligent in failing to observe warnings on the label of a paint can.**

**CONCISE RULE OF LAW: The defenses of contributory negligence and assumption of the risk may be invoked where the defendant's alleged breach of duty is based on a failure to warn.**

**FACTS:** Parris (P), a professional spray painter for twenty years, sued Bruder (D), seeking to recover damages for a disabling asthmatic condition allegedly contracted from exposure to fumes or vapors created in the spray application of an epoxy-base surface coating product manufactured by Bruder (D). Parris (P) contended that the product, Plytile, was dangerous, and that Bruder (D) was negligent in failing to give adequate instructions as to its use and failing to give warnings of the dangers Bruder (D) knew or should have known were involved in the use of the product. As one of its defenses, Bruder (D) asserted that the legend on the label of the product gave adequate notice that harm could arise from the use of its product under some conditions. Bruder (D) contended that if Parris's (P) condition was caused or aggravated by inhalation of fumes or vapors, his own negligence in failing to use a mask while spray painting contributed to the harm, precluding recovery. The jury returned a verdict in favor of Bruder (D), and Parris (P) then brought this motion for a new trial, contending that contributory negligence is not available as a defense in cases where a defendant's negligence consists of a failure to warn.

**ISSUE:** May the defenses of contributory negligence and assumption of the risk be invoked where the defendant's alleged breach of duty is based on a failure to warn?

**HOLDING AND DECISION:** (Luongo, J.) Yes. The defenses of contributory negligence and assumption of the risk may be invoked where the defendant's alleged breach of duty is based upon a failure to warn. The observation that to allow the defense of contributory negligence is to indulge in circular reasoning is perhaps valid in cases where the person harmed by the use of a product is neither aware nor is chargeable with knowledge that there is any risk of harm involved in the use of the product. That rationale would be of no help to Parris (P) in this case, for there was ample basis for a finding that Parris (P) had failed to exercise due care for his own safety and that his failure had contributed to the harm. Parris (P) had been a spray painter for more than twenty years. He testified that he was aware that a mask must be worn at all times during spray painting, particularly if the spraying was being done indoors as it was here. Parris's (P) employer furnished a mask for his use together with as many replacement filter cartridges as needed. It was clear that there was a substantial risk of harm from spray painting without a mask, although the precise nature of the harm was not testified to. Since there was evidence that Parris (P) was aware of risk of harm from failure to wear a mask while spray painting, the defense of contributory negligence became available. Denied.

**EDITOR'S ANALYSIS:** Parris's (P) argument was based upon a law review article that stated in part that: "Though these time-honored defenses (contributory negligence and assumption of risk) are frequently invoked to defeat recovery, they are theoretically inapplicable when the defendant's breach of duty is based on a failure to warn. To allow these defenses is to indulge in circular reasoning since usually the plaintiff cannot be said to have assumed a risk of which he was ignorant or to have contributed to his own injury when he had no way of reasonably ascertaining that the danger of injury existed." See, Dillard and Hart, Product Liability: Directions for Use and the Duty to Warn, 41 Va.L.Rev. 145, 163 (1955).

**NOTES:**

## McCOWN v. INTERNATIONAL HARVESTER CO.

463 Pa. 13, 342 A.2d 381 (1975).

**NATURE OF CASE: Appeal from award of damages for personal injuries.**

**FACT SUMMARY: Harvester (D) contended that contributory negligence should be a defense to actions in strict liability.**

**CONCISE RULE OF LAW: Contributory negligence is not an available defense to strict liability actions.**

**FACTS:** McCown (P) was injured while driving a tractor manufactured by Harvester (D). The design of the steering mechanism of the tractor made the vehicle unusually difficult to maneuver. Specifically, approximately 15% more mechanical effort than that normally expended had to be applied to the steering wheel to accomplish any given turn. McCown (P) struck a guardrail adjoining the Pennsylvania Turnpike, causing the steering wheel to spin rapidly in the direction opposite to the turn. The spokes of the spinning steering wheel struck McCown's (P) right arm, fracturing his wrist and forearm. McCown (P) brought suit in strict liability, and Harvester (D) asserted the defense of contributory negligence. The trial court found for McCown (P), and Harvester (D) appealed.

**ISSUE:** Is contributory negligence available as a defense to strict liability actions?

**HOLDING AND DECISION:** (Jones, J.) No. Contributory negligence is not an available defense to strict liability actions. A manufacturer, by marketing and advertising his products, impliedly represents that they are safe for their intended uses. Based on that implied representation is the consumer's assumption that a manufacturer's goods are safe. Recognition of consumer negligence as a defense to strict liability actions would contradict this normal expectation of product safety. The law should not require such inspection or caution when it has accepted as reasonable the consumer's anticipation of safety. Affirmed.

**CONCURRENCE:** (Pomeroy, J.) Defendants in strict liability actions are subjected to liability upon the belief that they are better able to bear the losses caused by defects in the products involved. It is a proper corollary to this principle that the lesser loss-bearing capacity of product users exists independently of their negligence or lack of it. It follows that such negligence should not ordinarily or necessarily operate to preclude recovery in a strict liability action.

**EDITOR'S ANALYSIS:** The majority opinion was based in part upon Comment N to § 402A of the Restatement (Second) of Torts. That section provides in relevant part: "Contributory negligence of the plaintiff is not a defense when such negligence consists merely in a failure to discover the defect in the product, or to guard against the possibility of its existence . . . (However) if the user or consumer discovers the defect and is aware of the danger, and nevertheless proceeds unreasonably to make use of the product and is injured by it, he is barred from recovery."

**NOTES:**

## DALY v. GENERAL MOTORS CORP.

20 Cal. 3d 725,144 Cal. Rptr. 380, 575 P.2d 1162 (1978).

**NATURE OF CASE: Appeal from award of damages for wrongful death.**

**FACT SUMMARY: General Motors (D) contended that Daly (P), the executor for the deceased, should not recover in a strict products liability action because the decedent had been contributorily negligent.**

**CONCISE RULE OF LAW: The principles of comparative negligence apply to actions founded on strict products liability.**

**FACTS:** In the early hours of October 31, 1970, decedent Kirk Daly (P), a thirty-six-year-old attorney, was driving his Opel southbound on the Harbor Freeway in Los Angeles, when it collided with and damaged fifty feet of metal divider fence. After the initial impact between the left side of the vehicle and the fence, the Opel spun counterclockwise, the driver's door was thrown open, and Daly was forcibly ejected from the car and sustained fatal head injuries. It was undisputed that had the deceased remained in the Opel, his injuries, in all probability, would have been relatively minor. In a wrongful death action brought by the executor of the deceased's estate, it was contended that the exposed push button on the door of the Opel constituted a design defect which caused injuries greatly in excess of those that Daly would otherwise have sustained. General Motors (D) was allowed to introduce evidence showing that the deceased had not used the car's shoulder harness system, and that he had been intoxicated at the time of the collision. The jury returned a verdict in favor of General Motors (D), holding that the executor could not recover because the deceased had been contributorily negligent. Daly (P) then brought this appeal.

**ISSUE:** Do the principles of comparative negligence apply to actions founded on strict products liability?

**HOLDING AND DECISION:** (Richardson, J.) Yes. The principles of comparative negligence apply to actions founded on strict products liability. The adoption of the comparative negligence concept is fair and equitable. Plaintiffs will continue to be relieved of proving that the manufacturer or distributor was negligent in the production, design, or dissemination of the article in question. A defendant's liability for injuries caused by a defective product remains strict. The principle of protecting the defenseless is likewise preserved, for a plaintiff's recovery will be reduced only to the extent that his own lack of reasonable care contributed to his injury. The manufacturer's liability, and therefore its incentive to avoid and correct product defects, remains. Its exposure will be lessened only to the extent that the trier finds that the victim's conduct contributed to his injury. Here, from the instructions given to the jury at trial, the jury could well have concluded that the decedent's negligent failure, induced by intoxication, to use the belts and locks constituted negligent conduct which reduces the culpability of GM (D). Reversed.

**CONCURRENCE:** (Clark, J.) A negligent plaintiff is responsible and should not recover as much as an innocent one.

**CONCURRENCE AND DISSENT:** (Jefferson, J.) According to reason, justice, and equity, the court should continue the existing legal principle that permits manufacturers to spread through society the costs of compensating injured plaintiffs fully, rather than the adoption of an untenable legal principle that will result in reducing the total costs to be borne by manufacturers, and thus decrease a plaintiff's recovery below the full losses sustained.

**DISSENT:** (Mosk, J.) Transferring the liability, or part of the liability, from the party responsible for putting the article in the stream of commerce to the consumer is precisely what the majority proposes to do. The result, however delicately described, is to dilute the defect of the article by elevating the conduct of the wounded consumer to an issue of equal significance.

**EDITOR'S ANALYSIS:** The majority opinion asserted as an additional justification for its position the fact that, under prior law, assumption of the risk was a complete defense to an action for strict products liability. Under that system, "the curious and cynical message is that it profits the manufacturer to make his product so defective that in the event of injury he can argue that the user had to be aware of its patent defects to the extent the incentives are inverted."

**NOTES:**

## COULTER v. AMERICAN BAKERIES CO.

Fla. Dist. App. Ct., 530 So. 2d 1009 (1988).

**NATURE OF CASE: Appeal of finding of comparative negligence in action seeking damages for personal injury.**

**FACT SUMMARY: A jury found Coulter (P) comparatively negligent for failing to protect herself against a harmful foreign substance she contended she could not reasonably have expected to find.**

**CONCISE RULE OF LAW: A consumer will not be comparatively negligent in falling to discover in food a foreign substance which he could not reasonably expect to find.**

**FACTS:** Coulter (P) purchased a doughnut from American Bakeries Company (D). Due to a painful dental condition, she did not chew the doughnut, but rather mixed it with milk in her mouth until it dissolved. A metal wire in the doughnut lodged in her throat, causing injury. A jury awarded her $12,500, but found comparative negligence and reduced the award to $2,500. Coulter (P) appealed.

**ISSUE:** May a consumer be comparatively negligent in failing to discover in food a foreign substance which he could not reasonably expect to find?

**HOLDING AND DECISION:** (Wigginton, J.) No. A consumer will not be comparatively negligent in failing to discover in food a foreign substance which he could not reasonably expect to find. In an action based on a harmful substance in food, the issue is whether the consumer could reasonably expect to find the substance in the food. If he could not, he is under no duty to consume the food in any particular manner so as to discover the substance. A consumer has no reason to expect a metal wire to be in a doughnut, and therefore Coulter's (P) failure to chew her food cannot be considered negligent. Reversed.

**EDITOR'S ANALYSIS:** A large issue in products liability law is whether comparative negligence shall be applied. Some commentators have likened this to comparing apples and oranges, as products liability supposedly is not based on negligence. Nonetheless, most jurisdictions do figure comparative negligence into products liability analysis.

**NOTES:**

## MORAN v. RAYMOND CORP.

484 F.2d 1008 (7th Cir. 1973), cert. denied, 415 U.S. 932 (1974).

**NATURE OF CASE: Appeal from damages awarded in personal injury complaint.**

**FACT SUMMARY: Moran (P) claimed that he thought he could safely operate a lift truck from outside the operator's cage because he had done so before, but Raymond Corp. (D) argued that he assumed the risk of injury so as to bar recovery when he hurt his arm doing so.**

**CONCISE RULE OF LAW: A plaintiff who knows a product is in a dangerous condition and proceeds in disregard of this known danger may not recover for resulting injuries.**

**FACTS:** While operating a sideloader (a type of fork lift), Moran (P) left the operator's cage and stood on the forks in order to retrieve part of a load he was moving. He then reached through an opening into the cage and pulled the control lever to lower the forks. He deliberately tried to bring his hand back quickly so the cross bar would not hit him, as he had successfully done in the past, but he was injured when it came down with a shearing action before he could get out of the way. He sued Raymond Corp. (D), the manufacturer of the lift truck, on negligence and strict liability theories. The jury awarded Moran (P) $250,000, and Raymond Corp. (D) appealed, arguing that Moran (P) had assumed the risk of his own injury.

**ISSUE:** May a plaintiff who knows a product is in a dangerous condition and proceeds in disregard of this known danger recover for resulting injuries?

**HOLDING AND DECISION:** (Pell, J.) No. A plaintiff who knows a product is in a dangerous condition and proceeds in disregard of this known danger may not recover for resulting injuries. In this case, Moran (P) admitted that he been told to stand in the cage when operating the controls. He clearly knew that there was a substantial risk involved in working with the machine. He knew the bar would hit him if he did not move out of the way. He took a calculated risk and therefore may not recover for resulting injuries. Reversed.

**EDITOR'S ANALYSIS:** The harshness of the assumption of risk doctrine counsels against its expansion or extension. Courts are loathe to apply the doctrine to children or even to adults lacking experience with the product in question. Some jurisdictions require a plaintiff to be subjectively aware of the nature, character, and extent of the danger posed by the specific defect in question; a general awareness that the product is somehow dangerous is not sufficient. See Mackowick v. Westinghouse Elec. Corp., 541 A.2d 749 (Pa. Super. Ct. 1988).

## HEIL CO. v. GRANT

Tx. Ct. of Civ. App., 534 W.W.2d 916 (1976).

**NATURE OF CASE: Appeal from award of damages for wrongful death.**

**FACT SUMMARY: Heil (D) contended that Grant (P) should be barred from recovering damages for wrongful death because the decedent had assumed the risk of harm.**

**CONCISE RULE OF LAW: A person may not recover for an injury received when he voluntarily exposes himself to a known and appreciated danger.**

**FACTS:** Valmarie Grant (P) and her children sued for the death of James Grant, their husband and father respectively. The decedent was killed on February 18, 1972, while assisting his brother, Vernon Grant, in making repairs on Vernon's dump truck. The dump truck was equipped with a telescopic sleeve hoist designed and sold by Heil (D) for the purpose of raising the bed of the truck. The hoist was operated by a mechanism consisting of a control valve with levers inside the cab, a hydraulic pump, and a partially exposed pullout cable running lengthwise beneath the bed. The decedent and Vernon were working beneath the raised bed when it somehow descended. Vernon jumped away but the decedent did not. Heil's (D) engineer found no malfunction in the hoist mechanism and concluded that the pullout cable had been tripped immediately before the accident, Vernon told the decedent that if he hit the pullout cable, the bed would come down. Grant (P) sued Heil (D) under a theory of strict liability for defective design of the hoist mechanism and for failure to warn of the hazard. The jury found for Grant (P), and Heil (D) brought this appeal, contending that the decedent had knowledge of the danger presented by the pullout cable, and therefore Grant (P) should be barred from recovery under the doctrine of assumption of the risk.

**ISSUE:** May a person recover for an injury received when he voluntarily exposes himself to a known and appreciated danger?

**HOLDING AND DECISION:** (Dunagan, J.) No. A person may not recover for an injury received when he voluntarily exposes himself to a known and appreciated danger. An injured person's knowledge of a dangerous condition or defect is measured subjectively, by that person's actual, conscious knowledge. The fact that the injured person should have known of the danger will not suppose the assumption of risk defense. Sometimes, however, a person may know such facts as to be charged with knowledge of the danger. This standard would be applied when it is difficult or impossible to determine the state of the injured person's mind, as it was in this case of fatal injury. Here, there was some evidence from which the jury could have found that the decedent knew of the danger, from the fact that he had been told of the effect of hitting the pullout cable. There is some evidence that the decedent might not have appreciated the danger of hitting the pullout cable. However, the decedent had previously made a living by building airplanes and doing construction work, and he was fifty-three years old at the time of the accident. By reason of the decedent's information, age, and experience, there was some evidence of probative force that he did appreciate the danger. Reversed and remanded for new trial.

**EDITOR'S ANALYSIS:** The court in this case noted that the warning of the risk does not have to come from the supplier of the defective product. "One who voluntarily chooses to use a chattel with a complete realization, regardless of how it was acquired, of the risks to which he thus exposes himself voluntarily assumes such risks . . .." 1 Hursh & Bailey, American Law of Products Liability 2d, § 2:107.

**NOTES:**

## JOHNSON v. CLARK EQUIPMENT CO.

274 Or. 403, 547 P.2d 132 (1976).

**NATURE OF CASE: Appeal from award of damages for personal injuries.**

**FACT SUMMARY: Johnson (P) contended that the doctrine of assumption of the risk should not bar him from recovering for personal injuries sustained in an accident because his decision to encounter the risk had not been unreasonable.**

**CONCISE RULE OF LAW: In a products liability action, a plaintiff will be barred from recovering if his decision to encounter the risk was unreasonable.**

**FACTS:** Johnson (P) brought suit to recover damages for injuries he sustained while operating a forklift truck manufactured and designed by Clark (D). Johnson (P) was employed as a forklift operator at the Warrenton Lumber Company. Because of his various responsibilities, the job was a hectic one. The accident occurred on June 24, 1971, shortly after Johnson's (P) shift began and while he was engaged in feeding the random planer. Johnson (P) was in a hurry and was carrying two banded bundles of wood. On the day of the accident, Johnson (P) had no one to help him cut the bands. Although he normally dismounted his machine and moved to the front to cut the bands, on this occasion Johnson (P) remained in the cab of the forklift and reached through its uprights with the cutters. While he was cutting the bands, his body came in contact with the ascent/descent lever controlling the movement of the forks. The forklift carriage descended and severed Johnson's (P) arms just below the elbows. In his complaint, Johnson (P) alleged faulty design and manufacture of the forklift. The jury, though, found for Clark (D) on the grounds that Johnson (P) had knowingly and voluntarily encountered the danger and was thus barred from recovering under the doctrine of assumption of the risk. Johnson (P), contending that his actions had been reasonable, appealed.

**ISSUE:** In a products liability action, will a plaintiff be barred from recovering if his decision to encounter a risk was unreasonable?

**HOLDING AND DECISION:** (Howell, J.) Yes. In a products liability action, unlike other tort actions, three elements must be shown before a plaintiff can be barred from recovery under the doctrine of assumption of the risk. The defendant must show, first, that the plaintiff himself actually knew and appreciated the particular risk or danger created by the defect. Second, it must be shown that the plaintiff voluntarily encountered the risk while realizing the danger. Third, it must be demonstrated that the plaintiff's decision to voluntarily encounter the known risk was unreasonable. In this case, the trial court's definition of assumption of risk was not complete. There was no discussion of the element of unreasonableness as it related to Johnson's (P) decision to encounter the risk. Although the court did mention the other two elements, proof of all three elements is essential to the assumption of the risk defense. The reasonableness of any decision to encounter a known danger must depend upon the circumstances surrounding that decision as well as on the relative probability and gravity of the risk incurred. Working conditions and related circumstances are a particularly relevant consideration in an inquiry into the reasonableness of a decision to encounter a job-related danger. Here, Johnson (P) testified that he was in a hurry at the time of the accident, and that, had he had time to think about it, he would not have reached through the uprights. Because the third element of the defense was not included in the jury instructions, the case must be reversed and remanded for a new trial.

**EDITOR'S ANALYSIS:** The court in this case noted that in determining whether the plaintiff's actions were reasonable, the decision to encounter a risk must be determined as of the time that the decision was made. In some jurisdictions, economic necessity, such as that demonstrated by this case, will not be an excuse for assuming a known hazard, unless protest by the worker would be futile.

**NOTES:**

# CHAPTER 14
# DAMAGES

## QUICK REFERENCE RULES OF LAW

1. **Personal Injury and Death.** No remittitur shall be granted if the trial judge determines that the jury verdict is within the maximum amount that the judge determines the jury could have reasonably awarded. (Anderson v. Sears, Roebuck & Co.)

2. **Emotional Distress.** When there is evidence of any injury, no matter how slight, the mental anguish suffered by the plaintiff becomes in important element in estimating the damages suffered. (Kroger Co. v. Beck)

3. **Emotional Distress.** No matter which theory in products liability is utilized, where a plaintiff alleges a product is defective, proof that the product has malfunctioned is essential to establish liability for an injury caused by the defect. (Khan v. Shiley, Inc.)

4. **Emotional Distress.** A bystander at a traumatic event or wrongful death may recover for emotional distress if the injury to the bystander from witnessing the event is foreseeable. (Pearsall v. Emhart Industries, Inc.)

5. **Economic Loss and Property Damage.** Manufacturers of a machines sold in commercial transactions are not liable in negligence or strict liability for economic loss caused by a failure of a component part of the machine which causes damage to the machine only. (Cooperative Power Association v. Westinghouse Electric Corp.)

6. **Economic Loss and Property Damage.** If the failure of a defective product causes economic loss only, injuring no person and damaging no other property, there is no cause of action in tort. (Casa Clara Condominium Association, Inc. v. Charley Toppino & Sons, Inc.)

7. **Punitive Damages.** (1) Punitive damages may properly be awarded in a strict liability action. (2) Defendant's compliance with an applicable federal safety standard does not preclude a punitive damages award. (Gryc v. Dayton-Hudson Corp.)

8. **Punitive Damages.** Reckless or outrageous conduct on the part of a defendant is the touchstone of punitive damages, and for behavior to be reckless, it must involve a risk of harm to others substantially in excess of that necessary to make the conduct negligent. (Acosta v. Honda Motors Co.)

9. **Punitive Damages.** Any amount awarded for punitive damages should bear a reasonable relation to the actual damages, but the amount may be left to the jury's sound discretion. (Vossler v. Richards Manufacturing Co.)

## ANDERSON v. SEARS, ROEBUCK & CO.

377 F.Supp. 136 (E.D.La. 1974).

**NATURE OF CASE: Motion for post-trial relief upon award of damages for personal injuries.**

**FACT SUMMARY: After a verdict in favor of Britain (P), who was severely burned by a fire ignited by a defective Sears (D) heater, Sears (D) moved for post-trial relief, including remittitur.**

**CONCISE RULE OF LAW: No remittitur shall be granted if the trial judge determines that the jury verdict is within the maximum amount that the judge determines the jury could have reasonably awarded.**

**FACTS:** Britain (P), an infant, was severely burned by a fire which swept her home, and which was ignited by a defective Sears (D) heater. After a jury verdict in favor of Britain (P), Sears (D) and the other defendants moved for post-trial relief including remittitur, with the question of whether the damages were excessive being the only one considered on appeal.

**ISSUE:** Shall remittitur be granted if, in the determination of the trial judge, the jury verdict is within the maximum amount that the jury could reasonably have awarded?

**HOLDING AND DECISION:** (Cassibry, J.) No. Remittittur shall not be granted if, in the determination of the trial judge, the jury verdict is within the maximum amount that the jury could reasonably have awarded. The case was fairly and properly tried, over a period of eight days, before a competent and attentive jury. After having received comprehensive and impartial charges, the jury deliberated for a reasonable time before returning its verdict. The legal standard on that to gauge a jury verdict for remittitur purposes is the "maximum recovery rule." This rule directs the trial judge to determine whether the verdict of the jury exceeds the maximum amount which the jury could reasonably find, and if it does, it may be reduced to the highest amount that the jury could have properly awarded. In this case, there are five cardinal elements of damages: past physical and mental pain; future physical and mental pain; future medical expenses; loss of earning capacity; and permanent disability and disfigurement. After totaling the estimated maximum recovery for each element, the jury award is shown not to be excessive. There was no error in the verdict because it exceeded the amount originally prayed for since the pleadings were amended subsequent to the verdict to conform to the proof and the verdict. The introduction of photographs of Britain (P) was not inflammatory nor was the child's presence in the courtroom inflammatory since she behaved properly. Motions denied.

**EDITOR'S ANALYSIS:** The "maximum recovery rule" cited in Anderson (there is no indication of why the case bears that name) requires the judge to make an independent determination of damages, it would seem, thus duplicating the work of the jury. The judge is not allowed to simply look at the verdict and decide that it is too high or too low. Although not mentioned as part of the rule, the decision did mention other factors to be considered in determining whether remittitur is proper: e.g., the length of the trial and the amount of time spent in deliberation.

**NOTES:**

## KROGER CO. v. BECK

Ind. App. Ct., 375 N.E.2d 640 (1978).

**NATURE OF CASE: Appeal from award of damages for mental anguish.**

**FACT SUMMARY: Kroger Co. (D) appealed the award of damages to Beck (P) for mental distress resulting from putting a piece of steak in her mouth with an inch-long piece of metal in it.**

**CONCISE RULE OF LAW: When there is evidence of any injury, no matter how slight, the mental anguish suffered by the plaintiff becomes in important element in estimating the damages suffered.**

**FACTS:** While eating a steak which had been prepackaged by and purchased from a Kroger (D) store, Beck (P) placed a piece in her mouth containing an inch-long piece of metal that caused her sharp pain and punctured her throat. After pulling the meat from her mouth, Beck (P) ran into the bathroom and vomited violently. She did not know if she bled and did not go to a doctor, but gargled with Listerine for a month. Although her mouth healed and she did not have a scar, she was afraid that such an incident would reoccur and was not able to enjoy eating meat thereafter. Beck (P) was awarded $2,700, and Kroger Co. (D) appealed, arguing that there was insufficient evidence of a contemporaneous physical injury to support an award of damages for mental anguish, and that the award was excessive.

**ISSUE:** When there is evidence of any injury, no matter how slight, does the mental anguish suffered by the plaintiff become an important element in estimating the damages sustained?

**HOLDING AND DECISION:** (Staton, J.) Yes. When there is evidence of any injury, no matter how slight, the mental anguish suffered by the plaintiff becomes an important element in estimating the damages sustained. Beck's (P) testimony was unrefuted, and it established the legally required injury as well as the causal connection with the emotional distress. A fact finder has the right to consider the mental suffering caused by the anxiety and fear of the ensuing consequences. Where realization of the physical effects that can be produced by the foreign object did produce the total emotional and physical result, recovery is allowed even if there is no showing that the fatal or deleterious consequence resulted in the particular case. Beck (P) thought she was going to choke to death. Also, her fear of eating meat was worthy of consideration by the court. The award is certainly not so great as to indicate a motivation of prejudice, passion, partiality, or corruption. Also, Kroger (D) gave no hint of what proper damages should have been. Affirmed.

**EDITOR'S ANALYSIS:** The vomiting, as well as the pin prick in the throat itself, might have been held to constitute a physical injury which alone, when coupled with emotional distress, could have supported recovery. The cases are conflicting. Way v. Tampa Coca Cola Bottling Co., 260 So. 2d 288, allowed recovery for a plaintiff who sucked on something like a rat and became ill. Harrison v. Canada Dry Corp., 245 A.2d 642, affirmed a directed verdict against a plaintiff who discovered cockroaches in his drink. However, he apparently did not ingest any of the insects.

**NOTES:**

## KHAN v. SHILEY INCORPORATED

Cal. Sup. Ct., 217 Cal. App. 3d 848 (1990).

**NATURE OF CASE: Appeal from the granting of a summary judgment motion.**

**FACT SUMMARY: Khan (P) contended that the trial court erred in holding that because the valve implanted in her heart had not yet malfunctioned, any grievances were speculative and her lawsuit premature.**

**CONCISE RULE OF LAW: No matter which theory in products liability is utilized, where a plaintiff alleges a product is defective, proof that the product has malfunctioned is essential to establish liability for an injury caused by the defect.**

**FACTS:** In 1983, Khan (P) had a Shiley (D) valve implanted in her heart which saved her life. After the implant, Khan's (P) life greatly improved. She had been told of the risks involved with the procedure and the side effects that could occur afterward. In 1985, Khan's (P) surgeon informed her that Shiley (D) had told him the implanted valve was within a group of valves being recalled due to a propensity to fracture. There had been numerous reports that the valves were falling apart and malfunctioning without notice, resulting in death to the patients. After the recall, Khan (P) claimed that her life had drastically changed. Khan (P) and her husband (P) brought suit against Shiley (D), alleging negligence, strict liability, fraud, and negligent infliction of emotional distress, among others. The trial court granted Shiley's (D) motion for summary judgment on the grounds that Khan's (P) lawsuit was premature. Khan (P) appealed.

**ISSUE:** If a plaintiff alleges that a product is defective, is proof that the product has malfunctioned essential to establish liability for an injury caused by the defect?

**HOLDING AND DECISION:** (Sonenshine, J.) Yes. No matter which theory in products liability is utilized, where a plaintiff alleges a product is defective, proof that the product has malfunctioned is essential to establish liability for an injury caused by the defect. The essential element of causation is missing here. Khan's (P) alleged injury was not caused by any defect in the valve. Rather, it was caused, if at all, by the knowledge the valve may, at some future time, fracture. In the absence of product malfunction, Khan (P) cannot establish that Shiley (D) breached any duty owed to her. Nor are Khan's (P) alleged emotional injuries a basis for recovery absent a ground for imposing liability pursuant to a recognized cause of action. As to the allegations of fraud, the Khans (P) have stated a cause of action, and Shiley (D) failed to meet their burden to establish there was no triable issue of material fact with respect to the fraud claim.

**EDITOR'S ANALYSIS:** Khan (P) testified in her deposition that the valve had not yet malfunctioned. She also responded affirmatively when asked if, to her knowledge, the valve had worked properly. The court reasoned that it would be unfair to award damages to a plaintiff who has not experienced any real injury caused by the product, which to the present day has worked splendidly.

**NOTES:**

## PEARSALL v. EMHART INDUSTRIES, INC.

U.S. Dist. Ct., E.D. Pa., 599 F. Supp. 207 (1984).

**NATURE OF CASE: Appeal from award of damages in products liability action.**

**FACT SUMMARY: Pearsall (P) sued Emhart Industries, Inc. (D), for damages and emotional distress allegedly caused by the malfunction of a smoke alarm in a fire in Pearsall's (P) home which claimed the lives of Pearsall's (P) husband and two children.**

**CONCISE RULE OF LAW: A bystander at a traumatic event or wrongful death may recover for emotional distress if the injury to the bystander from witnessing the event is foreseeable.**

**FACTS:** Pearsall (P) sued Emhart Industries, Inc. (D), for damages and emotional distress caused when a smoke alarm manufactured by Emhart (D) allegedly malfunctioned during a fire in Pearsall's (P) home which claimed the lives of Pearsall's (P) husband and two children. At trial, the jury found for Pearsall (P), but Emhart (D) appealed, claiming that Pearsall's (P) claim for emotional distress should not have been submitted to the jury since Pearsall (P) did not witness the deaths of her husband and children in the fire.

**ISSUE:** May a bystander at a traumatic event or wrongful death recover for emotional distress if the injury to the bystander from witnessing the event is foreseeable?

**HOLDING AND DECISION:** (Katz, J.) Yes. A bystander at a traumatic event or wrongful death may recover for emotional distress if the injury to the bystander from witnessing the event is foreseeable. The Supreme Court of Pennsylvania has applied a three-factor test to determine whether such injury is foreseeable. These factors are: (1) whether plaintiff was located near the scene of the accident; (2) whether the shock resulted from a direct emotional impact upon plaintiff from the sensory and contemporaneous observance of the accident; (3) and whether plaintiff and the victim were closely related. Here, the facts of the case support Pearsall's (P) claim of infliction of emotional distress. Pearsall (P), upon arriving home, witnessed the fire, stood near, and touched the bodies of her husband and children as they were being removed from the blaze. Thus, the emotional distress of this mother witnessing the fire and its carnage is foreseeable to a manufacturer of defective alarms and, therefore, meets the standards enunciated by the Pennsylvania Supreme Court.

**EDITOR'S ANALYSIS:** Like Pennsylvania, about half the states have adopted some form of foreseeability guidelines for the emotional distress of bystanders. However, there are only a small number of cases applying the guidelines in the products liability context. Some courts still apply the "zone of danger" test, and bystanders must prove the other elements of an emotional distress claim, including physical impact or injury.

**NOTES:**

## COOPERATIVE POWER ASSN. v. WESTINGHOUSE ELECTRIC CORP.

Sup. Ct. of N.D., 493 N.W.2d 661 (1992).

**NATURE OF CASE: Review of certified question from federal district court to determine whether contract or products liability law controls a product failure.**

**FACT SUMMARY: A transformer sold to a power generating station failed, damaging several internal components of the transformer.**

**CONCISE RULE OF LAW: Manufacturers of a machines sold in commercial transactions are not liable in negligence or strict liability for economic loss caused by a failure of a component part of the machine which causes damage to the machine only.**

**FACTS:** CPA (P) owned an electrical generating station. CPA (P) used step-up transformers to increase the voltage of electricity for transmission over power lines. Westinghouse (D) manufactured such transformers. Westinghouse (D) sold CPA (P) a defective transformer. The defect damaged the bushing and contaminated the transformer coils with metal particles, requiring replacement of the bushings and rewinding of the coils. Westinghouse (D) replaced the bushings, but refused to pay for rewinding the coils. CPA (P) sued, alleging breach of express warranty, breach of contract, negligence, and negligent misrepresentation, seeking damages of $1.6 million. Westinghouse (D) moved for summary judgment dismissal of the tort claims, asserting that since only the transformer was damaged, the sole remedy was in contract. The federal court certified the question about whether products liability was an appropriate legal theory.

**ISSUE:** May manufacturers of machines sold in a commercial transactions be held liable in tort for economic loss caused by the failure of a component part of the machine which caused direct damage to the machine only?

**HOLDING AND DECISION:** (Johnson, J.) No. Manufacturers of machines sold in commercial transactions are not liable in negligence or strict liability for economic loss caused by a failure of a component part of the machine which causes damage to the machine only. In East River Steamship Corp., 476 U.S. 858 (1986), the United States Supreme Court considered a similar issue in the context of admiralty law. In that case, the plaintiffs sought recovery under tort liability for defectively designed ship turbines which damaged themselves when operated. The Court unanimously held "that a manufacturer in a commercial relationship has no duty under either a negligence or strict products-liability theory to prevent a product from injuring itself." The Court considered three approaches for determining whether an action may be brought in tort for damage to the product itself: (1) the majority approach, which bars tort recovery if only the machine is damaged; (2) the minority approach, which permits tort recovery in all cases; and (3) the intermediate "degree-of-risk" approach, which differentiates between disappointed and endangered users. The Court chose the majority position, stating that the intermediate approach was too uncertain for business planning and that the minority position would blur the line between contract and tort law while inflating damage awards. Tort liability is designed to protect a consumer's right to be free from injury in the use of a product. Where a product damages only itself, it has not harmed the user. In this case, the transformer damaged only itself. Such a failure is properly understood as a warranty claim; the product failed to meet the expectations of the purchaser, CPA (P). This court adopts the U.S. Supreme Court majority position that contract law supplies the appropriate remedies in cases of product failure such as this.

**EDITOR'S ANALYSIS:** The position that economic losses cannot be recovered in tort law is, by far, the majority position. Some jurisdictions create an exception where the failure of the product has created an undue hazard to persons or other property. However, other courts have held so firmly to the majority position that tort damages were denied even in cases of highly dangerous machine failures, such as the violent, life-threatening explosion of a transformer.

**NOTES:**

## CASA CLARA CONDOMINIUM ASSOC., INC. v. CHARLEY TOPPINO & SONS, INC.

Sup. Ct. of Fla., 620 So. 2d 1244 (1993).

**NATURE OF CASE: Review of dismissal of tort damage claims.**

**FACT SUMMARY: Concrete house foundations with high salt content cracked, damaging the homes.**

**CONCISE RULE OF LAW: If the failure of a defective product causes economic loss only, injuring no person and damaging no other property, there is no cause of action in tort.**

**FACTS:** Toppino (D) supplied concrete for numerous construction projects. Some of the concrete it supplied had a high salt content that caused reinforcing steel to rust, which, in turn, caused the concrete to crack and break off. The Casa Clara Condominium Association (P) purchased condominium units and single-family homes built with the defective concrete. The failing concrete caused damage to the buildings. The homeowners filed suit against numerous defendants, including Toppino (D). The claims against Toppino (D) were for breach of warranty, products liability, and negligence. The circuit court dismissed all counts against Toppino (D). The district court applied the economic loss rule and held that no tort action against Toppino (D) was appropriate.

**ISSUE:** Can a homeowner recover for purely economic losses from a concrete supplier under a negligence theory?

**HOLDING AND DECISION:** (McDonald, J.) No. If the failure of a defective product causes economic loss only, injuring no person and damaging no other property, there is no cause of action in tort. For recovery in tort, there must be a showing of harm above and beyond disappointed expectations. Tort law does not protect a buyer's desire to enjoy a product. Tort law attempts to protect society's interest in being free from harm; contract law protects society's interest in the reliable performance of promises. In this case, the homeowners do not claim any personal injury or harm to any other property. The foundation of a home is integral to it, making the damage to the entire structure part of the failure of the entire product, which was the building. Since the only defect was to the property itself, and the only loss suffered by the homeowners was economic loss, tort damages are not an appropriate remedy. Affirmed.

**DISSENT:** (Barkett, J.) The homeowners are denied any remedy by this ruling. Their claim for breach of implied warranty has been denied for lack of privity with Toppino (D). In this case, the economic loss rule stretches too far, denying the homeowners any protection.

**DISSENT:** (Shaw, J.) The economic loss rule attempts to prevent parties that have bargained for the distribution of risk of loss to circumvent that bargain after loss occurs to property that was the subject of the bargain. This rationale fails when the injured party was not privy to the contract, but the third party's injury was foreseeable. The homeowners were never able to bargain for the allocation of risk; they are unprotected by this ruling.

**EDITOR'S ANALYSIS:** Courts usually have been more willing to justify recovery for damage to other property than the defective product itself. In this case, the court was unusually strict in defining the home as the product in question, denying that the foundation and structure above were separate items. Apparently, the homeowners would have had better luck had they stayed inside their crumbling homes until a piece of the house landed on them.

**NOTES:**

## GRYC v. DAYTON-HUDSON CORP.

Minn. Sup. Ct., 297 N.W.2d 727 (1980), cert. denied, 449 U.S. 921 (1980).

**NATURE OF CASE: Appeal from award of punitive damages in products liability case.**

**FACT SUMMARY: Dayton-Hudson Corp. (D) argued that punitive damages were not appropriate in Gryc's (P) action for injuries suffered when her pajamas caught fire and, alternatively, its compliance with the Flammable Fabrics Act of 1953 precluded such damages.**

**CONCISE RULES OF LAW: (1) Punitive damages may properly be awarded in a strict liability action. (2) Defendant's compliance with an applicable federal safety standard does not preclude a punitive damages award.**

**FACTS:** Four-year-old Gryc (P) was severely burned when her pajamas caught fire as she reached across an electric burner. The fabric, known as flannelette, ignited instantaneously and burned from hem to neck in four to five seconds. It was not treated with a chemical flame retardant but did meet the minimum federal standards of product flammability set forth in the Federal Flammable Fabrics Act of 1953. Gryc (P) sued the manufacturer, Riegel (D), and the dealer, Dayton-Hudson (D), contending that the untreated cotton flannelette was unreasonably dangerous for use as sleepwear. The jury agreed and awarded Gryc (P) $750,000 in compensatory damages and $1,000,000 in punitive damages. Riegel (D) appealed, arguing that punitive damages were not appropriate in products liability cases and that its compliance with the Act shielded it from liability.

**ISSUE:** (1) May punitive damages be awarded in a strict liability action? (2) Does defendant's compliance with an applicable federal safety standard preclude a punitive damages award?

**HOLDING AND DECISION:** (Todd, J.) (1) Yes. Punitive damages may properly be awarded in a strict liability action. Such damages are a legal tool to deter those manufacturers who would otherwise abuse their control over safety information and market defective products. (2) No. Defendant's compliance with an applicable federal safety standard does not preclude a punitive damages award. Riegel (D) was aware that the test employed in the Flammable Fabrics Act was invalid and that unreasonably dangerous fabrics, including newspaper, passed the test. Therefore compliance with the Act does not protect Riegel (D) from punitive damages. Moreover, there was no clear congressional intent to preempt the private state remedy of punitive damages. Since Gryc (P) provided evidence that flannelette was hazardous, that flame retardant could have reduced the hazard, and that Riegel (D) chose not to use the retardant because it would be too costly, the $100,000,000 award was not excessive as a matter of law. Affirmed.

**EDITOR'S ANALYSIS:** The Restatement (Second) of Torts § 908(2) states that punitive damages may be awarded for outrageous conduct, evil motive, or reckless indifference to the rights of others. Strict products liability is not mentioned. Courts and commentators have differed on whether to imply preclusion or permission to award punitives in those cases. Critics of the awards contend that such damages upset the delicate balance struck in the creation of strict products liability regime and that the goals of punitives are unachievable in that context and will have undesirable economic and social consequences.

**NOTES:**

## ACOSTA v. HONDA MOTOR CO., LTD.

717 F.2d 828 (3d Cir. 1983).

**NATURE OF CASE: Appeal from award of punitive damages in products liability action.**

**FACT SUMMARY: Acosta (P) sued Honda Motor Company, Ltd. (D), alleging defects in design and manufacture and failure to warn, after Acosta (P) was thrown from a motorcycle made by Honda (D) and injured.**

**CONCISE RULE OF LAW: Reckless or outrageous conduct on the part of a defendant is the touchstone of punitive damages, and for behavior to be reckless, it must involve a risk of harm to others substantially in excess of that necessary to make the conduct negligent.**

**FACTS:** Acosta (P) sued Honda Motor Company, Ltd. (D), alleging defects in design and manufacture and failure to warn, after Acosta (P) was thrown from a motorcycle made by Honda (D) and injured. At trial, the jury returned a verdict against Honda (D) for both compensatory and punitive damages. The judge denied Honda's (D) motion for judgment n.o.v., and Honda (D) appealed, contending that the evidence was insufficient as a matter of law to sustain the award of punitive damages, and that the court erred in submitting the issue to the jury in the first place.

**ISSUE:** Is reckless or outrageous conduct on the part of a defendant the touchstone of punitive damages, and for behavior to be reckless, must it involve a risk of harm to others substantially in excess of that necessary to make the conduct negligent?

**HOLDING AND DECISION:** (Becker, J.) Yes. Reckless or outrageous conduct on the part of a defendant is the touchstone of punitive damages, and for behavior to be reckless, it must involve a risk of harm to others substantially in excess of that necessary to make the conduct negligent. Also, such behavior must involve an easily perceptible danger of death or substantial physical harm, and the probability that it will so result must be substantially greater than is required for ordinary negligence. Here, viewing the evidence in the light most favorable to Acosta (P), the conduct of Honda (D) was not outrageous or reckless. Indeed, this court discerns no basis upon which the jury could have concluded that Honda (D) knew or had reason to know that the rear wheel of Acosta's (P) motorcycle was defective in design or manufacture and that they decided not to remedy the defect in conscious disregard of or with indifference to the risk thereby created. In short, a jury could not have reasonably concluded that the evidence showed Honda (D) to have acted with reckless disregard for the safety of users of the motorcycle. Accordingly, the district court should have granted Honda's (D) motion for directed verdicts on the punitive damage claim. Reversed and remanded.

**EDITOR'S ANALYSIS:** In addition to punishment, punitive or "exemplary" damages also work to maximize compliance with the rules of law and to compensate plaintiffs. They are often criticized as a method of giving plaintiffs undeserved windfalls as they are awarded in addition to compensatory damages. Most courts will not award such damages in contract cases.

**NOTES:**

## VOSSLER v. RICHARDS MANUFACTURING CO., INC.

Cal. App. Ct., 143 Cal. App. 3d 952 (1983).

**NATURE OF CASE: Appeal from award of damages in products liability action.**

**FACT SUMMARY: Vossler (P) sued Richards Manufacturing Company, Inc. (D), for compensatory and punitive damages in products liability when Vossler (P) discovered that a prosthetic device implanted in his knee had been improperly manufactured and that the defect had been concealed from the public.**

**CONCISE RULE OF LAW: Any amount awarded for punitive damages should bear a reasonable relation to the actual damages, but the amount may be left to the jury's sound discretion.**

**FACTS:** Richards Manufacturing Company, Inc. (D), produced prosthetic devices used to make artificial knee joints. Vossler (P) had one of these devices implanted in his right knee which eventually caused impingement on Vossler's (P) kneecap. This necessitated eventual removal of the kneecap, among other damages. Vossler (P) sued Richards (D) when Vossler (P) discovered that Richards (D) knew that components of the prostheses had been manufactured improperly, and concealed this fact from the medical profession and the public. Vossler (P) requested compensatory and punitive damages, and the jury returned a verdict for Vossler (P), awarding compensatory damages of $25,000 and punitive damages of $500,000. Richards (D) appealed the sufficiency of the evidence justifying award of the punitive damages.

**ISSUE:** Should any amount awarded for punitive damages bear a reasonable relation to the actual damages, but may the amount be left to the jury's sound discretion?

**HOLDING AND DECISION:** (Andreen, J.) Yes. Any amount awarded for punitive damages should bear a reasonable relation to the actual damages, but the amount may be left to the jury's sound discretion. Here, it was undisputed at trial that Richards (D) purposely concealed the manufacturing defect in the protheses from the medical profession, its own sales personnel, and the public solely to protect its market position. Richards (D) further attempted to capitalize on its concealment of its manufacturing error by advertising components that had originally been correctly designed as newly designed components. Richards' (D) conduct to protect its profits threatened excruciating pain and crippling immobility to thousands of arthritic patients and anguish to their physicians and their families. Insofar as the reprehensibility of conduct was concerned, the jury's award of punitive damages in this case was fully justified. Affirmed.

**EDITOR'S ANALYSIS:** A very difficult problem for courts and juries has been the determination of appropriate amounts for punitive damages awards. The Restatement (Second) formulation is widely accepted, however, in making the determination. The Restatement directs the fact finder to consider (1) the character of the defendant's act, (2) the nature and extent of the plaintiff's harm, and (3) the defendant's wealth.

**NOTES:**

# CHAPTER 15
# SPECIAL TYPES OF DEFENDANTS

## QUICK REFERENCE RULES OF LAW

1. **Retailers, Wholesalers, and Distributors.** Restatement (Second) § 402A, by its literal terms, imposes strict liability for any sale of a defective product, and the sale of the product may trigger strict liability. (Zamora v. Mobil Corp.)

2. **Component Part Manufacturers and Assemblers.** The manufacturer and supplier of a defective component part is subject to strict liability for harm caused by the defect where there is no change in the component part itself, but it is merely incorporated into something larger. (City of Franklin v. Badger Ford Truck Sales, Inc.)

3. **Component Part Manufacturers and Assemblers.** A component part manufacturer who has no role in designing the finished product and who supplied a nondefective part cannot be held liable for defective design. (Lee v. Butcher Boy)

4. **Component Part Manufacturers and Assemblers.** A manufacturer of a safe, raw-material component is not liable for injury caused by the final product if the final assembly is what renders the product dangerous and the manufacturer warns the final product assembler of any nonobvious risks in the product usage. (Apperson v. E.I. DuPont de Nemours & Co.)

5. **The Federal Government.** No liability shall lie, under the Federal Torts Claims Act, for any claim based upon the performance of a discretionary function on the part of a federal agency or employee, whether or not the discretion involved is abused. (Berkovitz v. United States)

6. **Government Contractors.** State law which holds government contractors liable for design defects in military equipment does in some circumstances present a significant conflict with federal policy and must be displaced. (Boyle v. United Technologies Corp.)

7. **Parent and Apparent Manufacturers.** (1) If a parent company observes corporate formality in its dealings with its subsidiary, and the subsidiary is financially able to operate independently, the parent corporation is not liable for the subsidiary's acts under an alter ego theory. (2) A parent corporation is not liable for the actions of its subsidiary, under agency theory, where the parent corporation has taken no action to indicate that the subsidiary acts as its agent. (3) A parent company that puts out as its own product a chattel manufactured by its independent subsidiary is subject to liability as though it were the actual manufacturer. (Fletcher v. Atex, Inc.)

8. **Certifiers and Endorsers.** An endorser who, for financial gain, induces the public to purchase a product which is defective and not as represented in the endorsement is liable to a purchaser relying on the endorsement. (Hanberry v. Hearst Corp.)

9. **Successor Corporations.** The liabilities of a selling predecessor corporation are not imposed on the successor corporation unless the successor expressly assumes liability, the transaction is a de facto merger, the successor is a mere continuation of the predecessor, or the transaction is a fraudulent attempt to avoid liability. (Guzman v. MRM/Elgin)

10. **Employers.** The dual-capacity doctrine provides that an employer may become liable in tort to an injured employee when the employer assumes an identity separate and apart from his role as employer. (Rader v. United States Rubber Reclaiming Co.)

11. **In General.** Among wrongdoers, the one whose fault is secondary may receive indemnity from the primary wrongdoer. (DiGregorio v. Champlain Valley Fruit Co.)

12. **In General.** An intermediate distributor in a chain of distribution must indemnify the ultimate distributor when both are strictly liable in tort for the injuries to the plaintiff. (Promaulayko v. Johns Manville Sales Corp.)

13. **Work-Related Injuries.** In a case involving injury to his employee, which is covered by workers' compensation, the amount of liability of that employer for contribution to a third-party tortfeasor should he limited to his workers' compensation liability to the employee. (Lambertson v. Cincinnati Corp.)

14. **Partial Settlements.** When one joint tortfeasor defendant settles with the plaintiff, the remaining codefendant or codefendants are chargeable with the total verdict less that attributable to the settling defendant's percentage share. (Cartel Capital Corp. v. Fireco of New Jersey)

## ZAMORA v. MOBIL CORP.

Wash. Sup. Ct., 104 Wash. 2d 199 (1985).

**NATURE OF CASE: Appeal of summary judgment grant denying damages in products liability action.**

**FACT SUMMARY: Zamora (P) sued Mobil (D) and Cal Gas (D) in negligence and strict liability when a propane gas leak, which involved propane manufactured by Mobil (D) and distributed by Cal Gas (D), went undetected because insufficient odorant had been added to the gas, resulting in a fire which killed five of Zamora's (P) children.**

**CONCISE RULE OF LAW: Restatement (Second), § 402A by its literal terms, imposes strict liability for any sale of a defective product, and the sale of the product may trigger strict liability.**

**FACTS:** A propane gas leak in Zamora's (P) house went undetected because insufficient odorant had been added to the gas by its manufacturer, Mobil Corporation (D). A resulting fire killed five of Zamora's (P) children. Zamora (P) sued Mobil (D) and Cal Gas (D), the distributor, in negligence and strict products liability. Cal Gas (D) moved for summary judgment, and the trial court granted the motion. Zamora (P) appealed.

**ISSUE:** Does Restatement (Second), § 402A, by its literal terms, impose strict liability for any sale of a defective product, and may the sale of the product trigger strict liability?

**HOLDING AND DECISION:** (Pearson, J.) Yes. Restatement (Second), § 402A, by its literal terms, imposes strict liability for any sale of a defective product, and the sale of the product may trigger strict liability. Here, Cal Gas (D) had no possession of the propane, but sold the gas completely as a paper transaction. However, Cal Gas (D) is properly regarded as a member in the chain of distribution of the propane. The primary policy justification recognized by this court for the extension of strict liability to all sellers in the chain of distribution is provision of the "maximum of protection" to the consumer. The sellers are then required to argue among themselves any questions as to their respective liability. Accordingly, Cal Gas (D) is appropriately included within the chain of distribution to Zamora (P). Reversed and remanded.

**EDITOR'S ANALYSIS:** Most courts have held that a retailer does not have a duty to test or inspect in the absence of notice that a product could be dangerous. However, the courts have also held that the retailer does have a duty to warn in certain circumstances. Such circumstances include where the retailer knows or should know that the product is likely to be dangerous when put to normal use.

**NOTES:**

## FRANKLIN v. BADGER FORD TRUCK SALES, INC.

Wis. Sup. Ct., 207 N.W.2d 866 (1973).

**NATURE OF CASE: Action in strict tort liability for property damages.**

**FACT SUMMARY: A fire truck purchased by the city of Franklin (P) from Badger Ford (D) was damaged when it tipped over while negotiating a turn due to a defective wheel.**

**CONCISE RULE OF LAW: The manufacturer and supplier of a defective component part is subject to strict liability for harm caused by the defect where there is no change in the component part itself, but it is merely incorporated into something larger.**

**FACTS:** The city of Franklin (P) sued the following, alleging each liable under products liability for the sale to Franklin (P) of a fire truck chassis with a defective wheel: Badger Ford Truck Sales, Inc. (D), the sales company; Ford (D), the chassis maker; and Gunite (D), the wheel maker. The fire truck was damaged when it tipped over while negotiating a turn while responding to a fire call. The case against all three went to the jury on the basis of strict liability. Ford (D) and Gunite (D) contended that they were manufacturers of component parts and, as such, were not subject to the rule of strict liability.

**ISSUE:** Is the manufacturer and supplier of a defective component part subject to strict liability for harm caused by the defect where there is no change in the component part itself, but it is merely incorporated into something larger?

**HOLDING AND DECISION:** (Hansen, J.) Yes. The manufacturer and supplier of a defective component part is subject to strict liability for harm caused by the defect where there is no change in the component itself, but it is merely incorporated into something larger. Where the component part is subject to further processing or substantial change, or where the causing of injury is not directly attributable to defective construction of the component part, the result might be different. The question is essentially one of whether the responsibility for discovery and prevention of the dangerous defect is shifted to the intermediate party who is to make the changes. The responsibility for the defective construction of the wheel should not be shifted from the maker of the wheel or from the assembler of wheel and chassis so as to make only the seller, who was in no position to detect the hidden defect, strictly liable. Remanded for trial so that the relative negligence of defendants for purposes of contribution may be determined.

**EDITOR'S ANALYSIS:** As stated in the Franklin decision, the maker of a component part which is subject to further processing or substantial change might not be liable if the cause of the injury is not directly attributable to a defect of that part. An example of where the maker of a component part would still be strictly liable even if the part were substantially changed might be the supplier of the material out of which the defective wheel in Franklin was made. Even though changed around, if that material was of such inferior quality that the damage was attributable to it, its manufacturer might be liable.

## LEE v. BUTCHER BOY

Cal. App. Ct., 169 Cal. App.3d 375, 215 Cal. Rptr. 195 (1985).

**NATURE OF CASE: Appeal from grant of defense motion for summary judgment in personal injury case.**

**FACT SUMMARY: When Lee (P) was injured by a meat grinder machine, she sued not only the manufacturer of the grinder (D), but also the manufacturer of the motor (D) used in the grinder.**

**CONCISE RULE OF LAW: A component part manufacturer who has no role in designing the finished product and who supplied a nondefective part cannot be held liable for defective design.**

**FACTS:** Mrs. Lee (P) was injured when her hand caught in a meat grinding machine manufactured by Butcher Boy (D). The Lees (P) contended that the motor should have stopped immediately when turned off and, since it did not, the motor's manufacturer (D) should be held liable, in addition to Butcher Boy (D), for defectiveness and for a failure to warn. The court granted the motor's manufacturer (D) motion for summary judgment, and the Lees (P) appealed.

**ISSUE:** May a component part manufacturer who has no role in designing the finished product and who supplied a nondefective part be held liable for defective design?

**HOLDING AND DECISION:** (Thompson, J.) No. A component part manufacturer who has no role in designing the finished product and who supplied a nondefective part cannot be held liable for defective design. In this case, the motor manufacturer (D) had no role in the design of the grinder and it relied on Butcher Boy (D) to make the grinder safe. Therefore the motor manufacturer's (D) design of the nondefective motor could not have proximately caused Lee's (D) injury. Affirmed.

**EDITOR'S ANALYSIS:** The court also held that the motor's manufacturer had no duty to warn because it gave no input and had no control over the design and packaging of the grinder. Courts are reluctant to impose component part liability where another manufacturer does the packaging, labeling, and marketing. In Walker v. Stauffer Chemical Corp., 96 Cal. Rptr. 803 (Ct. App. 1971), for example, the court found that the manufacturer of sulfuric acid supplied to the manufacturer of a drain cleaner had no duty to warn consumers.

**NOTES:**

## APPERSON v. E.I. DU PONT DE NEMOURS & CO.

41 F.3d 1103 (7th Cir. 1985).

**NATURE OF CASE: Consolidated appeal of summary judgments in products liability actions.**

**FACT SUMMARY: A temporomandibular joint prosthesis failed in numerous patients, abrading bone surfaces and triggering immune system reactions.**

**CONCISE RULE OF LAW: A manufacturer of a safe, raw-material component is not liable for injury caused by the final product if the final assembly is what renders the product dangerous and the manufacturer warns the final product assembler of any nonobvious risks in the product usage.**

**FACTS:** The Proplast TMJ implant was designed, manufactured, and sold by Vitek, Inc. Proplast is a material designed to encourage tissue ingrowth. Proplast is made of carbon, soluble ingredients, and polytetraflourethylene (better known as Teflon). DuPont (D) supplied Vitek with Teflon for the implant. DuPont (D) informed Vitek that Teflon had shown poor results when used in hip implants. DuPont (D) conditioned the sale of the Teflon on acknowledgement of disclaimers and an agreement that Vitek would use its own medical judgment as to the safety of Teflon in the TMJ implant. Vitek used the Teflon in TMJ implants. The jaw implants abraded bone in patients, necessitating numerous removal procedures. Patients who had been injured by the implants filed suit against DuPont (D) under products liability theories. The district court granted summary judgment to DuPont (D), finding that it owed no duty of care to the plaintiffs.

**ISSUE:** Can a manufacturer of a raw material be held liable for injuries which resulted from the end use of the material when the raw material only became dangerous because of the particular use?

**HOLDING AND DECISION:** (Cudahy, J.) No. A manufacturer of a safe, raw-material component is not liable for injury caused by the final product if the final assembly is what renders the product dangerous and the manufacturer warns the final product assembler of any nonobvious risks in the product usage. While manufacturers of inherently dangerous raw materials may be held liable for injury caused by the use of those materials in end products, manufacturers of inherently safe raw materials are not liable if it was the particular use of the material which caused the final product to be dangerous. In this case, Teflon had been proven to have a wide range of safe applications. Teflon was not dangerous; it was its use by Vitek that caused harm or risk of harm to patients. Additionally, manufacturers of raw materials must warn of any nonobvious risks that depend on the use of the material. In this case, DuPont (D) warned Vitek that Teflon may have been unsuitable as a jaw implant. DuPont (D) cited studies that showed Teflon to be unsuitable in hip implants. DuPont (D) complied with its obligation to warn of improper uses for Teflon, and it owed no duty to patients by virtue of the fact that Teflon is a safe raw material. Affirmed.

**EDITOR'S ANALYSIS:** This case tackles the issue of how responsible a raw component manufacturer should be in determining the dangers of potential end uses of its product. It is argued that imposing liability where the manufacturer was to some degree aware of the potential use of the material would promote ignorance on the part of the manufacturer, turning a blind eye to known risky uses to avoid liability. At least in this case, DuPont (D) supplied Vitek with current scientific evaluations of a similar use of Teflon.

**NOTES:**

## BERKOVITZ v. UNITED STATES

486 U.S. 531 (1988).

**NATURE OF CASE: Appeal from denial of motion to dismiss action for damages under the Federal Tort Claims Act.**

**FACT SUMMARY: Berkovitz (P), and his parents, sued the government (D) under the Federal Tort Claims Act after Berkovitz (P) contracted polio from ingesting polio vaccine manufactured by Lederle Laboratories and allegedly wrongfully licensed by the Division of Biologic Standards.**

**CONCISE RULE OF LAW: No liability shall lie, under the Federal Torts Claims Act, for any claim based upon the performance of a discretionary function on the part of a federal agency or employee, whether or not the discretion involved is abused.**

**FACTS:** Berkovitz (P) ingested a dose of polio vaccine manufactured by Lederle Laboratories in 1979. He developed a severe case of polio soon thereafter, became almost completely paralyzed, and was unable to breathe without a respirator. Berkovitz (P) and his parents then sued the government (D) after it was determined that Berkovitz (P) contracted polio from the vaccine. The claim was filed under the Federal Tort Claims Act and alleged that the Division of Biologic Standards (DBS), then a part of the National Institute of Health, had acted wrongfully in licensing Lederle to produce the vaccine. The government (D) moved to dismiss the suit for lack of subject matter jurisdiction on the grounds that agency actions fell within the discretionary exception of the FTCA. The district court denied this motion, concluding that the licensing of the drug was not a "discretionary function" within the meaning of the FTCA. At the government's (D) request, the district court certified its decision for immediate appeal to the Third Circuit, and the court reversed. Berkovitz (P) appealed.

**ISSUE:** Shall liability lie, under the Federal Torts Claims Act, for any claim based upon the performance of a discretionary function on the part of a federal agency or employee, whether or not the discretion involved is abused?

**HOLDING AND DECISION:** (Marshall, J.) No. No liability shall lie, under the Federal Torts Claims Act, for any claim based upon the performance of a discretionary function on the part of a federal agency or employee, whether or not the discretion involved is abused. This exception, however, protects discretionary functions rather than regulatory functions. The significance of Congress's choice of language is supported by the legislative history. The discretionary function exception applies only to conduct that involves the permissible exercise of policy judgment. Here, the DBS, as a precondition to licensing, must receive certain test data from the manufacturer relating to a product's compliance with regulatory standards. The DBS has no discretion to issue a license without first receiving the required test data; to do so would violate statutory directive. Accordingly, to the extent that Berkovitz's (P) licensing claim is based on a decision of the DBS to issue a license without having received the required test data, the discretionary function exception poses no bar. Reversed and remanded.

**EDITOR'S ANALYSIS:** The Federal Torts Claims Act generally authorizes suits against the United States for damages. Such damages include injury or loss of property, or personal injury or death caused by negligent or wrongful behavior on the part of a government employee. The injury must occur under circumstances where the United States, if a private person, would be liable to the claimant in accordance with the law of the place where the injury occurred.

**NOTES:**

## BOYLE v. UNITED TECHNOLOGIES CORP.

487 U.S. 500 (1988).

**NATURE OF CASE: Appeal from reversal of denial of judgment n.o.v. in products liability action.**

**FACT SUMMARY: Boyle (P) sued United Technologies Corporation (UTC) (D) for a design defect allegedly existing in a series of helicopters manufactured by UTC (D) after Boyle's (P) son, who was trapped in a UTC (D) helicopter after a crash, drowned because of the way the escape hatch was designed.**

**CONCISE RULE OF LAW: State law which holds government contractors liable for design defects in military equipment does in some circumstances present a significant conflict with federal policy and must be displaced.**

**FACTS:** Boyle's (P) son, David, a U.S. Marine helicopter co-pilot, was killed when the helicopter in which he was flying crashed off the coast of Virginia Beach, Virginia, during a training exercise. David survived the impact of the crash, but was unable to escape from the helicopter and drowned. Boyle (P) then brought an action against United Technologies Corporation (D), which built the helicopter for the United States. Boyle (P) alleged that UTC (D) defectively designed the co-pilot's emergency escape system. The jury returned a verdict for Boyle (P), and the court denied UTC's (D) motion for judgment notwithstanding the verdict. The court of appeals reversed and entered judgment for UTC (D) on the basis that UTC (D) could not be held liable for the design defect because the evidence presented satisfied the requirements of the military contractor defense. Boyle (P) appealed.

**ISSUE:** Does state law which holds government contractors liable for design defects in military equipment in some circumstances present a significant conflict with federal policy and, if so, must it be displaced?

**HOLDING AND DECISION:** (Scalia, J.) Yes. State law which holds government contractors liable for design defects in military equipment does in some circumstances present a significant conflict with federal policy and must be displaced. Here, the state-imposed duty of care that is the asserted basis of UTC's (D) liability (specifically, the duty to equip helicopters with the sort of escape-hatch mechanism Boyle (P) claims was necessary) is precisely contrary to the duty imposed by the government contract — the duty to manufacture and deliver helicopters with the sort of escape-hatch mechanism shown by the specifications. The imposition of liability on government contractors will directly affect the terms of government contracts: either the contractor will decline to manufacture the design specified by the government, or it will raise its price. Either way, the interests of the United States will be directly affected. Thus, the circumstances of this case present a significant conflict between state policy and federal policy; state law must be displaced and federal law must control. This action must be remanded to the court of appeals for determination of whether a reasonable jury could have found for Boyle (P), on the facts presented, consistent with the government contractor defense. Judgment vacated.

**DISSENT:** (Brennan, J.) While a legislator, this judge would probably vote against any law absolving multibillion-dollar private enterprises from answering for their tragic mistakes, at least if that law were justified by no more than the unsupported speculation that their liability might ultimately burden the U.S. Treasury. Some other members of this court would evidently vote otherwise, but that should not matter here. Being judges, not legislators, the vote is not ours to cast.

**DISSENT:** (Stevens, J.) When the novel question of policy involves a balancing of conflicting interests in the efficient operation of a massive governmental program and the protection of the rights of the individual, this court should defer to the expertise of Congress. The Court's failure to so defer makes the majority's decision today especially distressing.

**EDITOR'S ANALYSIS:** In the Boyle case, the U.S. Supreme Court adopted a test used by the Fourth and Ninth Circuits to decide whether liability could be imposed upon government contractors for design defects in military equipment. Liability cannot be imposed if the United States approved reasonably precise specific cautions. The contractor will also not be liable if the equipment conformed to those specifications, and the contractor warned the United States about the dangers in the use of the equipment that were known to the contractor but not to the United States.

**NOTES:**

## FLETCHER v. ATEX, INC.

68 F.3d 1451 (2d Cir. 1995).

**NATURE OF CASE: Review of summary judgment dismissing tort claims against a parent corporation.**

**FACT SUMMARY: Kodak (D) owned Atex (D), a manufacturer of keyboards alleged to have caused repetitive stress injuries to users.**

**CONCISE RULE OF LAW: (1) If a parent company observes corporate formality in its dealings with its subsidiary, and the subsidiary is financially able to operate independently, the parent corporation is not liable for the subsidiary's acts under an alter ego theory. (2) A parent corporation is not liable for the actions of its subsidiary, under agency theory, where the parent corporation has taken no action to indicate that the subsidiary acts as its agent. (3) A parent company that puts out as its own product a chattel manufactured by its independent subsidiary is subject to liability as though it were the actual manufacturer.**

**FACTS:** Kodak (D) owned Atex (D) as a subsidiary corporation. Atex (D) was financially independent, capable of surviving on its own. Furthermore, Kodak (D) and Atex (D) observed proper corporate formalities, respecting the structure and form of management of each company. Atex (D) manufactured computer keyboards. The keyboards were sold under the Atex (D) label, and nowhere on the packaging was Kodak (D) mentioned as being involved. The keyboards were alleged to have caused repetitive stress injuries due to their defective design. Fletcher (P) and others sued Atex (D) and Kodak (D) under various tort theories. The district court granted summary judgment for Kodak (D).

**ISSUE:** (1) Can a parent corporation be held liable for a defective product sold by its wholly independent subsidiary? (2) Is a subsidiary an agent of the parent company for the purpose of extending vicarious liability to the parent company? (3) Can a parent company be held liable if it is the "apparent" manufacturer of the products made by its subsidiary?

**HOLDING AND DECISION:** (Cabranes, J.) (1) No. If a parent company observes corporate formality in its dealings with its subsidiary, and the subsidiary is financially able to operate independently, then the parent corporation is not liable for the subsidiary's acts under an alter ego theory. Corporate law allows for the piercing of the corporate veil where an injustice would result otherwise. If a parent corporation uses a subsidiary to shield itself from liability, then a plaintiff may reach through the subsidiary to the parent. In this case, Kodak (D) observed proper corporate formalities with Atex (D). Atex (D) managed its own affairs, and no injustice will result if Kodak (D) does not suffer the same liability claims as Atex (D). Affirmed. (2) No. A parent corporation is not liable for the actions of its subsidiary, under agency theory, where the parent corporation has taken no action to indicate that the subsidiary acts as its agent. The subsidiary alone cannot bind the parent corporation to liability by acting as though it represents the parent; the parent corporation must give some indication of the representational capacity of the subsidiary. In this case, Kodak (D) made no such representation. No evidence exists that Kodak (D) gave Atex (D) the apparent or implied authority to act on its behalf. Affirmed. (3) Yes. A parent company that puts out as its own product a chattel manufactured by its independent subsidiary is subject to liability as though it were the actual manufacturer. One of the many goals of the tort law is to protect the consumer. If a seller claims a product as its own, then it also warrants the product and assumes liability as though it were its own. In this case, Kodak (D) did not sell, distribute, or manufacture the keyboards. Furthermore, Kodak (D) did not permit its logo to be affixed to the packages or keyboards. There is no evidence that any purchaser relied on the belief that Kodak (D) was the source of the keyboards. There can be no liability in this case under an apparent manufacturer theory. Affirmed.

**EDITOR'S ANALYSIS:** The apparent manufacturer theory arose from the concept of estoppel. By embracing a product as its own and inducing a purchaser to rely on the seller's reputation, the seller could not then claim that it was not liable as the manufacturer after so implying in the course of dealing. The doctrine becomes more important as corporate structures become increasingly complex.

**NOTES:**

## HANBERRY v. HEARST CORP.

276 Cal. App. 2d 680, 81 Cal. Rptr. 519 (1969).

**NATURE OF CASE: Appeal from dismissal of action for negligent endorsement.**

**FACT SUMMARY: Hearst (D) published a magazine called "Good Housekeeping" which placed its "Seal" upon a pair of shoes which Hanberry (P) purchased and alleged were defective.**

**CONCISE RULE OF LAW: An endorser who, for financial gain, induces the public to purchase a product which is defective and not as represented in the endorsement is liable to a purchaser relying on the endorsement.**

**FACTS:** Hearst (D) was the publisher of a magazine called "Good Housekeeping" which endorsed certain products with its "Seal." The magazine stated that the seal meant that the products approved were good ones and that the advertising claims in the magazine were truthful. Hanberry (P) purchased a pair of shoes bearing the seal and alleged that she relied upon the Hearst (D) advertisement. The shoes were alleged to be defective in that they were slippery when worn on vinyl and other floor coverings. Hanberry (P) further alleged that she slipped and fell while wearing the shoes, sustaining severe personal injuries. The trial court sustained Hearst's (D) general demurrer to the causes of action against it, and Hanberry (P) appealed. (The manufacturer and retailer of the shoes were parties defendant who answered and were not involved in this appeal.)

**ISSUE:** Is an endorser who, for financial gain, induces the public to purchase a product which is defective and not as represented in the endorsement liable to a purchaser relying upon the endorsement?

**HOLDING AND DECISION:** (Ault, J.) Yes. Hearst (D) is not just a publisher of a magazine which accepts advertisements. To enhance the value of its magazine, it offers its "Consumers' Guaranty Seal" to products meeting standards the magazine chooses to impose. Implicit in the seal is the representation that the magazine has taken reasonable steps to examine the products endorsed and has found them satisfactory. Hanberry (P) has alleged that such steps were not taken and that she relied on the endorsement in purchasing the shoes in question. Hearst's (D) acceptance (by endorsing the product) of a duty to use ordinary care in issuing its seal is furthermore not limited by its offer (in describing the meaning of the seal) merely to replace the product or refund the money for it if defective. An endorser who, for financial gain, induces the public to purchase a product which is defective and not as represented in the endorsement is liable to a purchaser relying upon the endorsement. The fact that Hearst (D) is not in privity of contract with Hanberry (P) does not preclude this liability. Reversed as to those causes of action alleging negligent misrepresentation, which are reinstated.

**EDITOR'S ANALYSIS:** As the opinion indicates in dicta, merely printing an advertisement in a magazine is not necessarily an endorsement of the type which gives rise to a representation of safety or fitness. Something further is required, which would reasonably give the public the impression that the publication is lending its identity and reputation to the fitness and safety of the product.

**NOTES:**

## GUZMAN v. MRM/ELGIN

Sup. Jud. Ct. of Mass., 409 Mass. 563, 567 N.E.2d 929 (1991).

**NATURE OF CASE: Ruling by the U.S. District Court on a certified question in a products liability suit.**

**FACT SUMMARY: Guzman (P) was injured by a machine manufactured by MRM, which was later purchased by Cozzoli (D) and operated as a subsidiary called MRM/Elgin (D).**

**CONCISE RULE OF LAW: The liabilities of a selling predecessor corporation are not imposed on the successor corporation unless the successor expressly assumes liability, the transaction is a de facto merger, the successor is a mere continuation of the predecessor, or the transaction is a fraudulent attempt to avoid liability.**

**FACTS:** MRM was a manufacturer and seller of various machinery. After selling a machine to Guzman (P), MRM's assets were sold and then resold to Cozzoli Machine Co. (D). Cozzoli (D) continued to manufacture and sell machines of the same basic design through a subsidiary called MRM/Elgin (D). Guzman (P) was injured by the machine and sued the successor corporation and parent. The question of whether Massachusetts recognized a product line exception to successor immunity from liability was certified in district court.

**ISSUE:** When a corporation is purchased, is the corporate successor liable for injuries resulting from defective products manufactured and sold by the predecessor if the successor continues the product line of the predecessor?

**HOLDING AND DECISION:** (Lynch, J.) No. The liabilities of a selling predecessor corporation are not imposed on the successor corporation unless the successor expressly assumes liability, the transaction is a de facto merger, the successor is a mere continuation of the predecessor, or the transaction is a fraudulent attempt to avoid liability. Several jurisdictions have allowed an exception to successor liability immunity where the successor continues the product line. It is argued that the plaintiff's remedies are destroyed by a sale. Also, the successor is in the same position to spread the risk as was the predecessor. Finally, the successor gains both the benefit of continuing the operation with the attached good will and the burden of assuming the same responsibility. The first argument fails, because it is the demise of the predecessor that deprived a plaintiff of a remedy, not the subsequent purchase by the successor corporation. The second fails on fairness grounds; the entity which placed the product into the market should be the one which bears the liability risk. The third argument fails to recognize that the successor paid for the good will when it bought the assets of the predecessor. In this case, Cozzoli (D) purchased a corporation's assets, thus ending the life of the purchased corporation. Cozzoli (D) then used the assets to create a subsidiary which began operations where the predecessor left off. MRM/Elgin (D) did not make the defective product which harmed Guzman (P), and there has been no sound argument offered as to why an exception in liability immunity for the successor should be made.

**EDITOR'S ANALYSIS:** The successor corporation took no part in bringing the predecessor's product and the product user together. The primary reason that plaintiffs continue to sue successor corporations is that the successor is still in business and generally has access to substantial cash assets. The court failed to acknowledge that if a product line exception was recognized the by courts, companies could simply adjust the price in asset sales to reflect possible future liability.

**NOTES:**

## RADER v. U.S. RUBBER RECLAIMING CO., INC.

617 F. Supp. 1045 (S.D. Miss. 1985).

**NATURE OF CASE: Action for damages under the dual-capacity doctrine for products liability.**

**FACT SUMMARY: Rader (P), an employee of U.S. Rubber (D), was injured in the scope of his employment and alleged that not only was he entitled to workers' compensation benefits, but also entitled to recover independently from U.S. Rubber (D) for his injuries.**

**CONCISE RULE OF LAW: The dual-capacity doctrine provides that an employer may become liable in tort to an injured employee when the employer assumes an identity separate and apart from his role as employer.**

**FACTS:** Rader (P), an employee of U.S. Rubber (D), was injured in the scope of his employment. Rader (P) was burned when a machine he was operating malfunctioned. Rader (P) contended that U.S. Rubber (D) designed the machine and was liable for the injuries he sustained under the dual-capacity doctrine. U.S. Rubber (D), at trial, moved for summary judgment on the basis that workers' compensation was Rader's (P) exclusive remedy. Rader (P) responded that the dual-capacity doctrine, under which an employer assumes a role independent of his status as an employer, permits recovery despite the exclusive provisions of workers' compensation.

**ISSUE:** Does the dual-capacity doctrine provide that an employer may become liable in tort to an injured employee when the employer assumes an identity separate and apart from his role as employer?

**HOLDING AND DECISION:** (Barbour, J.) Yes. The dual-capacity doctrine provides that an employer may become liable in tort to an injured employee when the employer assumes an identity separate and apart from his role as employer. However, the vast majority of courts have rejected the dual-capacity doctrine and have held that an employer who designs, manufactures, or distributes a product used by its employees cannot be held liable to an injured employee on the theory of products liability. The states that acknowledge the doctrine limit its applicability to products that are not only furnished to the employee but also sold to the public. Here, Rader (P) has not alleged that U.S. Rubber (D) sold its machine to the public. Even if he did, this court's conclusion would be the same. The Mississippi Supreme Court has consistently rejected attempts to circumvent the exclusive remedy of workers' compensation. This court is also of the opinion that the Mississippi Supreme Court could likewise reject Rader's (P) attempt to circumvent the workers' compensation act on the basis of the dual-capacity doctrine. Judgment for U.S. Rubber (D).

**EDITOR'S ANALYSIS:** The dual-capacity doctrine, in spite of widespread attempts to invoke it as a way to defeat exclusiveness, was acknowledged in only two states, Ohio and California, and even there for only a few years, from 1977 to 1983. In 1982, the California legislature effectively abolished the doctrine. In 1983, the Ohio Supreme Court so restricted the doctrine as to make it ineffective.

**NOTES:**

**DiGREGORIO v. CHAMPLAIN VALLEY FRUIT CO.**
Vt. Sup. Ct., 255 A.2d 183 (1969).

**NATURE OF CASE: Appeal from dismissal of action for negligent endorsement.**

**FACT SUMMARY: DiGregorio (P), the operator of a market which sold a banana which contained a glass fruit thermometer which had been inserted by Champlain (D), a wholesaler, called upon Champlain (D) to enter and defend the action brought by the purchaser of the banana and, after a settlement was reached with the purchaser, sought indemnity from Champlain (D).**

**CONCISE RULE OF LAW: Among wrongdoers, the one whose fault is secondary may receive indemnity from the primary wrongdoer.**

**FACTS:** DiGregorio (P), the operator of a market, purchased some bananas from Champlain Valley Fruit Co. (D), a wholesaler. One of the bananas contained a glass fruit thermometer, which had been inserted by Champlain (D), and was retailed to a customer who injured her teeth endeavoring to eat the banana, and sued DiGregorio (P), which called upon Champlain (D) to enter and defend the action, which it refused to do. Champlain (D) was later joined as a party defendant. The action was settled, and DiGregorio (P) sought to recover its contribution to the settlement and reasonable expenses. Champlain (D) appealed the judgment for DiGregorio (P) on the ground that DiGregorio (P) had only the standing of joint tortfeasor.

**ISSUE:** Among wrongdoers, may one whose fault is secondary recover indemnity from the primary wrongdoer?

**HOLDING AND DECISION:** (Holdren, J.) Yes. Among wrongdoers, one whose fault is secondary may recover indemnity from the primary wrongdoer. The most that can be said for DiGregorio's (P) misconduct is a failure to discover, in its retail operation, the presence of the thermometer which, of itself, will not defeat DiGregorio's (P) right to indemnity against the seller who put the harmful cause in motion. Under the Uniform Sales Act, the sale of the bananas, first by Champlain (D) and later by DiGregorio (P), carried an implied warranty that the food was wholesome and fit for human consumption at the time of purchase. The fact that the injured consumer had a right of action against either the wholesaler or retailer or both does not disrupt Champlain's (D) undertaking with DiGregorio (P). There is no policy of law which prevents DiGregorio (P) from holding Champlain (D) to its implied warranty for such damage as it sustained from the purchase and resale of the dangerous commodity. Thus, the parties were not equally at fault, so indemnity is not precluded by the rule against contribution among wrongdoers. Nor does the fact that DiGregorio (P) settled preclude indemnity since Champlain (D) was asked to defend and did become a party to the action. Affirmed.

**EDITOR'S ANALYSIS:** The Uniform Commercial Code provides a "vouching in" procedure under which the buyer of a product, e.g. a retailer who is sued for breach of warranty for which his seller is answerable, can give the seller written notice that if he does not come in and defend he will be bound in any action against him by his buyer by any determination of fact common to the two litigations. Then, if he does not defend, he is bound U.C.C. 2-07(5).

**NOTES:**

## PROMAULAYKO v. JOHNS MANVILLE SALES CORP.

Sup. ct. of N.J., 116 N.J. 505, 562 A.2d 202 (1989).

**NATURE OF CASE: Review of appellate reversal of grant of indemnification for a tort damage award.**

**FACT SUMMARY: Promaulayko (P) contracted asbestosis from exposure to asbestos sold to his employer, Ruberoid, from a chain of distribution starting in the Soviet Union.**

**CONCISE RULE OF LAW: An intermediate distributor in a chain of distribution must indemnify the ultimate distributor when both are strictly liable in tort for the injuries to the plaintiff.**

**FACTS:** Promaulayko (P) worked for Ruberoid. Ruberoid purchased asbestos from Leonard Buck (D), Asbestos Corporation Limited (D), and various other suppliers. Included in the asbestos sold by Buck (D) to Ruberoid was 96.5 tons of Soviet asbestos, which Buck (D) purchased from Amtorg Trading (D). The asbestos was in hundred-pound bags that failed to warn of the dangers of asbestosis. Promaulayko (P) contracted asbestosis and died. A jury found that Amtorg (D) had supplied all of the Soviet asbestos that caused the injuries and death. Buck (D) was awarded indemnification from Amtorg (D). Buck (D) and Amtorg (D) appealed the distribution of the damage award.

**ISSUE:** Must an intermediate distributor in a chain of distribution indemnify the ultimate distributor when both are strictly liable in tort to the injured plaintiff?

**HOLDING AND DECISION:** (Pollack, J.) Yes. An intermediate distributor in a chain of distribution must indemnify the ultimate distributor when both are strictly liable in tort for the injuries to the plaintiff. The primary goals of strict liablity in tort are to allocate the risk of loss to the party best able to distribute it and to allocate the risk of loss to the party best able to control it. Shifting risk up the chain of distribution toward the manufacturer serves both goals. First, the distributor closest to the manufacturer can spread the cost of risk over all purchasers. Second, the distributor closest to the manufacturer is in the best position to pressure the manufacturer to produce a safe product. In this case, Amtorg (D) can best meet both goals. Amtorg (D) was the primary distributor of the Soviet asbestos. And Amtorg (D) could shift the risk premium to all purchasers of asbestos that it distributed. Reversed.

**EDITOR'S ANALYSIS:** The court acknowledged that there may be cases in which the distributor closest to the end point of sale will be in a better position to allocate risk or pressure for safety. But the court indicated that such an argument would be dealt with on a case-by-case basis; the presumption will always be that entities higher on the distribution chain should indemnify those lower on it.

## LAMBERTSON v. CINCINNATI CORP.

Minn. Sup. Ct., 257 N.W.2d 679 (1977).

**NATURE OF CASE: Appeal from denial of contribution to defendant in personal injury action.**

**FACT SUMMARY: Cincinnati (D), the manufacturer of a machine which injured Lambertson (P), was found liable to Lambertson (P) and sought contribution from Lambertson's (P) employer.**

**CONCISE RULE OF LAW: In a case involving injury to his employee, which is covered by workers' compensation, the amount of liability of that employer for contribution to a third-party tortfeasor should he limited to his workers' compensation liability to the employee.**

**FACTS:** Lambertson (P) was injured by a press brake during the course of his employment with Hutchinson Manufacturing and Sales, Inc. After recovering workers' compensation from Hutchinson, Lambertson (P) sued Cincinnati Corp. (D), the manufacturer of the press. The jury found all parties causally negligent and apportioned their comparative negligence. Cincinnati (D) sought indemnity or contribution from Hutchinson and appealed the denial of its claim.

**ISSUE:** In a case involving injury to his employee which is compensated by workers' compensation, should the amount of liability of the employer for contribution to a third-party tortfeasor be limited to his workers' compensation liability to his employee?

**HOLDING AND DECISION:** (Sheran, J.) Yes. In a case involving injury to his employee which is compensable by workers' compensation, the amount of liability of that employer for contribution to a third-party tortfeasor should be limited to the amount of his workers' compensation liability to his employee. There has been great controversy over the rights of parties in the workers' compensation system: employers, employees, and third-party tortfeasors. Their interests are as follows: that of the employer in limiting his liability to the workers' compensation schedule; that of the employee in receiving full workers' compensation benefits and a common law recovery from any third party who has contributed to his injury; and that of the third party in limiting its liability to no more than its established fault. By allowing the third party to receive contribution from the employer up to the amount of his workers' compensation liability, the employers' interest in not paying more than his workers' compensation liability is preserved, while allowing the third party to receive limited contribution. Cincinnati (D) to be granted contribution from Hutchinson in an amount proportional to its percentage of negligence up to its total workers' compensation liability to Lambertson (P).

**EDITOR'S ANALYSIS:** The rule of Lambertson is a minority position, with most courts denying contribution by employers to manufacturers. In fact, the employer is usually permitted to recover the amount of the workers' compensation he has paid when the employee collects from a third-party manufacturer.

## CARTEL CAPITAL CORP. v. FIRECO OF NEW JERSEY

N.J. Sup. Ct. 81 N.J. 548 (1980).

**NATURE OF CASE: Appeal from award of damages in products liability action.**

**FACT SUMMARY: Cartel Capital Corporation (P) and Country Burger (P) sued Fireco of New Jersey (D), the retailer, installer, and service of Country Burger's (P) fire extinguishing equipment in strict liability for property damage caused by a fire during which the equipment allegedly failed to operate.**

**CONCISE RULE OF LAW: When one joint tortfeasor defendant settles with the plaintiff, the remaining codefendant or codefendants are chargeable with the total verdict less that attributable to the settling defendant's percentage share.**

**FACTS:** Cartel Capital Corporation (P) and Country Burger (P) sued Fireco of New Jersey (D), the retailer, installer, and service of Country Burger's (P) fire extinguishing equipment, and Ansul, Inc. (D), the manufacturer of that equipment, in strict liability for property damage caused by a fire during which the equipment allegedly failed to operate. Fireco (D) and Ansul (D) assessed cross-claims against each other. At the outset of the trial, Ansul (D) settled with Country Burger (P), voluntarily dismissed its cross-claims and successfully moved for dismissal of Fireco's (D) cross-claims. Country Burger (P) then proceeded against Fireco (D) alone. The jury found that Fireco (D) was liable, but also determined that Country Burger (P) was guilty of negligence. The jury fixed the percentages of fault as: Country Burger (P) -41%; Fireco (D) -30%; and Ansul (D) -29%. The court then entered judgment in favor of Country Burger (P) for $34,020, plus interest and costs. Fireco (D) appealed.

**ISSUE:** When one joint tortfeasor defendant settles with the plaintiff, is the remaining codefendant or codefendants chargeable with the total verdict less that attributable to the settling defendant's percentage share?

**HOLDING AND DECISION:** (Schreiber, J.) Yes. When one joint tortfeasor defendant settles with the plaintiff, the remaining codefendant or co-defendants are chargeable with the total verdict less that attributable to the settling defendant's percentage share. Applying the foregoing principles, this court finds that the total relevant fault is that of Ansul (D) and Fireco (D), there being no contributory negligence as a matter of law. Ansul's (D) 29% and Fireco's (D) 30%, or 59%, constitute the total fault in this case. In a sense, the 59% is 100%. Thus, Fireco's (D) responsibility is 30/59ths of 50.8% and Ansul's (D) is 29/59ths, or 49.2%. It follows that Fireco's (D) proportionate share of the entire damages of $113,400 is $57,661.01, and Ansul's (D) share is $55,738.99. Ansul (D), however, settled its obligation to Country Burger (P) for $50,000. Fireco (D) remains liable for its share, however. The cause is thus remanded to the trial court for entry of judgment in Country Burger's (P) favor.

**EDITOR'S ANALYSIS:** In many jurisdictions, basic settlement rules are now governed by statute. The approach of New Jersey, as in the Fireco case, reflects that of § 6 of the Uniform Comparative Fault Act, which reduces a plaintiff's recovery against nonsettling defendants by the percentage fault of any settling defendants. By comparison, in California, the plaintiff's claim is reduced by the dollar value of a "good faith" settlement.

**NOTES:**

# CHAPTER 16
# SPECIAL TYPES OF PRODUCTS AND TRANSACTIONS

## QUICK REFERENCE RULES OF LAW

1. **Leases and Bailments.** Strict lability applies to commercial lessors primarily in the business of leasing the type of product causing the injury. (Samuel Friedland Family Enterprises v. Amoroso)

2. **Leases and Bailments.** A store is not liable under the doctrine of strict liability for mishaps resulting from the use of articles which it provides for the convenience of its customers. (Keen v. Dominick's Finer Foods, Inc.)

3. **Services.** Strict products liability does not apply to hospital or medical personnel for defects in a medical device. (Cafazzo v. Central Medical Health Services, Inc.)

4. **Services.** Implied-at-law warranties do not arise from the sale of a service unattached to a product. (Lewis v. Big Powderhorn Moutain Ski Corp.)

5. **Used Products.** Strict liability is applicable against the seller of a used product. (Jordan v. Sunnyslope Appliance Propane & Plumbing Supplies Co.)

6. **Real Estate.** An in-ground swimming pool is not a "product" for purposes of strict liability in tort. (Menendez v. Paddock Pool Construction Co.)

7. **Miscellaneous "Products."** An animal cannot be a "product" for purposes of strict liability. (Latham v. Wal-Mart Stores, Inc.)

8. **Miscellaneous "Products."** Products liability law does not apply to the contents of a book. (Winter v. G.P. Putnam's Sons)

9. **Miscellaneous "Products."** Strict products liability applies to the provider of electrical service. (Bryant v. Tri-County Electric Membership Corp.)

# Notes

## SAMUEL FRIEDLAND FAMILY ENTERPRISES v. AMOROSO

Fla. Sup. Ct., 630 So. 2d 1067 (1994).

**NATURE OF CASE: Certified question following order reversing directed verdict in favor of defendents in personal injury action.**

**FACT SUMMARY: The Amorosos (P) argued that a hotel and a sailboat rental stand should be held strictly liable for leasing them a defective sailboat.**

**CONCISE RULE OF LAW: Strict lability applies to commercial lessors primarily in the business of leasing the type of product causing the injury.**

**FACTS:** The Diplomat Hotel (D), as a service to guests, contracted with Sunrise Water Sports (D) to operate a sailboat rental facility. Sunrise (D) in turn subcontracted with Atlantic Sailing Center (D) to effect the rentals. Mrs. Amoroso (P) was injured while using a rented sailboat. Mr. and Mrs. Amoroso (P) brought a personal injury action against Diplomat (D), Sunrise (D), and Atlantic (D), alleging a strict liability cause of action. The trial court directed a defense verdict, ruling that strict liability did not apply to commercial lease transactions. The court of appeals certified a question to the Florida Supreme Court regarding whether the doctrine of strict liability extended to commercial lease transactions of defective products.

**ISSUE:** Does strict liability apply to commercial lessors primarily in the business of leasing the type of product causing the injury?

**HOLDING AND DECISION:** (Grimes, J.) Yes. Strict liability applies to commercial lessors primarily in the business of leasing the type of product causing the injury. The policy rationale behind imposing strict liability onto the manufacturers and sellers of a product is that these persons are in the best position vis-à-vis the consumer to make the products safe, and strict liability creates an incentive to do so. Also, it allows the risk of harm to be somewhat borne by society as a whole, not by individual victims. This rationale applies equally to lessors; they are in the best position to ensure product safety and to spread risk, provided that leasing such products is a substantial part of their business. Therefore, provided that criterion is met, strict liability will be applied to lessors. Here, renting sailboats was a substantial part of the business of all three defendants, so strict liability is applicable. Affirmed.

**CONCURRENCE AND DISSENT:** (McDonald, J.) The Diplomat Hotel (D) is not primarily in the business of leasing sailboats and should not, therefore, be held strictly liable in this case.

**EDITOR'S ANALYSIS:** Products liability law recognizes the "occasional seller" rule, which holds that products liability will not be applied against an occasional, informal seller of a product. An example often cited is the housewife who makes and sells preserves on an occasional basis. The court grafted this rule onto its application here by limiting products liability to lessors engaged in the business of leasing the allegedly defective product.

**NOTES:**

## KEEN v. DOMINICK'S FINER FOODS, INC.

Ill. Ct. of App., 364 N.E.2d 502 (1975).

**NATURE OF CASE: Appeal from dismissal of count for strict liability in tort.**

**FACT SUMMARY: Keen (P), who was injured while shopping in Dominick's (D) store when a shopping cart tipped over, appealed the dismissal of a count in her complaint which alleged a cause of action is strict liability in tort.**

**CONCISE RULE OF LAW: A store is not liable under the doctrine of strict liability for mishaps resulting from the use of articles which it provides for the convenience of its customers.**

**FACTS**: Keen (P) was injured while using a shopping cart which tipped over on her in Dominick's (D) store, and her complaint alleged a cause of action in strict liability. Keen (P) appealed the granting of Dominick's (D) motion to strike the count in strict liability in tort.

**ISSUE:** Is a store liable under the doctrine of strict liability for mishaps resulting from the use of articles which it provides for the convenience of its customers?

**HOLDING AND DECISION:** (McNamara, J.) No. A store is not liable under the doctrine of strict liability for mishaps resulting from the use of articles which it provides for the convenience of its customers. Liability will not be imposed upon a defendant who is not a part of the original producing and marketing chain. Unlike a seller of gas who was held strictly liable for injuries resulting from a defective tank which it supplied for storage of the gas, the market is not strictly liable for injuries resulting from use of the shopping cart. While the tank was an incident of the sale of the gas, the shopping cart is only a convenient receptacle which the customer may temporarily utilize to move groceries. The shopping cart was placed into the stream of commerce by the parties responsible for its distribution to Dominick's (D). Public policy considerations do not demand that the duty of a storekeeper to keep its premises in a safe condition be elevated beyond the traditional standard of reasonable care. Dominick's (D) cannot be considered to be part of the distributive chain within the ambit of the principles of strict products liability. Affirmed.

**EDITOR'S ANALYSIS:** Whether or not strict liability attaches to injuries resulting from the use of a product often depends on whether or not the court finds the product has been placed in the stream of commerce. Tires which were supplied to a tire-testing facility to be used on vehicles which were testing other tires were held not to be in the stream of commerce, and their manufacturer was not liable for the death of a test driver resulting from a blowout of one of the tires. Armstrong Rubber Co. v. Urquidez, 570 S.W.2d 374. (Tex. 1978). However, the Supreme Court of Alabama found that the doctrine of strict liability in tort should apply to an aircraft manufacturer because it placed a defective aircraft in the stream of commerce by demonstration, even though no sale was made.

## CAFAZZO v. CENTRAL MEDICAL HEALTH SERVICES, INC.

Pa. Sup. Ct., ___ Pa .___, 668 A.2d 521 (1995).

**NATURE OF CASE: Review of order dismissing action based on strict products liability.**

**FACT SUMMARY: Cafazzo (P) sought to assert a strict liability claim concerning a defective prosthetic device against the hospital and the physician who implanted it.**

**CONCISE RULE OF LAW: Strict products liability does not apply to hospital or medical personnel for defects in a medical device.**

**FACTS:** Cafazzo (P) underwent surgery for implantation of a mandibular prosthesis. The device later turned out to be defective. Cafazzo (P) brought suit based on strict liability against Central Medical (D), the hospital, and the physician (D) who had installed the device. The trial court sustained the defendants' demurrer and dismissed. The court of appeals affirmed, and the Pennsylvania Supreme Court granted review.

**ISSUE:** Does strict products liability apply to hospitals or medical personnel for defects in a medical device?

**HOLDING AND DECISION:** (Montemuro, J.) No. Strict products liability does not apply to hospitals or medical personnel for defects in a medical device. Superficially, medical personnel fall within the ambit of products lability law as enunciated in § 402A of the Restatement (Second) of Torts, in that they are in the business of selling a product: the patient does "buy" the product from the medical provider. However, this court is not inclined to slavishly follow the letter of the law if doing so does not advance the policy reasons underlying it. The basic policy behind the imposition of strict liability is (1) to encourage manufacturers to make their products safer, and (2) to spread the risk of loss throughout society. Medical personnel do not have the ability to make medical devices safer. Also, they do not have the resources to be agents of risk spreading. Consequently, it would be improper to impose strict liability upon them. Affirmed.

**DISSENT:** (Cappy, J.) The court is incorrect in saying that medical personnel are not in a position to improve the safety of medical products.

**EDITOR'S ANALYSIS:** Products liability is supposed to apply to products, but not to services. As the present case illustrates, however, the distinction between a service and a product is not always clear. The defendants here, for instance, were arguably supplying both a product and a service.

**NOTES:**

## LEWIS v. BIG POWDERHORN MOUNTAIN SKI CORP.

Mich. App. Ct., 245 N.W.2d 81 (1976).

**NATURE OF CASE: Action for damages for personal injuries.**

**FACT SUMMARY: After being injured while riding a rope-tow at Big Powderhorn's (D) ski facility, Lewis (P) sued, alleging alternative theories of liability, and appealed the dismissal of the count for breach of implied warranties.**

**CONCISE RULE OF LAW: Implied-at-law warranties do not arise from the sale of a service unattached to a product.**

**FACTS:** Lewis (P) claimed to have been injured while riding a rope-tow at Big Powderhorn Mountain Ski Corp.'s (D) ski facility. Lewis (P) alleged three alternative theories of liability, but only the one based on negligence was presented to the jury, which found no cause of action. Lewis (P) appealed dismissal of the count for breach of implied warranties.

**ISSUE:** Do implied-at-law warranties arise from the sale of a service unattached to a product?

**HOLDING AND DECISION:** (Burns, J.) No. Implied-at-law warranties do not arise from the sale of a service unattached to a product. Since the sale of goods is not involved, the implied warranties contained in the Uniform Commercial Code do not apply. Where implied warranties have been applied to services, there have been products involved. For example, Buckeye Union Fire Insurance Co. v. Detroit Dison Co. involved a "service," the sale of electricity, inseverably linked to a tangible (and defective) "product," electricity, sold by the kilowatt. The product liability concepts of implied warranties of merchantability and fitness for use are meaningless when applied to the rope-tow since Lewis (P) was unable to provide any evidence as to defectiveness or unfitness of the rope-tow apparatus. The implied warranty claimed is as to safety in the operation of the rope-tow. However, any "implied warranty of safety" can be nothing other than an implied promise not to operate the rope-tow in a negligent manner. And the question of negligent operation is precisely that which the jury was properly allowed to determine. Affirmed.

**DISSENT:** (Burns, J.) The perceived requirement that the sale of a product must accompany the provision of a service before implied warranties will arise does not make sense. When the rendition of a service does not meet the legitimate expectations of the person being served, a proper cause of action arises. The action is contractual in foundation and distinct from the negligence action.

**EDITOR'S ANALYSIS:** Although the decision in Hoffman accepts the concept of an implied warranty for services, it finds little distinction between implied liability and negligence under the circumstances. In Lewis, the court simply rejects the implied warranty concept completely and insists that the issue be posed in terms of negligence. The Hoffman court might have accepted a cause of action in the Lewis fact situation since the only com- plaint with the jury instruction in Hoffman was that it did not permit the defense of contributory negligence and assumption of the risk, and there was at least no question of contributory negligence in Lewis.

**NOTES:**

## JORDAN v. SUNNYSLOPE APPLIANCE PROPANE & PLUMBING SUPPLIES CO.

Ariz. Ct. of App., 135 Ariz. 309, 660 P.2d 1236 (1983).

**NATURE OF CASE: Appeal from summary judgment dismissing strict products liability action.**

**FACT SUMMARY: Jordan (P) asserted that Sunnyslope Appliance (D), a dealer that sold a used propane tank that exploded, should be held strictly liable for the destruction of his house.**

**CONCISE RULE OF LAW: Strict liability is applicable against the seller of a used product.**

**FACTS:** Jordan's (P) house was destroyed when a used propane tank his father had purchased exploded and caused a fire. He brought an action against Sunnyslope Appliance Propane & Plumbing Supplies Co. (D), the dealer that had sold the used tank. The trial court, ruling that strict products liability did not apply to sellers of used products, entered summary judgment dismissing the action. Jordan (P) appealed.

**ISSUE:** Is strict liability applicable against the seller of a used product?

**HOLDING AND DECISION:** (Meyerson, J.) Yes. Strict liability is applicable against the seller of a used product. It is true that the connection of an aftermarket dealer to a product's stream of commerce is more attenuated than the manufacturer or the original seller. However, for strict liability to apply to a product, it must have been, under Arizona law, "unreasonably dangerous." A purchaser of a used product cannot expect its quality to be as good as it was when brand new, but he does have a right to expect it not to be unreasonably dangerous. Also, like the manufacturer and original seller, the aftermarket seller is in a better position than the consumer to prevent a product from being dangerous and also to spread the risk of loss. Therefore, the better view is that strict liability in tort should extend to the seller of used products. Reversed.

**EDITOR'S ANALYSIS:** There is a good deal of disagreement among the states as to the liability of used-product vendors. Some take the same approach as taken by the court here. Others agree with the reasoning of the trial court. Still others split the baby and impose liability for patent defects and not for those of a latent nature.

## MENENDEZ v. PADDOCK POOL CONSTRUCTION CO.

Ariz. Ct. of App., 172 Ariz. 258, 836 P.2d 968 (1991).

**NATURE OF CASE: Appeal from dismissal of strict tort claim in personal injury action.**

**FACT SUMMARY: Menendez (P) brought a strict liability claim against Paddock Pool (D), the builder of a custom-built swimming pool, after he was thrown into the shallow end, resulting in quadriplegia.**

**CONCISE RULE OF LAW: An in-ground swimming pool is not a "product" for purposes of strict liability in tort.**

**FACTS:** Menendez (P) suffered serious spinal injuries after being thrown into a swimming pool. The pool had been custom designed as a nondiving lap pool. Menendez (P) brought a strict liability claim against the builder of the pool, Paddock Pool Construction Co. (D). The trial court held strict liability inapplicable since an in-ground pool is not manufactured and then introduced into the stream of commerce for sale, and hence is not a "product" per se, and dismissed the strict tort claim. Menendez (P) appealed.

**ISSUE:** Is an in-ground swimming pool a "product" for purposes of strict liability in tort?

**HOLDING AND DECISION:** (Taylor, J.) No. An in-ground swimming pool is not a "product" for purposes of strict liability in tort. Therefore, strict products liability does not apply against the builder of a custom swimming pool. The usually cited policy reasons behind strict liability are cost shifting, public safety, and facilitation of recovery. These goals are advanced when mass-produced products are involved. However, when a unique product is involved, these concerns have less force. Also, a pool is less a product than a structural improvement to real estate. For these reasons, a custom pool should not be considered a product. Affirmed.

**EDITOR'S ANALYSIS:** Products liability has been asserted against structures. This is most commonly found in the tract home situation. As homes produced en masse are conceptually not that different from other mass-produced items, such as automobiles, courts have on numerous occasions considered them amenable to strict liability. See, e.g., Schipper v. Levitt and Sons, Inc., 207 A.2d 314 (N.J. 1965).

**NOTES:**

## LATHAM v. WAL-MART STORES, INC.

Mo. Ct. of App., 818 S.W.2d 673 (1991).

**NATURE OF CASE: Appeal from dismissal of products liability action.**

**FACT SUMMARY: The Lathams (P) argued that an animal was a "product" in their strict liability claim against Wal-Mart (D), which had sold them a diseased parrot.**

**CONCISE RULE OF LAW: An animal cannot be a "product" for purposes of strict liability.**

**FACTS:** Latham (P) contracted a disease which had been carried by a parrot his wife (P) had purchased from Wal-Mart Stores, Inc. (D). The Lathams (P) brought a products liability suit against Wal-Mart (D), contending that the parrot was a "product" within the meaning of strict liability. The trial court disagreed and dismissed. The Lathams (P) appealed.

**ISSUE:** Can an animal be a "product" for purposes of strict liability?

**HOLDING AND DECISION:** (Gaertner, J.) No. An animal cannot be a "product" for purposes of strict liability. One of the characteristics a thing must have to be considered a "product" for purposes of strict liability is that it must leave the seller's hands in an essentially immutable condition, which is to say, it must not be subject to much change while in the possession of the consumer. An animal, by its nature, is quite mutable; it is subject to a constant process of internal development and growth while in the consumer's possession. Consequently, an animal is not a "product" in the strict liability sense. Affirmed.

**EDITOR'S ANALYSIS:** Some courts do place animals partly within the ambit of products liability. These cases generally hold that an animal is not a defective product if it does what comes naturally (e.g., a dog bites), but can be a defective product if something is wrong with it that cannot not reasonably contemplated by the purchaser (e.g., it is diseased).

**NOTES:**

## WINTER v. G.P. PUTNAM'S SONS

938 F.2d 1033 (9th Cir. 1991).

**NATURE OF CASE: Appeal from summary judgment dismissing products liability action.**

**FACT SUMMARY: Winter (P) contended that a book containing erroneous information about wild mushrooms was a defective product.**

**CONCISE RULE OF LAW: Products liability law does not apply to the contents of a book.**

**FACTS:** Winter (P) and a companion (P) became very ill after eating wild mushrooms they had picked, and eventually required liver transplants. They had allegedly eaten the mushrooms based on representations in a book distributed by G.P. Putnam's Sons (D) that that particular mushroom was safe to eat. They sued Putnam (D), contending that the book was a defective product. The trial court entered summary judgment dismissing the case, and Winter (P) appealed.

**ISSUE:** Does products liability law apply to the contents of a book?

**HOLDING AND DECISION:** (Sneed, J.) No. Products liability law does not apply to the contents of a book. Products liability law is geared toward the tangible world. It was not created to apply to intangible matters such as words and ideas. To attempt to do so would be problematic, to say the least. Our society places a high priority on the unfettered exchange of ideas, and any attempt to apply products liability law to the written word would be antithetical to this. Winter (P) argues that facts can be incorrect, as opposed to ideas, and can give rise to liability. However, where facts end and ideas begin is unknowable and not an appropriate area for judicial inquiry. Affirmed.

**EDITOR'S ANALYSIS:** The rule stated here is almost universally followed. The main exception lies in the area of aviation. Courts have imposed strict liability for incorrect aeronautical charts.

**NOTES:**

## BRYANT v. TRI-COUNTY ELECTRIC MEMBERSHIP CORP.

844 F. Supp. 347 (W.D. Ky. 1994).

**NATURE OF CASE: Action in negligence and strict liability seeking damages for destruction to property.**

**FACT SUMMARY: Bryant (P) sought to recover against Tri-County (D), a public utility company, after an electrical fire, contending that strict liability applied to injuries caused by defective electricity.**

**CONCISE RULE OF LAW: Strict products liability applies to the provider of electrical service.**

**FACTS:** A fire destroyed a sawmill owned by Bryant (P). Investigation showed that a machine switch had exploded. Bryant (P) sued the local electrical utility, Tri-County Electric Membership Corp. (D), contending that numerous power surges coming over transmission wires had caused the switch to fail. The claim was based on strict products liability. Tri-County (D) moved to dismiss, contending that electricity was not subject to strict liability.

**ISSUE:** Does strict products liability apply to the provider of electrical service?

**HOLDING AND DECISION:** (Heyburn, J.) Yes. Strict products liability applies to the provider of electrical service. Electricity is a somewhat unusual substance (if it can be called that) to be designated a "product," but the same policy reasons underlying products liability generally apply to electricity. The average consumer is in no position, vis-à-vis the provider, to "inspect" the product for safety; he must rely on the superior knowledge of the provider. Also, the provider is in a better position to promote safety and to spread the risk of providing service. For this reason, products liability will be applied to electrical service. Motion denied.

**EDITOR'S ANALYSIS:** Some products liability cases focus on "tangible" as opposed to "intangible" items in deciding what may be a product. In some instances this test would be of little help. While one can "feel" the effects of electricity, it is not tangible in the commonly accepted sense of the term.

# CHAPTER 17
# SPECIAL ISSUES IN AUTOMOTIVE LITIGATION

## QUICK REFERENCE RULES OF LAW

1. **Crashworthiness.** To establish a prima facie case with respect to a design defect claim, a plaintiff must show that an alternative design was safer or more capable of preventing the harm suffered than the allegedly defective design. (Burgos v. Lutz)

2. **Crashworthiness.** The "second-collision" doctrine imposes liability upon a manufacturer in a vehicular collision case for design defects that do not cause the initial accident but that cause additional injuries when the driver or passenger subsequently impacts with a defective interior or exterior of the vehicle. (Sumnicht v. Toyota Motor Sales, U.S.A., Inc.)

3. **Crashworthiness.** Compliance with the mandates of the Safety Act does not shield an automaker from design defect liability. (Tebbetts v. Ford Motor Co.)

4. **Driver Fault.** Evidence of a failure to use a seat belt may be admissible to support an affirmative defense of comparative negligence. (Lowe v. Estate Motors, Ltd.)

5. **Punitive Damages.** A corporate decision to forego inexpensive modifications that considerably reduce the risk of serious injury is sufficient grounds for punitive damages. (Grimshaw v. Ford Motor Co.)

6. **Recall.** A common-sense approach must be used in construing the term "unreasonable." (United States v. General Motors Corp.)

# Notes

## BURGOS v. LUTZ

N.Y. Sup. Ct., App. Div., 128 A.D. 2d 496 (1987).

**NATURE OF CASE: Appeal from denial of damages in products liability action.**

**FACT SUMMARY: Burgos (P) sued Lutz (D) for negligence and Honda (D) for products liability and defective design when Burgos's (P) decedent was killed when his Honda Civic was struck by Lutz's (D) automobile at an intersection.**

**CONCISE RULE OF LAW: To establish a prima facie case with respect to a design defect claim, a plaintiff must show that an alternative design was safer or more capable of preventing the harm suffered than the allegedly defective design.**

**FACTS:** Burgos's (P) decedent was killed while driving his Honda Civic 1200 when he made a left turn at an intersection, and his car was struck by an oncoming vehicle driven by Lutz (D). The decedent apparently suffered a laceration of his thoracic aorta and died instantly. Burgos (P) then brought an action against Lutz (D) for negligence and Honda (D) for defective design of the seat belt system and steering column of the Honda. After a three-month jury trial, the jury returned a verdict in Lutz's (D) and Honda's (D) favor. Burgos (P) appealed.

**ISSUE:** To establish a prima facie case with respect to a design defect claim, must a plaintiff show that an alternative design was safer or more capable of preventing the harm suffered than the allegedly defective design?

**HOLDING AND DECISION:** (Per curiam) Yes. To establish a prima facie case with respect to a design defect claim, a plaintiff must show that an alternative design was safer or more capable of preventing the harm suffered than the allegedly defective design. Here, Burgos's (P) evidence about the defective seat belt system consisted of expert testimony to the effect that, upon inspection of the actual seat belt in the decedent's Honda, the locking device performed erratically. Burgos (P) failed to establish that the erratic performance was caused by the design of the locking device. Accordingly, Burgos (P) failed to establish a prima facie case of a defectively designed seat belt system. Also, regarding the design of a steering column, although Burgos's (P) expert testified to the characteristics and qualities of an alternative steering column energy absorption system, the expert failed to explain how the proposed design would have prevented any of the decedent's injuries under the circumstances of the actual collision. Thus, Burgos (P) failed to show that an alternative design was any safer or more capable of preventing the harm that the decedent suffered than Honda's (D) design and has failed to establish a prima facie case with regard to this alleged design defect. Affirmed.

**EDITOR'S ANALYSIS:** A typical automobile defect case usually involves a complicated interrelationship of proof of design defect. This might include the feasibility of alternative designs, the role of safety devices, and issues of causation. All cases of this type require extensive expert testimony on what are often speculative questions, such as what would have happened had the plaintiff been wearing a seat belt or had the steering column absorbed more energy.

**NOTES:**

## SUMNICHT v. TOYOTA MOTOR SALES, U.S.A., INC.

Wis. Sup. Ct., 121 Wis. 2d 338 (1984).

**NATURE OF CASE: Appeal from award of damages in products liability action.**

**FACT SUMMARY: Sumnicht (P) sued Toyota Motor Sales, U.S.A., Inc. (D), alleging strict products liability when Sumnicht (P) was severely injured in an automobile accident, riding as a passenger in a Toyota Corona.**

**CONCISE RULE OF LAW: The "second-collision" doctrine imposes liability upon a manufacturer in a vehicular collision case for design defects that do not cause the initial accident but that cause additional injuries when the driver or passenger subsequently impacts with a defective interior or exterior of the vehicle.**

**FACTS:** Sumnicht (P) was involved in an automobile accident which rendered him a quadriplegic. Sumnicht (P) was apparently lying down in the back seat of the auto with his head behind the driver's seat immediately prior to the accident. One of Sumnicht's (P) friends, O'Connor, was driving the auto, a Toyota Corolla, which left the road and hit a tree. Upon impact, Sumnicht (P) was apparently propelled forward, and his head became entrapped in the cut-out portion of the back of the driver's seat, while his lower torso swung forward, smashing into the back of the front passenger's seat. Sumnicht (P) suffered a fractured dislocation of his cervical spine at C-7, which caused his quadriplegia. Sumnicht (P) brought suit against Toyota (D), alleging strict products liability and that the front seat system of the auto was both defective and unreasonably dangerous. At trial, the jury found that the auto was designed defectively and awarded Sumnicht (P) damages. Toyota (D) appealed.

**ISSUE:** Does the "second-collision" doctrine impose liability upon a manufacturer in a vehicular collision case for design defects that do not cause the initial accident but that cause additional injuries when the driver or passenger subsequently impacts with a defective interior or exterior of the vehicle?

**HOLDING AND DECISION:** (Ceci, J.) Yes. The "second-collision" doctrine imposes liability upon a manufacturer in a vehicular collision case for design defects that do not cause the initial accident but that cause additional injuries when the driver or passenger subsequently impacts with a defective interior or exterior of the vehicle. In a "second collision" case, the plaintiff must show proof that the alleged defect was a substantial factor in causing the injury. Here, there is credible evidence to suppose a finding that the defective seat design was a substantial factor in causing Sumnicht's (P) injuries. The jury chose to believe Sumnicht's (P) theory of causation — that the entrapment and capturing capability of the seat backs of the Corolla and the failure of the seat bracket to keep the passenger seat back stable — enhanced and created the injury mechanism. It is, thus, rational to hold that Toyota's (D) seat system was not as safe as it reasonably could have been. Affirmed.

**DISSENT:** (Steinmetz, J.) It is incomprehensible that the jury found under the facts of this case that Sumnicht (P) was not negligent for his own care and safety by failing to wear the available rear seat belt.

**EDITOR'S ANALYSIS:** The test for defectiveness in crash worthiness or "second collision" cases involves the same basic considerations arising in defect cases generally. Courts in such cases have noted the importance of considering price in the crashworthiness risk-benefit calculus. In fact, it has been observed that if changes in design would appreciably add to cost, add little to safety, and take an article out of the price range of the market to which it was intended to appeal, it may be unreasonable as well as impractical for the courts to require a manufacturer to adopt such changes.

**NOTES:**

## TEBBETTS v. FORD MOTOR CO.

N.H. Sup. Ct., 665 A.2d 345, cert. denied, 116 S. Ct. 1036 (1996).

**NATURE OF CASE: Appeal from summary judgment dismissing wrongful death action.**

**FACT SUMMARY: Ford Motor Co. (D) contended that compliance with the National Traffic and Motor Vehicle Safety Act shielded it from liability for failure to install airbags in its cars.**

**CONCISE RULE OF LAW: Compliance with the mandates of the Safety Act does not shield an automaker from design defect liability.**

**FACTS:** Rebecca Tebbetts was killed in an automobile collision. Her mother (P) sued Ford Motor Co. (D), the manufacturer, alleging that the failure to include a driver's side airbag was a design defect. Ford (D) contended that it had complied with the design mandates of the National Traffic and Motor Vehicle Safety Act of 1966 and that such compliance precluded state tort liability for alleged design defects. The trial court granted summary judgment dismissing the action, and Tebbetts (P) appealed.

**ISSUE:** Does compliance with the mandates of the Safety Act shield an automaker from design defect liability?

**HOLDING AND DECISION:** (Batchelder, J.) No. Compliance with the mandates of the Safety Act does not shield an automaker from design defect liability. Congress may preempt state tort liability either by: express preemption, occupation of the field, or by implied preemption. Here, the Safety Act did not expressly preempt state tort law with respect to design defect. With respect to occupation of the field and implied preemption, it should be noted that tort law is an area generally left to the states, and evidence of intent to preempt must be clear. Here, this is far from the case. In fact, there is some indication in the congressional record that there was no intent to preempt. Based on this, this court concludes that the dictates of the Safety Act were meant to be a minimum standard with respect to auto safety, but not the only standard. Reversed.

**EDITOR'S ANALYSIS:** The most significant recent case regarding preemption was Cippollone v. Liggett Group, Inc., 505 U.S. 504 (1992). That action involved the extent to which federal cigarette warning requirements preempted state failure-to-warn liability. The Court held that congressional intent was the sole factor relevant to a preemption issue.

**NOTES:**

## LOWE v. ESTATE MOTORS, LTD.

Mich. Sup. Ct., 428 Mich. 439 (1987).

**NATURE OF CASE: Appeal from reversal of denial of award of damages.**

**FACT SUMMARY: Lowe (P), who was severely injured while her son was driving her Mercedes 300D, claimed the accident was attributable to a defectively designed floor mat which wedged under the brake pedal, causing her son to lose control of the auto and crash, but Mercedes (D) argued that Lowe (P) was comparatively negligent for failure to wear her seat belt.**

**CONCISE RULE OF LAW: Evidence of a failure to use a seat belt may be admissible to support an affirmative defense of comparative negligence.**

**FACTS:** Lowe (P) sued Mercedes-Benz of North America (D), Estate Motors Limited (D), and Newark Auto Products (D) in products liability, contending that an accident in which Lowe (P) was severely injured while her son was driving Lowe's (P) Mercedes 300D was attributable to a defectively designed floor mat which wedged under the brake pedal, causing her son to lose control of the car and crash. At trial, Mercedes (D) asserted an affirmative defense of comparative negligence on the basis of Lowe's (P) failure to use the available three-point seat restraint. Lowe (P) then moved to strike that affirmative defense and to exclude at trial the admission of any evidence concerning that safety device and Lowe's (P) failure to use it, as the failure to wear a seat belt did not contribute to the cause of the accident. The trial court denied Lowe's (P) motions. Lowe (P) appealed, and the court of appeals reversed. Mercedes (D) then appealed.

**ISSUE:** May evidence of a failure to use a seat belt be admissible to support an affirmative defense of comparative negligence?

**HOLDING AND DECISION:** (Riley, J.) Yes. Evidence of a failure to use a seat belt may be admissible to support an affirmative defense of comparative negligence. If competent evidence is proffered, the issue may be appropriately submitted for jury consideration. The decision of the court of appeals in this case is inconsistent with the foregoing principles. The rationale of that court is that one need not anticipate the negligence of others, even if foreseeable, that a high percentage of automobile occupants do not use seat belts, that seat belt effectiveness is highly speculative, and that the imposition of a duty to use them for purposes of the common law doctrine of comparative negligence is merely appropriate for legislative consideration. Such a policy is flawed and inconsistent with modern and traditional principles of negligence law. Thus, this court reverses the decision of the court of appeals and reinstates the trial court's decision. Reversed.

**DISSENT:** (Archer, J.) Retaining the rule of inadmissibility of seat belt use is particularly important in a products liability case because the types of conduct being considered are usually varied and different.

**SEPARATE OPINION:** (Levin, J.) The view expressed in the lead opinion that evidence concerning the seat-restraint system may be considered by the trier of fact in determining whether a motor vehicle was defective in design where the plaintiff asserts the crashworthiness doctrine as a theory of liability is the proper approach.

**EDITOR'S ANALYSIS:** A large majority of statutes requiring adults to wear seat belts either provide that a violation cannot be grounds for reducing an award on the basis of comparative negligence, or limit the possible reduction to a small percentage of the award. Of the twenty-six states that have statutes in effect, three limit the possible reduction to a small percentage. Of the twenty-three other states, sixteen provide either that evidence of nonuse is not admissible in a civil action, or that it cannot be used to reduce an award.

**NOTES:**

## GRIMSHAW v. FORD MOTOR CO.

119 Cal. App. 3d 757, 174 Cal. Rptr. 348 (1981).

**NATURE OF CASE: Cross-appeal from award of damages in action for personal injuries.**

**FACT SUMMARY: Grimshaw (P) was seriously injured when the Ford Pinto in which he was a passenger exploded when rear-ended.**

**CONCISE RULE OF LAW: A corporate decision to forego inexpensive modifications that considerably reduce the risk of serious injury is sufficient grounds for punitive damages.**

**FACTS:** Ford (D) conceived the Pinto as a low-cost, subcompact vehicle. The requirements imposed by Ford (D) had the effect of placing the fuel tank in a vulnerable location. Evidence showed that on several occasions it was brought to the attention of Ford (D) management that inexpensive modifications to the design could substantially reduce the danger presented by the gas tank, but that Ford (D) management decided to forego the modifications. Grimshaw (P) was seriously burned when the Pinto in which he was riding was rear-ended. The trial court instructed the jury that punitive damages could be awarded if Ford (D) had acted with oppression, fraud, or malice. "Malice" included in its definition conscious disregard for the safety of others. The jury brought in an award of $2,841,000 in compensatory damages and $125,000,000 in punitive damages, reduced to $3,500,000 by the court. Ford (D) appealed the award of punitive damages and Grimshaw (P) appealed the reduction.

**ISSUE:** Is a corporate decision to forego inexpensive modifications that considerably reduce the risk of serious injury sufficient grounds for punitive damages?

**HOLDING AND DECISION:** (Tamura, J.) Yes. A corporate decision to forego inexpensive modifications that considerably reduce the risk of serious injury is sufficient grounds for punitive damages. Traditionally, punitive damages generally were awarded in the case of intentional torts. However, the term "malice" encompasses a conscious disregard for the rights of others and the actual desire to harm others is unnecessary. Recklessness will suffice. The actions of Ford's (D) management here were consistent with a jury's determination that Ford's (D) management had indeed acted with conscious disregard for the safety of the public. As to the amount awarded, while it was much higher than any amount heretofore given, the net worth of Ford (D) made it not unreasonable as a matter of law. To serve their deterrent purpose, they are meant to be onorous. As far as the reduction is concerned, this is within the power of the trial court and, absent clear abuse, which has not been shown, it will not be disturbed. Affirmed.

**CONCURRENCE:** (Kaufman, J.) While agreeing with the disposition of each issue, there were some problems with the court's conclusions regarding certain testimony and instructions, and for that reason the whole opinion cannot be endorsed.

**EDITOR'S ANALYSIS:** As the court stated, punitive damages traditionally were awarded for only intentional conduct. Many, if not most jurisdictions, still follow this rule. The awarding of punitive damages for nonintentional torts started in the 1970s, and first received the approval from a major state supreme court in Taylor v. Superior Court, 24 Cal. 3d 890, 598 P.2d 854 (1979).

**NOTES:**

## UNITED STATES v. GENERAL MOTORS CORP.

565 F.2d 754 (D.C. Cir. 1977).

**NATURE OF CASE: Appeal from imposition of civil penalty.**

**FACT SUMMARY: General Motors (D) contended that a defect in certain carburetors, which could result in engine fires, did not pose an unreasonable risk of accidents or injuries.**

**CONCISE RULE OF LAW: A common-sense approach must be used in construing the term "unreasonable."**

**FACTS:** On December 19, 1974, the administrator of the National Highway Traffic Safety Administration (NHTSA), acting pursuant to his authority under the National Traffic and Motor Vehicle Safety Act, determined that Rochester Quadrajet carburetors installed in 1965 Chevrolets and 1966 Chevrolets and Buicks contained a "defect which relates to motor vehicle safety," and that the manufacturer was therefore required to notify owners of the potential danger. The carburetor in question contained a fuel inlet plug which could become dislodged during operation of the vehicle, resulting in gasoline spilling directly into the engine, causing fires under the hood. General Motors (D) did not comply with the notice order, but rather filed suit to have the order declared null and void. At the same time, the administrator (P) brought suit to enforce the order and to impose a civil penalty on General Motors (D) for its failure to comply. The district court granted the administrator's (P) motion for summary judgment, and General Motors (D) then brought this appeal, contending that material questions of fact existed as to whether the defect in the carburetor "relates to motor vehicle safety."

**ISSUE:** Must a common-sense approach be used in construing the term "unreasonable?"

**HOLDING AND DECISION:** (Wright, J.) Yes. A common-sense approach must be adopted in construing the Safety Act and particularly, the term "unreasonable." Applying such an approach, there is no question but that engine fires, which may occur on thoroughfares where pulling over and standing outside the car is difficult or dangerous, or which may take the driver by surprise and quickly spread to the passenger compartment, are extremely dangerous for all involved and should be considered an unreasonable risk to safety. The basic purpose of the Safety Act is to reduce motor vehicle accidents, injuries, and property damage. Where a defect, a term used in the sense of error or mistake, has been established in a motor vehicle, and where this defect results in hazards as potentially dangerous as a sudden engine fire, and where there is no dispute that at least some such hazards, in this case fires, can definitely be expected to occur in the future, then the defect must be viewed as one "related to motor vehicle safety," and the Act's basic purpose of protecting the public requires that notification be provided. Remanded for a hearing on the amount of the penalty.

**EDITOR'S ANALYSIS:** The Safety Act referred to in this case sets certain minimum standards which manufacturers must meet in their recall notices to consumers. The recall notice must clearly describe the defect, evaluate the risk, specify measures to remedy the defect, and inform the purchaser that repairs will be made without charge.

**NOTES:**

# CHAPTER 18
# SPECIAL ISSUES IN TOXIC SUBSTANCE LITIGATION

## QUICK REFERENCE RULES OF LAW

1. **The Nature of Toxic Substance Litigation.** A product is unreasonably dangerous only when it is dangerous to an extent beyond that contemplated by the ordinary consumer who purchases it. (Borel v. Fibreboard Paper Products Corp.)

2. **Class Actions: Certification.** Nicotine-dependent smokers constitute a certifiable class. (Castano v. American Tobacco Co.)

3. **Class Actions: Management.** Due process in the asbestos context should not be analyzed in the narrow, traditional, one-sided view of defendants but should also encompass the impact on plaintiffs and even the obvious societal interest involved. (Cimino v. Raymark Industries, Inc.)

4. **The Capacity of the Agent to Cause Plaintiff's Disease.** An expert's opinion need not be based on techniques generally accepted in the scientific community in order to be admissible in a federal court. (Daubert v. Merrell Dow Pharmaceuticals, Inc.)

5. **The Capacity of the Agent to Cause Plaintiff's Disease.** Testimony of experts need not be based on generally accepted methodologies to be admissible, but rather must be based on scientific knowledge that will assist the trier of fact. (Hopkins v. Dow Corning Corp.)

6. **Whether Plaintiff's Disease Was Caused by the Agent.** The uncertainties and legal obstacles that would accompany years of protracted litigation must be considered in assessing the fairness of a settlement of a mass exposure case. (In re Agent Orange Product Liability Litigation)

7. **Identifying the Party Responsible for the Agent.** Market share liability may not replace proof of causation-in-fact in a products liability action. (Smith v. Eli Lilly & Co.)

8. **Statutes of Limitations, Res Judicata, and Damages.** (1) A plaintiff in an asbestos action may not recover based on the possibility of contracting cancer. (2) Punitive damages are not recoverable in an asbestos action. (Jackson v. Johns-Manville Sales Corp. (Jackson I))

9. **Statutes of Limitations, Res Judicata, and Damages.** For a case to be deemed "uniquely federal" so that a substantive federal rule will be imposed, the interest at stake must relate to an articulated federal policy or directly implicate the authority and duties of the federal government. (Jackson v. Johns-Manville Sales Corp. (Jackson II))

10. **Statutes of Limitations, Res Judicata, and Damages.** None given. (Jackson v. Johns-Manville Sales Corp. (Jackson II 1/2))

11. **Statutes of Limitations, Res Judicata, and Damages.** In a mass tort litigation, damages may be awarded for mental anguish and probable future medical consequences, and punitive damages may also be awarded. (Jackson v. Johns-Manville Sales Corp. (Jackson III))

## BOREL v. FIBREBOARD PAPER PRODUCTS CORP.

493 F.2d 1076 (5th Cir. 1973), cert. denied,
419 U.S. 869, 95 S. Ct. 127, 42 L. Ed. 2d 107 (1974).

**NATURE OF CASE: Appeal from award of damages for negligence.**

**FACT SUMMARY: Fibreboard (D) contended that it should not be held liable in negligence for damage caused by asbestos dust because the dangers posed by asbestos dust were not known at the time the products containing asbestos were sold.**

**CONCISE RULE OF LAW: A product is unreasonably dangerous only when it is dangerous to an extent beyond that contemplated by the ordinary consumer who purchases it.**

**FACTS:** Borel (P) developed pulmonary asbestosis, and eventually a form of lung cancer known as mesothelioma, from the inhalation of asbestos dust over the thirty-four years he worked as an industrial insulation worker. Borel (P) was aware of the heavy concentrations of asbestos dust in the air but failed to wear a respirator because it made breathing difficult, was uncomfortable, and had to be specially requested. Respirators were not available at all in his earlier years on the job. Instead, he would sometimes use Mentholatum in his nostrils or would sometimes wear a wet handkerchief over his face. Borel (P) brought suit against Fibreboard (D) and other manufacturers of insulation materials containing asbestos for their failure to warn of the dangers of inhaling the dust. Fibreboard (D) defended on the grounds that the dangers of inhaling asbestos dust were not reasonably foreseeable at the time the products causing Borel's (P) injury were sold. The jury returned a verdict for Borel (P), and Fibreboard (D) appealed.

**HOLDING AND DECISION:** (Wisdom, J.) Yes. A product is unreasonably dangerous only when it is dangerous to an extent beyond that contemplated by the ordinary consumer who purchases it. A seller is under a duty to warn of only those dangers that are reasonably foreseeable. The requirement of foreseeability coincides with the standard of due care in negligence cases in that a seller must exercise reasonable care and foresight to discover a danger in his product, and to warn users and consumers of that danger. Unavoidably unsafe products are those which, in the present state of human knowledge, are incapable of being made safe for their ordinary and intended use, but from which important benefits may be derived, such as experimental drugs. However, even when the marketing of such a product is justified, the seller still has a responsibility to inform the user or consumer of the risk of harm. The failure to give adequate warnings in these circumstances renders the product unreasonably dangerous. The rationale for this rule is that the user or consumer is entitled to make his own choice as to whether the product's utility or benefits justifies exposing himself to the risk of harm. Here, because Fibreboard (D) had a duty to test its product, and because it is held to have the knowledge and skill of an expert, the jury was entitled to find that the danger to Borel (P) and other insulation workers from inhaling asbestos dust was foreseeable to Fibreboard (D) at the time the products causing Borel's (P) injuries were sold. Affirmed.

**EDITOR'S ANALYSIS:** As Judge Wisdom notes in this case, a manufacturer in cases such as this is held to the knowledge and skill of an expert. The manufacturer's status as expert means that at a minimum, he must keep abreast of scientific knowledge, discoveries, and advances and he is presumed to know the information imparted thereby. Additionally, the manufacturer under those circumstances has a duty to test and inspect his product.

**NOTES:**

**CASTANO v. AMERICAN TOBACCO CO.**

160 F.R.D. 544, rev'd, ___ F.3d ___ (E.D. La. 1995).

**NATURE OF CASE: Motion for class certification in mass tort litigation.**

**FACT SUMMARY: In an action against American Tobacco Co. (D) and other members of the tobacco industry, class certification was sought with respect to nicotine-dependent smokers (P).**

**CONCISE RULE OF LAW: Nicotine-dependent smokers constitute a certifiable class.**

**FACTS:** A massive tort action was brought against American Tobacco (D) and other members of the tobacco industry, alleging that various tobacco companies had conspired to addict cigarette users through nicotine manipulation. Causes of action were based on fraud, state consumer protection violations, breach of warranties, and strict products liability. The plaintiffs sought damages for economic loss, emotional distress, and punitive damages, excluding, however, personal injury damages. Class certification was sought by motion.

**ISSUE:** Do nicotine-dependent smokers constitute a certifiable class?

**HOLDING AND DECISION:** (Jones, J.) Yes, nicotine-dependent smokers constitute a certifiable class. Fed.R.Civ.P 23(a) states four requirements for class certification. These are numerosity, commonality, typicality, and adequacy of representation. These four criteria are met in this case. The proposed class is certainly high in number, perhaps as high as fifty million persons. Commonality, meaning all plaintiffs have common characteristics relevant to the suit, is also clearly present. The third criterion requires that the claims of each class member be relatively similar. This is also clearly the case. Finally, unnamed class members must be adequately represented by the named class members. Here, counsel for the plaintiffs clearly are able to adequately represent the class. The certification of a class under Rule 23(a) is not the end of the matter; certification must be present as to each cause of action, meaning that class action rather than individual issues must predominate each cause. [The court went on to hold that class action issues predominated with respect to punitive damages, fraud, breach of warranty, intentional tort, negligence, and strict liability. It found a lack of predominance with respect to issues of causation, comparative negligence, and compensatory damages.] Motion granted in part, denied in part.

**EDITOR'S ANALYSIS:** The plaintiffs here won this round, but lost the next. On interlocutory appeal, the Fifth Circuit reversed the district court's order and decertified the class. The main reason for the reversal was the fact that state, as opposed to federal law, governed the action, and differences in state law made class certification improper.

**CIMINO v. RAYMARK INDUSTRIES, INC.**

751 F. Supp. 649 (E.D. Texas 1990).

**NATURE OF CASE: Review of the procedure used in asbestos class actions.**

**FACT SUMMARY: The court tried to analyze past asbestos cases in order to provide a fair and cost-effective means of trying large numbers of asbestos cases.**

**CONCISE RULE OF LAW: Due process in the asbestos context should not be analyzed in the narrow, traditional, one-sided view of defendants but should also encompass the impact on plaintiffs and even the obvious societal interest involved.**

**FACTS:** [Not included in casebook excerpt. This was a case analysis.]

**ISSUE:** Should due process in the asbestos context be analyzed in the narrow, traditional, one-sided view of defendants?

**HOLDING AND DECISION:** (Parker, J.) No. Due process in the asbestos context should not be analyzed in the narrow, traditional, one-sided view of defendants but should also encompass the impact on plaintiffs and even the obvious societal interest involved. In Cimino, 160 damages cases were litigated together. Despite the variables inherent in the different cases, there is a 99% likelihood that the average result would have been similar if each case had been tried separately. The 1% chance of a significant difference does not raise due process concerns. To take defendant's argument is to embrace perfection as the benchmark. Therefore, due process does not entitle defendants to traditional one-on-one trials.

**EDITOR'S ANALYSIS:** In the asbestos litigation cases being decided in the Eastern District of Texas, over 448 members of the asbestos class have died waiting for their cases to be heard. By arguing the need for one-on-one trials, the defendants in these litigations have an advantage in that, the longer they wait and draw out the process, many more plaintiffs will die, and their cases will die with them. Out of fairness to these plaintiffs, justice mandates that similar claims be tried in a class form.

**NOTES:**

## DAUBERT v. MERRELL DOW PHARMACEUTICALS, INC.

508 U.S. 579 (1993).

**NATURE OF CASE: Review of dismissal of products liability action.**

**FACT SUMMARY: Merrell (D) contended that Daubert's (P) expert witness testimony regarding birth defects should not be admitted because it had not been subject to peer review and thus did not pass the "general acceptance" test.**

**CONCISE RULE OF LAW: An expert's opinion need not be based on techniques generally accepted in the scientific community in order to be admissible in a federal court.**

**FACTS:** Daubert (P) filed an action against Merrell Dow Pharmaceuticals (D), contending that his birth defects had been due to maternal ingestion of the drug Bendectin. Merrell (D) moved for summary judgment, introducing evidence showing no connection between Bendectin and birth defects. In opposition, Daubert (P) filed declarations from eight different experts claiming that such a link existed. These conclusions were based on animal studies, pharmacological studies, and reanalysis of previously published epidemiological studies. The district court refused to admit Daubert's (P) evidence, contending that it was based on methodologies not generally accepted in the scientific community. It granted Merrell's (D) summary judgment motion. The Ninth Circuit affirmed. The Supreme Court granted review.

**ISSUE:** Must an expert's opinion be based on techniques generally accepted in the scientific community in order to be admissible in a federal court?

**HOLDING AND DECISION:** (Blackmun, J.) No. An expert's opinion need not be based on techniques generally accepted in the scientific community in order to be admissible in a federal court. The admissibility of expert testimony in a federal trial is governed by Federal Rule of Evidence 702. This rule allows evidence if it will assist the trier of fact, is relevant, and rests on a reliable foundation. Nothing in Rule 702 demands that the methodology underlying the scientific testimony be generally accepted, and such a requirement should not be read into the rule. This is not to say that any allegedly expert opinion is admissible. The subject of an expert's testimony must be "scientific knowledge," meaning it must be derived by the scientifc method and subject to scientific processes such as peer review, testability, and, as a factor, community acceptance. Rule 702 would not allow a crackpot theory by a self-appointed expert.

**EDITOR'S ANALYSIS:** Rule 702 is not the only Federal Rule of Evidence applicable to expert scientific testimony. Rule 703 provides that expert opinions based on otherwise inadmissable hearsay are to be admitted only if the facts or data are reasonably relied on by experts in the relevant field. Rule 706 permits the court to appoint an expert of its own choosing, and Rule 403 permits the exclusion of relevant evidence if its probative value is outweighed by the danger of unfair prejudice.

## HOPKINS v. DOW CORNING CORP.

33 F.3d 1116 (9th Cir. 1994).

**NATURE OF CASE: Appeal from verdict awarding compensatory and punitive damages for personal injury in action alleging fraud, strict products liability, and breach of warranties.**

**FACT SUMMARY: Dow (D) contended that expert testimony regarding breast implants should not have been admitted because the experts' methodologies were not generally accepted in the scientific community.**

**CONCISE RULE OF LAW: Testimony of experts need not be based on generally accepted methodologies to be admissible but rather must be based on scientific knowledge that will assist the trier of fact.**

**FACTS:** Hopkins (P) sued Dow Corning Corp. (D), contending that breast implants that had been manufactured by Dow (D) had made her ill. At trial, she introduced expert testimony by a toxicologist, a rheumatologist, and an immunologist. A jury returned a special verdict finding Dow (D) liable and awarded $840,000 in compensatory damages and $6.5 million in punitive damages. Dow (D) appealed, contending that the opinions given by the experts had been based on methodologies not generally accepted in the scientific community.

**ISSUE:** Must expert testimony be based on generally accepted methodologies to be admissible?

**HOLDING AND DECISION:** (Hug, J.) No. Testimony of experts need not be based on generally accepted methodologies to be admissible but rather must be based on scientific knowledge that will assist the trier of fact. Under Federal Rule of Evidence 702, expert testimony may be admitted if it is reliable and would tend to help a trier of fact deal with issues beyond the knowledge of a lay jury. The key to reliability is not the opinion itself, but the methods used to reach the opinion. If the methods are scientifically sound, the opinion is admissible. Here, the opinions of the various experts were based on clinical records, animal studies, and medical literature. These are reliable bases for opinions when no epidemiological data is available, so the testimony was properly admitted. Affirmed.

**EDITOR'S ANALYSIS:** The result here was largely dictated by the Supreme Court case Daubert v. Merrell Dow, 509 U.S. 579 (1993). That opinion rejected the standard urged here by Dow (D). Under Daubert, "general acceptance" can be a factor of admissibility, but not the sina que non thereof.

## IN RE AGENT ORANGE PRODUCT LIABILITY LITIGATION

597 F. Supp. 740, aff'd, 818 F.2d 145 (2d Cir. 1987).

**NATURE OF CASE: Motion to approve settlement in mass tort litigation.**

**FACT SUMMARY: Representatives of tens of thousands of veterans (P) who came in contact with the herbicide Agent Orange during the Vietnam War reached a settlement with the federal government (D) and the chemical industry (D) on the eve of trial.**

**CONCISE RULE OF LAW: The uncertainties and legal obstacles that would accompany years of protracted litigation must be considered in assessing the fairness of a settlement of a mass exposure case.**

**FACTS:** In 1979, Vietnam War veterans (P) commenced a class action against the federal government (D) and chemical manufacturers (D) for damages for injuries suffered by the veterans (P) following contact with the herbicide Agent Orange. After five years of extensive discovery, the parties' representatives proposed a tentative settlement regarding the case against the chemical companies (D). The court was asked to approve the settlement over the objections of those veterans (P) who wanted a jury to once and for all demonstrate the connection between Agent Orange and their physical and mental maladies.

**ISSUE:** Must the uncertainties and legal obstacles that would accompany years of protracted litigation be considered in assessing the fairness of a settlement of a mass exposure case?

**HOLDING AND DECISION:** (Weinstein, C.J.) Yes. The uncertainties and legal obstacles that would accompany years of protracted litigation must be considered in assessing the fairness of a settlement of a mass exposure case. In this case, the veterans (P) face enormous legal problems before they might succeed in obtaining relief. The problem of the "indeterminate plaintiff," the heavy burden placed on the veterans (P) by the preponderance rule, and the inadequacy of a plaintiff-by-plaintiff solution must be assessed. Courts must attempt to devise the most effective and equitable means of dealing with the vexing problem of toxic torts in the absence of appropriate legislation. The settlement proposed here gives the veterans (P) more than they would be likely to achieve by attempting to litigate to the death. It provides funds to help at least some of the veterans (P) and their children. The settlement is tentatively approved.

**EDITOR'S ANALYSIS:** Because of the epidemiological nature of evidence against Agent Orange, no individual veteran (P) would likely be able to prove that his adverse health effects are due to exposure to the chemical. In dicta, Judge Winstein proposed that one way to deal with this problem would be shift the burden to the chemical companies (D) to prove that Agent Orange was not responsible for the veterans' injuries. Another solution would be to try all the veterans' (P) claims together in a class action and arrive at a single, class-wide determination of the total harm. The chemical companies (D) would then be liable to each exposed veteran (P) for a pro rata share of that veteran's (P) injuries.

**NOTES:**

## SMITH v. ELI LILLY & COMPANY

137 Ill. 2d 222, 148 Ill. Dec. 22, 560 N.E. 2d 324 (1990).

**NATURE OF CASE: Appeal from denial of summary judgment.**

**FACT SUMMARY: Smith (P) contended that market share liability should be substituted for the element of causation in fact because she could not identify the specific manufacturer of the drug that allegedly gave her cancer.**

**CONCISE RULE OF LAW: Market share liability may not replace proof of causation-in-fact in a products liability action.**

**FACTS:** Smith (P) suffered from vaginal cancer and contended that the drug DES, prescribed for her mother while Smith (P) was in utero, caused her cancer. Smith (P) knew the color, size, and dosage of the drug her mother took, but she was unable to identify the specific manufacturer of the product. After naming 138 drug companies that manufactured DES in Smith's (P) original complaint, only 20 companies, including Eli Lilly (D), remained in the suit after various motions were resolved. Counts IX and X of Smith's (P) complaint alleged theories of negligence and strict liability and invoked market share as the means for apportioning damages. Smith (P) contended that the drug companies failed to properly test DES and to adequately warn of its dangers. The trial court granted Eli Lilly's (D) motion for summary judgment on the first nine counts but denied the motion on the strict liability action and adopted market share liability. The appellate court likewise adopted a theory of market share liability and extended its application to the negligence action, count IX. Eli Lilly (D) appealed.

**ISSUE:** Should market share liability replace proof of causation-in-fact in a products liability action?

**HOLDING AND DECISION:** (Ryan, J.) No. Market share liability may not replace proof of causation-in-fact in a products liability action. The concept that liability may be imposed based merely on a breach of duty, without causation being established, has long been rejected in American tort law. As illustrated in this case, the majority of plausible defendants have not been or cannot be brought before the court. Those who are present have the difficult burden of establishing their share of a market. The companies which cannot prove their share will be made to pay the unattributed portion of the damages, thus paying the damages which rightfully belong to companies which are insolvent, not amenable to suit in the jurisdiction, or for some other reason are not before the court. Market share liability makes the entire drug industry an insurer of all injuries attributable to defective drugs of uncertain or unprovable origin, including those injuries manifesting themselves a generation later, and regardless of whether particular defendants had any part whatever in causing the claimed injury. Market share liability is an unreasonable overreaction in attempting to achieve what is perceived as a socially satisfying result. This is too great a deviation from a tort principle which we have found to serve a vital function in the law, causation in fact, especially when market share liability is a flawed concept. Reversed.

**DISSENT:** (Clark, J.) This court should adopt the theory of market share liability established in Hymowitz v. Eli Lilly & Co., 73 N.Y. 2d 487. Because liability under the Hymowitz theory is based on the overall risk produced and not causation in a single case, a defendant who was a part of the market that DES sold for pregnancy use cannot escape liability merely because the defendant can show that its DES could not in fact have been the DES that caused the plaintiff's injuries. However, a defendant can escape liability if the defendant can show that it was not a member of the national market of DES marketed for pregnancy.

**EDITOR'S ANALYSIS:** DES was a drug created in 1937 that was used as a miscarriage preventative. By the end of 1952, up to 191 companies were manufacturing and distributing DES. In 1971, two medical studies suggested that there was an association between the outbreak in young women of cancer and the maternal ingestion of DES during pregnancy. In the 1970s, hundreds of lawsuits were filed by women known as "DES daughters." However, a great debate followed because the manufacturers argued that a high incidence of cancer was not found in these so-called DES daughters. That issue was one for the finder of fact and not the appellate court.

**NOTES:**

## JACKSON v. JOHNS-MANVILLE SALES CORP. (JACKSON I)

727 F2d 506 (5th Cir. 1984).

**NATURE OF CASE: Appeal from award of damages in asbestos-related personal injury action.**

**FACT SUMMARY: Jackson (P), who worked in a shipyard where he was exposed to asbestos products manufactured by Johns-Manville (D) and other manufacturers consistently over eighteen years, contracted asbestosis and introduced evidence of his increased risk of cancer.**

**CONCISE RULE OF LAW: (1) A plaintiff in an asbestos action may not recover based on the possibility of contracting cancer. (2) Punitive damages are not recoverable in an asbestos action.**

**FACTS:** Jackson (P) worked in various capacities at a shipyard over the span of eighteen years. He was frequently exposed to asbestos products made by Johns-Manville (D) and other manufacturers. The products contained no warnings. Jackson (P) eventually developed asbestosis. He had not developed cancer at the time he brought suit against Johns-Manville (D) and the other manufacturers, although his statistical probability of contracting it had substantially increased. The jury awarded Jackson (P) $391,000 in compensatory damages and $625,000 in punitive damages. Jackson (P) had been permitted to introduce evidence concerning his risk of future cancer.

**ISSUE:** (1) May a plaintiff in an asbestos action recover based on the possibility of contracting cancer? (2) Are punitive damages recoverable in an asbestos action?

**HOLDING AND DECISION:** (Clark, J.) No. (1) A plaintiff in an asbestos action may not recover based on the possibility of contracting cancer. It is true that a plaintiff may recover for future damages. However, this can occur only when it is reasonably certain future damages will occur. The possibility that Jackson (P) will develop cancer is just that — a possibility. If it does develop, then the cause of action will arise. If it does not, then the cause of action will not. This is analogous to statute of limitation rules. The statute will not begin to run until the cancer develops, if it does in fact develop. Thus, the cause of action will not accrue until then. (2) Punitive damages are not recoverable in an asbestos action. Punitive damages are a questionable proposition at best in a strict liability action, since the emphasis is on the product, not the conduct of the manufacturer. In mass asbestos litigation, they present a serious possibility that they will bleed the defendants to death, thus drying up the compensation sources for future plaintiffs. The whole purpose of strict liability is to compensate, and to assess punitive damages against the defendants can seriously impair the defendants' ability to provide such compensation. Reversed.

**EDITOR'S ANALYSIS:** It is the essential purpose of punitive damages to punish a defendant and to thus deter like conduct. This is inherently at odds with our civil justice system, which is based on compensation. The court here obviously was of the opinion that where deterrence and compensation could not coexist, deterrence had to be sacrificed.

**NOTES:**

**JACKSON v. JOHNS-MANVILLE SALES CORP.**
**(JACKSON II)**
750 F.2d 1314 (5th Cir. 1985),
cert. denied, 478 U.S. 1022 (1986).

**NATURE OF CASE: Appeal in action for damages for asbestos inhalation.**

**FACT SUMMARY: Jackson (P) and other shipyard workers (P) filed suit against Johns-Manville (D) for injuries suffered during the years they worked with asbestos products.**

**CONCISE RULE OF LAW: For a case to be deemed "uniquely federal" so that a substantive federal rule will be imposed, the interest at stake must relate to an articulated federal policy or directly implicate the authority and duties of the federal government.**

**FACTS**: Jackson (P) sued Johns-Manville (D) for injuries relating to the inhalation of asbestos products during his years working in a shipyard. At trial, Jackson (P) introduced the so-called Sumner Simpson letters into evidence; which purported to show that Johns-Manville (D) knew or should have known of the dangers asbestos products posed to shipyard workers. Johns-Manville (D) argued that the letters were of no probative value because they referred only to the danger faced by plant workers and miners exposed to raw asbestos, not shipyard workers such as Jackson (P) who handled only finished asbestos products. Jackson (P) also introduced expert witness testimony that his exposure to asbestos significantly increased his chances of developing cancer. The district court admitted the Sumner Simpson letters and the expert testimony, and a verdict was returned in favor of Jackson (P). Johns-Manville (D) appealed. The court of appeals reversed on the admissibility of both the letters and the expert testimony, then granted a rehearing of the case en banc to determine the admissibility of the letters and the expert testimony, and to determine whether the case was an appropriate one for the imposition of federal common law.

**ISSUE**: For a case to be deemed "uniquely federal" so that a substantive federal rule will be imposed, must the interest at stake relate to an articulated federal policy or directly implicate the authority and duties of the federal government?

**HOLDING AND DECISION**: (Randall, J.) Yes. For a case to be deemed "uniquely federal" so that a substantive federal rule will be imposed, the interest at stake must relate to an articulated federal policy or directly implicate the authority and duties of the federal government. Displacement of state law is primarily a decision for Congress. However, Congress has yet to take any action on the problems of asbestos exposure. Although asbestos-related injuries have been evidenced throughout the country, it does not follow that a uniquely federal interest is at stake. Additionally, the district court acted properly in admitting the Sumner Simpson letters. The letters meet the threshold test for relevancy, and any distinction as to the types of workers they refer to goes to weight rather than admissibility. A decision on the admissibility of the expert testimony regarding the risk of cancer must be delayed until the certified question regarding damages is answered. It is most appropriate that the nature of the actionable injury and the availability of damages be certified to the Mississippi Supreme Court.

**CONCURRENCE:** (Rubin, J.) Although diversity cases should not be reheard en banc, the majority is correct in remanding the case for certification on the state-law issues.

**DISSENT:** (Clark, J.) The majority's contention that the issues must be decided by state law is ridiculous. The number of asbestos claims is rising exponentially, and the only just resolution would be to certify this case to the U.S. Supreme Court for a determination of whether federal common law must be developed to govern this uniquely interdependent mass of tort litigation.

**EDITOR'S ANALYSIS**: Since this case was decided in the mid 1980s, the number of asbestos-related cases has continued to increase drastically. A number of states have enacted legislation that allows more leniency in asbestos cases in regard to the discovery laws and the statutes of limitation. Similar statutes have also been enacted to protect individuals exposed to other toxic substances and women suffering from conditions caused by breast implants.

**NOTES:**

## JACKSON v. JOHNS-MANVILLE SALES CORP. (JACKSON II 1/2)

Miss. Sup. Ct., 469 So. 2d 99 (1985).

**NATURE OF CASE: Response to certified question of law in asbestos products liability action.**

**FACT SUMMARY: The Fifth Circuit certified a question of law to the Mississippi Supreme Court regarding the types of damages available in one claim in a mass tort case.**

**CONCISE RULE OF LAW: None given.**

**FACTS:** In a tort case arising out of asbestos exposure, the Fifth Circuit certified the following questions of law to the Mississippi Supreme Court: (1) Are mental anguish damages available in asbestos products liability actions?; (2) Are damages available for fear of an increased risk of cancer?; and (3) Are punitive damages available in such actions?

**ISSUE:** None given.

**HOLDING AND DECISION:** (Per curiam, en banc) [The court declined to accept the Fifth Circuit's invitation to rule on the legal issues posed to it, leaving the issues unresolved.]

**EDITOR'S ANALYSIS:** Federal courts sitting in diversity must follow state substantive law. This can be conflicting or nonexistent. One approach to dealing with this problem is issue certification, as the Fifth Circuit did here. The problem, of course, is that state courts are not obligated to honor such requests. In such an instance, the federal courts must do their best to divine what state law might be.

**NOTES:**

## JACKSON v. JOHNS-MANVILLE SALES CORP. (JACKSON III)

781 F.2d 394 (5th Cir. 1986).

**NATURE OF CASE: Appeal from judgment awarding damages for personal injury in strict liability action.**

**FACT SUMMARY: Johns-Manville (D) contended that (1) mental anguish damages, (2) punitive damages, and (3) damages for probable future medical consequences were not available in a mass tort litigation.**

**CONCISE RULE OF LAW: In a mass tort litigation, damages may be awarded for mental anguish and probable future medical consequences, and punitive damages may also be awarded.**

**FACTS:** In 1978, Jackson (P), an asbestosis victim, filed a class action, along with other victims, that was not certified. He subsequently obtained a judgment on his own complaint against asbestos manufacturer Johns-Manville Sales Corp (D). The judgment included compensatory damages for mental anguish and probable future contraction of cancer, as well as punitive damages. Johns-Manville (D) appealed, contending that these damages were unavailable as a matter of law.

**ISSUE:** In a mass tort litigation, may damages be awarded for mental anguish and probable future medical consequences, and may punitive damages also be awarded?

**HOLDING AND DECISION:** (Randall, J.) Yes. In a mass tort litigation, damages may be awarded for mental anguish and future medical consequences, and punitive damages may also be awarded. With respect to future medical consequences, the actionable tortious conduct is the exposure of the plaintiff to the toxic substance. Once any injury manifests itself, the statute of limitations begins to run, and since a cause of action may not be split, any injury resulting from the exposure must be litigated. While a probable future prospect of cancer is not the same as cancer, it is a legitimate item of damages if it can be proven. It therefore must be raised when injury is first manifested. With respect to mental anguish over the prospect of future cancer, emotional pain over the fact one will likely die of a painful cancer (mesothelioma, the cancer associated with asbestos exposure, is almost always fatal) is very real to the victim. With respect to punitive damages, Johns-Manville's (D) argument seems to be that such exposure in a potential mass tort case constitutes excessive punishment, no matter how egregious its conduct might have been. Restated, the argument is that because its conduct affected many people rather than a few, such conduct should not give rise to punitive damages liability. This is a weak argument, to say the least. Johns-Manville (D) could have argued to the jury, as it does to this court, that exemplary damages should not be awarded because such might drive it into insolvency, denying recovery to future plaintiffs. It chose not to do so, and it is not an issue to be decided now. Affirmed.

**DISSENT:** (Clark, J.) Because of the national scope of asbestos litigation, federal law, rather than state law, should be the basis for the decision here.

**EDITOR'S ANALYSIS:** Toxic tort cases have been a major problem for the court system, particularly the federal judiciary. Quite simply courts were not designed to deal with cases involving such litigant numerosity. The courts have all but begged Congress to enact a statutory compensation scheme for some toxic substance exposure including asbestos. However, Congress has never done so, leaving the courts to sort things out as best they can.

**NOTES:**

# Notes